AN HONOURABLE DECEPTION?

New Labour, Iraq, and the Misuse of Power

CLARE SHORT

*f*P

FREE PRESS

First published in Great Britain by The Free Press in 2004
An imprint of Simon & Schuster UK Ltd
A Viacom company

1 3 5 7 9 10 8 6 4 2

Simon & Schuster UK Ltd
Africa House
64–78 Kingsway
London WC2B 6AH

Simon & Schuster Australia
Sydney

www.simonsays.co.uk

A CIP catalogue for this book is available
from the British Library.

ISBN: 0-7432-6392-8

Typeset by M Rules
Printed and bound in Great Britain by
Mackays of Chatham plc

For my mother and father
and the values they taught us

CONTENTS

CONTENTS

'Never tell each other lies'
—*Paul's letter to the Colossians*

INTRODUCTION

Everywhere I go, in Britain and overseas, people ask me why Tony Blair did what he did on Iraq. This book is my attempt to answer that question as fully and honestly as I can. I have written it so that the discussion of how such a disastrous mistake came to be made can be more fully informed, and in the hope that we can begin to learn the lessons and start to put things right.

The most spectacular thing that went wrong with New Labour was Iraq, and this is the focus of the book. But the question of how Tony Blair came to adopt such a misjudged policy towards Iraq is partly answered by analysing the nature of New Labour. From the start it was obsessed with presentation rather than content and willing to be economical with the truth. New Labour was also the project of a small group that captured power in the Labour Party and had little respect for democratic and constitutional decision-making. The book puts the decision to support the US neoconservatives' policy on Iraq in this wider context.

There are those who argue that it is the duty of members of the Labour Party, and Labour MPs in particular, to be loyal and supportive of their leader, come what may. I cannot accept this. The world is in trouble, and the policies of the British Labour government are part of the problem. It is essential that we understand how these mistakes came to be made in order to correct them. We must also take back the right to engage in discussion and to seek to change Labour policy when we believe the leadership has got things wrong. Loyalty is a good quality, but loyalty to a terrible error simply entrenches that error.

The book begins with a brief account of how I became involved in politics and my experience of Labour's years in Opposition. However, the book is not a memoir or a Labour history. The personal material is provided in order to explain where my politics come from. My account of the years of Opposition seeks to correct the New Labour myth that Labour could not have won in 1997 without Blair. There is no doubt that Labour was set to win the forthcoming General Election under John Smith. Blair almost certainly added to the majority, but the reforms carried through under Neil Kinnock and John Smith, and the failings of the Tory party in power, meant that Labour was poised to win, with John Smith becoming the first Labour Prime Minister since Jim Callaghan lost in 1979. Smith's tragic heart attack in 1994 deprived us of a leader who would very probably have made a great Prime Minister.

This part of the story is also important because it was after the 1992 defeat that New Labour was created by a very small group of people who went on to take over the reins of power and to restrict and diminish the democracy of the party. The idea of New Labour was an imitation of President Clinton's New Democrats, and focused completely on presentational questions. It became clear during Blair's second term that neither Blair nor New Labour had any significant guiding principles, philosophy or values. The achievements of the government on economic management, public expenditure and tackling child poverty flow from the Treasury. Gordon Brown was originally part of the New Labour project but is increasingly distanced from it. The 'Third Way' was an attempt to turn triangulation – the identification of two opposing views so the middle position can be pursued – into a philosophy. But triangulation was a tactic and contained no guiding principles. New Labour was and is a ruthless, power-winning project. It has little idea what it wants power *for* and because it is focused on winning media approval, tends to drift steadily in a direction approved by the Murdoch press.

My account of Blair's first term is not intended to provide a full history. I summarise some of the reforms that flowed from long-standing Labour commitments, of which we can continue to be proud. But I also give an account of how Blair's leadership style has steadily undermined the checks and balances of our constitutional system and the democracy of the Labour Party. It is this leadership style that is the fundamental explanation of the serious errors of the second term. My account of the development of Blair's foreign policy in the first term also paves the way for the later errors in Iraq. The outline of our approach to international development contains the core of an alternative foreign policy.

Chapter 3 brings me to Blair's second term and the frail electoral base on which the massive Commons majority is constructed. The second term has been dominated by Blair's determination to join Bush in his war in Iraq. In this part of the book, I have quoted extensively from the diary I kept at the time. I have reflected upon whether it is right to reveal these accounts of private meetings and conversations, and have decided that what happened in Iraq is so serious that people are entitled to know how we got there. In addition, No. 10 provides accounts to the media of private meetings and exchanges when it suits them to do so, and has therefore opened up these questions for public discussion.

Chapter 5 tells the story of how I was persuaded to remain in the government despite the failure to obtain UN authorisation for war; and of my efforts to build international support for the reconstruction of Iraq. It also shows how the promises Tony Blair made to me on a UN lead on reconstruction and the implementation of the 'Road Map' to the establishment of a Palestinian state were not fulfilled – and, it seems, were not sincerely meant. Chapter 6 covers my resignation and the arguments over foundation hospitals and top-up fees, as well as the findings of the Hutton and Butler reports.

The title of the book comes from my reflections in this period. I was asked in June 2003, when giving evidence to the Foreign

Affairs Committee inquiry into the decision to go to war in Iraq, whether I thought the Prime Minister had deceived me, the Cabinet and Parliament deliberately, or on the basis of wrong information. I said then that the Prime Minister 'must have concluded that it was honourable and desirable to back the US in military action in Iraq, and that it was therefore honourable for him to persuade us through the various ruses and devices he used to get us there, so I presume he saw it as an honourable deception'. This argument mirrors the claims of good faith made by the No. 10 machine after the Butler Report made clear that the intelligence on Iraq had been misused and exaggerated in Prime Ministerial statements to the House of Commons, and in the notorious dossier of September 2002. Butler said at his press conference that 'we have no reason, found no evidence, to question the Prime Minister's good faith'. We were thereafter constantly told that whatever Butler said did not matter, because there was 'good faith'. The Prime Minister himself said that the Butler Report showed that government and intelligence services acted 'in good faith'. He went on to tell the House of Commons, 'For any mistakes made, as the report finds, in good faith, I of course take full responsibility, but I cannot honestly say that I believe that getting rid of Saddam was a mistake at all. Iraq, the region, the wider world, are better and safer places without him.'

The question we must all address is whether it is acceptable for the Prime Minister to deceive us in the making of war and the taking and sacrificing of human life because he personally believed it was the right thing to do. Do we want to live under a constitutional system that allows decisions to be made in this highly personalised way? And although the Prime Minister constantly insists that his policy has been beneficial because it has removed Saddam Hussein from power, there are few serious people who accept that the region and the wider world are better and safer as a consequence of the war and its aftermath. In Iraq, relief at the removal of Saddam Hussein has turned sour in the killing and chaos of occupation. The polling evidence shows that a majority of Iraqis, who are overwhelmingly pleased that Saddam has gone, believe the invasion has done more harm than good. The Coalition Provisional Authority's own polling, leaked in May 2004, showed that 92 per cent of those surveyed saw the coalition forces as occupiers, and 55 per cent believed they would feel safer if those forces left immediately.

My final chapter outlines the way forward. I argue that the world is in considerable trouble and that without a change of policy, the Middle East will continue to burn with anger and al-Qaeda continue to strengthen. I suggest that a change in UK policy on the Middle East would leave the US isolated at a time when it needs allies and could therefore help change US policy, and bring about both the establishment of a Palestinian state and a handover in Iraq that could lead to a period of progress in the region. As I write, the outcome of the US presidential election is unknown and the US electorate almost evenly divided. Whatever the result, a change in US policy towards Israel and the Palestinians is essential to progress in the Middle East. If there is no change, we are almost certainly looking ahead to decades of bloodshed.

The rest of the chapter calls for a reassessment of UK and EU foreign policy in order to build a multilateral system based on a commitment to justice and fair rules as the only way to govern the post-Cold War world. I also call for a renewed focus on the need to reduce poverty and instability and the loss of environmental resources if we are to prevent catastrophic turmoil in the years to come.

My conclusion is that the major errors made by both the Thatcher and Blair governments flow from a spirit of hubris that develops from big majorities in the House of Commons which do not reflect the balance of opinion in the country. These exaggerated majorities and the tradition of party loyalty have led to a weakening of Cabinet government and a marginalisation of Parliament. The most urgent reform needed to improve our constitutional arrangements is a change to our electoral system. A balance of representation in the Commons which reflected public opinion would mean that governments could not take Parliament for granted, and would have to consult and listen in order to win support. This would reinstate the authority of Parliament and the Cabinet and prevent the system of personalised decision-making that has led to so many serious errors. Labour fought the 1997 election on a promise of a referendum on proportional representation, but the promise was not kept. The Labour leadership is unlikely to embrace electoral reform in the future because the electoral system is now massively biased in Labour's favour. This helps explain Blair's unwillingness to adjust his attitude or policies after very bad results in the 2004 local and European elections and in the by-elections in Leicester South and Birmingham Hodge Hill.

There is no immediate solution available to the problems we face. The likelihood is that Labour will win the next election and Blair will continue with his current policies. But this is not inevitable. The future is a matter of will and choice. I know many lifelong Labour voters and former party members who are voting Liberal Democrat to try to bring in a hung Parliament and a Labour–Lib Dem coalition. They calculate that this is the best way to win a change of policy in the Middle East, a commitment to electoral reform and a renewal of the Labour Party. Those of us who are unwilling to abandon the Labour Party have an urgent duty to organise to restore its integrity and to reinstate its traditional values in relation to both international and domestic policy. I take the view that it would be easier to make this change if Blair could be persuaded to step down, but whether he steps down now or later, the reclaiming for the Labour Party of the values for which it has always proudly stood is an urgent necessity. The country does not want Conservative values and is unwilling to express its disgruntlement with New Labour by voting Conservative. But many New Labour policies are indistinguishable from those of the Conservative Party and the country lacks an electoral vehicle to obtain what it seems to want, which is a government committed to social justice and the rule of law, at home and overseas. It is a terrible irony that at a time when the country is moving firmly towards social democratic values, New Labour is moving in a different direction.

I hope that this book will contribute to the growing debate as to how we can put right what has gone so terribly wrong, and restore the effectiveness of our constitutional system and the honour of our country.

I

THE YEARS OF OPPOSITION:
1983–97

Getting into politics

I was elected to Parliament to represent Birmingham Ladywood in 1983, at the age of thirty-seven. I was determined to try to help make the world a better place. My politics were very strongly shaped by my family and childhood.

I was born and grew up in my constituency. I am the second of seven children. My mother is the great-granddaughter of Thomas O'Loughlin, who came to Birmingham from County Clare in the 1840s to escape the Irish famine. The city gave us work and education and a strong sense of community. For all of this, my family love our city and its history of welcoming incomers and embracing the diversity of its people. My father came from Crossmaglen in Northern Ireland. He was the eldest boy of eleven children and, like many eldest sons in Irish families, destined to be a priest. He decided the priesthood was not for him and came to England to train as a teacher. He caught TB teaching in the East End, joined the Navy because the doctor said he needed a cruise, read widely and saw a lot of China before and during the Communist revolution. He then came to Birmingham to teach, and met and married my mother.

He was a dedicated teacher and a father we loved and admired. He minded greatly about the partition of Ireland, which happened when he was seventeen, and was deeply critical of Britain's colonial history. My father's school served a poor community and I can remember him rushing off at weekends to try to rescue families that had been evicted on to the streets, because in those days housing was in such short supply that rooms were rented out to whole families without any security of tenure. My mother was and is a deeply loving and caring person, with a deep religious commitment. She is the daughter of a toolmaker who was an active trade unionist and, in between caring for seven of us, she worked as a book-keeper and was a community and Labour Party activist. We grew up with a natural commitment to social justice and support for the Labour Party as the instrument of advance. We had a happy, noisy Catholic childhood. We played in the street, got on with our neighbours, and in the good years went to Ireland for our holidays where we swam in the sea, roamed in the fields and met up and bonded with our cousins.

My interest in politics and decision to become a politician came from a desire to care for people and make life fairer. These values came from my parents. We were brought up to try to help people and make the world more just. None of my sisters and brothers has stood for elected office but all have similar values and an engagement in politics as a way of making the world fairer. Most of my cousins are the same. My political values are basically deeply embedded family values, and my father's international view of the world was always part of that reality. I remember the Suez crisis when I was ten and having to explain to classmates that Nasser was entitled to nationalise the Suez Canal. But I also remember the awfulness of the Russian invasion of Hungary the same year. My father stuck on the wall a picture of a weeping boy beside a tank. I can still recall the excitement and enthusiasm we felt when Ghana became independent in 1957 – the signal that the colonial era was coming to an end.

I decided to study political science at university because that was what interested me – moral and political philosophy, sociology, economics, international relations and political history. I had no idea what job this would lead to, but found the subjects immensely interesting and enjoyed my years of study very much. This was part of the joy of those times, learning for learning's sake – most of us worked hard and I learned an enormous amount. I lived on my grant, worked in the holidays, and like most of that 1960s generation felt that my university education was a great privilege and that I should try to give something back to society in return for what I had been given.

I did not involve myself in student politics. I went to the occasional meeting when notorious politicians from the Monday Club visited. This led to demonstrations against their racist views. I shared the objection but didn't like the semi-violent protests. Jack Straw was President of the Student Union when I was at Leeds. The only memory I have of him then was proudly reading out telegrams of congratulation when Leeds students organised a sit-in following the example of LSE where, if I remember correctly, evidence had been found that the administration was keeping political files on the students. I went to have a look at the Leeds sit-in and found a hundred or so students sitting on the floor outside the library. I was not impressed – a university keeping files on the political opinions of students is a serious matter, but the sit-in in Leeds was purely imitative and it fizzled out after a day or two.

I did involve myself in Labour Party politics and joined the local party in Chapeltown, which was in Keith Joseph's constituency. I spent some months during the summer of 1970 working in Leeds North East in the General Election. We had a very enthusiastic campaign and were convinced we had a good chance of defeating a Conservative Cabinet minister, but instead, on election night, we shared the misery of so many Labour Party workers who had no idea that Harold Wilson was set to lose and Edward Heath take over in Downing Street.

After university, I took the exams to enter the Civil Service. I had no intention of spending my life as a bureaucrat, but was very keen to go and have a look at the British establishment at work. I worked in the Home Office from 1970 to 1975. The Assistant Principal grade was seen as a training grade, leading to promotion to the Senior Civil Service. My first job was in Prison Planning, when the prison population reached the all-time high of 40,000. The size of the prison population was causing deep concern. I was engaged in long-term prison planning and reviewing the experiments there had been with various prison regimes. I became a visitor at a Pentonville pre-release scheme and also visited and was very impressed with the therapeutic regime at Grendon Underwood. But the research was clear that, whatever the regime, prison did not rehabilitate and was a very expensive way of making it more likely that people would re-offend. I can only imagine what my bosses in those days would make of us reaching a prison population of as much as 80,000 just thirty years later.

I then moved on to the Criminal Department, reviewing the law on vagrancy and street offences. For this I hunted out old files and found one where a school teacher had got into trouble and gone to prison. He wrote an eloquent and beautifully handwritten letter to the then Home Secretary, Winston Churchill, about how the prisons were training camps for young criminals. And in those days, the Home Secretary saw and read the letter and commented on how important it was. I am afraid that today a letter from a member of the public would not get to a junior minister, let alone the Home Secretary.

After that I went to the Immigration Department during the Ugandan Asian crisis when Robert Carr, as Home Secretary, stood by our obligations to the Ugandan Asians who were expelled by Idi Amin and had been given a promise of entitlement to come to Britain at the time of Uganda's independence. This generated an enormous quantity of abusive, racist mail and I worked in a special unit to deal with ministerial correspondence.

My next job was Private Secretary to Mark Carlisle, the Minister of State responsible for the criminal departments. He was a decent man and we got on very well. It was during this time that we had the miners' strike and the three-day week. I still remember, almost nostalgically, the power cuts which brought London into darkness, so that I had to find my way out of the old Home Office in Whitehall, lit with hurricane lamps, back to my flat in Clapham lit with candles. As the days went on, the government started to crumble and Mark Carlisle would sit in his room with his Parliamentary Private Secretary, Alan Haselhurst (now Sir Alan and Deputy Speaker) and, for the first time, we had political conversations. Edward Heath called an election in February 1974, and the people decided to return a Labour government without an overall majority. During the campaign, we had sat in the private office waiting for the outcome, silent and almost paperless. The only documents that were circulated were the manifestos of the major parties.

My new minister was Alex Lyon and the new Home Secretary Roy Jenkins – the recidivist Home Secretary, as he joked. Alex had responsibility for the Criminal Department and Immigration. It was the immigration work that was the most onerous. At this time, the wives and children of the workers who had been recruited from India, Pakistan, Bangladesh and the Caribbean in the 1950s and 1960s were trying to join their menfolk. The climate generated by Enoch Powell and those who followed him was nasty, and there were more and more obstacles to family reunion. Alex was determined to use his authority to get families reunited, but this meant he had to take on the ever-cautious department and read all the details of vast numbers of family cases. He worked enormously hard at this and brought a lot of happiness to many people. I came to respect him very much, he was a man of complete honesty who was committed to making life fairer, especially for those who suffered most. We became entangled, then broke off the relationship, but we came together again and married in 1982.

I was promoted after private office to become a Principal in the Urban Deprivation Unit set up by Robert Carr to try to work out why there were such deep levels of deprivation in the inner city. Good work was done in the unit, the most important being an analysis of census information which showed that there was a concentration of deprivation in the inner city but, on every indicator, more deprived people living elsewhere. Thus the basic problem was inequality rather than a special feature of the inner city. This was not a particularly welcome finding. Later, the work of the unit was rightly transferred to the Department of the Environment, but I had decided it was time to bring my bureaucratic career to an end, return to Birmingham and work more closely with local people.

For the next few years I worked as the Director of a community organisation based in Handsworth called AFFOR (All Faiths for One Race). It had been established by representatives of all the different faiths in Birmingham coming together to combat racism. We worked against the rising tide of electoral support for the National Front and also to combat some of the terrible abuse young black people were receiving from the police. I became involved with the then Chief Constable, Sir Philip (now Lord) Knights, in trying to change this and move the West Midlands police to a new style of community policing. I also established advice sessions for families who were divided by the working of the immigration rules and wrote a handbook on immigration law for community advisers. People still approach me in Birmingham to remind me of those days and to introduce young members of their families who they say would not have been here if we had not succeeded in reuniting their family.

I continued to be active in local Labour Party politics. Brian Walden was my local MP and tried to block my transfer into the tiny local party. He did not know me and I had already served on national Labour Party advisory committees, helping to draw up Labour Party policy. I suspect he thought anyone under thirty was potentially dangerous. It was in this period that Roy Jenkins stood down from his Stechford seat to become the President of the European Commission. I worked in the by-election, but clashed with the party hierarchy when the National Front planned a march in an area of the constituency which had a substantial Asian population. We were determined to show our support for local people. In the end there wasn't violence as the party had feared, but the seat, which had a large Labour majority, was lost to the Conservatives.

In 1979 I was appointed Director of Youthaid, a campaign and pressure group focused on combating youth unemployment which was rising steadily. We undertook research and campaigned for better provision for the young unemployed. It was in this period that I first met Peter Mandelson. He was Chair of the British Youth Council and Youthaid was housed in a different part of the same building. He was very annoyed when I was invited to represent youth organisations on the Special Programmes Board of the Manpower Services Commission. The Board was thought to be prestigious because it supervised all special programmes for the unemployed and included representatives of government, business, training and education and the TUC. Mandelson badly wanted the job and went to great efforts to replace me. I resisted and he failed. I used to say later, if only the Labour Party had resisted his blandishments in the same way, it would be much happier and in better shape! As unemployment continued its relentless rise, we established the Unemployment Unit which had both a charitable and a non-charitable arm. This meant we were free to comment on the underlying causes of the rise in unemployment, which were of course economic and political.

I had continued to be active in local Labour politics in Clapham and then Battersea and was beginning to think I would like to put myself forward to possibly be selected as a parliamentary candidate. It had been whilst I was working in the Home Office that I had first formed the idea that I would like to be an MP. As a Private Secretary I worked with ministers of successive parties. This would involve going to the House of Commons to provide back-up to my minister for debate, question time and in committee stages of Bills. When I saw the kind of people that were MPs, I realised that someone like me could become one. I was a member of the Labour Party and strongly committed to social justice at home and abroad and realised I might be able to stand for election and commit my life to working for these values. Alex Lyon, who became my partner and then husband, supported and encouraged me very strongly.

The most difficult step was to actually say this was what I wanted. I felt somehow ashamed of the ambition. But the Labour Party had a system for local parties to nominate individuals as suitable MP material, and when I tentatively put my name forward to my local party in Battersea, they interviewed me and gave me a strong endorsement. Following that, my name was put on a list that was circulated and I received invitations to selection conferences in two or three seats, including Bermondsey on the famous occasion when Peter Tatchell became the Labour candidate and Labour lost a previously rock-solid seat to the Liberals. But my real dream was to represent Handsworth, the place where I was born and grew up and where my parents lived. And then Sheila Wright, who was an old family friend, announced that she would not stand for Parliament again and a selection began in Handsworth. I was lucky in all of this. Some of the big Labour names, who had lost their seats in 1979 when Mrs Thatcher swept to power, sniffed at the seat, but realising it would be affected by boundary changes, decided to stay away. Rudy Narayan, the flamboyant Guyanese barrister, showed an interest, but got into trouble for offering inappropriate hospitality, and at the end of the process I won the selection with a large majority. It was not long after that a date for the boundary changes to be implemented was announced and this meant the candidates for Ladywood and Handsworth had to compete for the support of the new Ladywood. The candidate for Ladywood was Albert Bore, now Sir Albert Bore and former Leader of Birmingham Council. He had been selected in an unpleasant clash with the sitting MP, and the result was that the mainstream members divided between us and those who had supported the previous MP came to me and I won fairly easily.

Then suddenly the election date was announced. We had to work very hard to get organised. The Conservative Party put up a well-heeled Asian candidate thinking that the Asian community would vote for an Asian. We had an old-fashioned rally in Birmingham Town Hall to launch the campaign with Michael Foot, our leader, and I spoke as the local candidate. After a whirlwind campaign, I was elected.

It was with no triumphalism that I entered the House of Commons. My husband Alex Lyon lost his seat in York, which he had held for seventeen years, and I was therefore well aware of how badly Labour had done. I was elected the same year as Gordon Brown and Tony Blair. In that election, Labour polled 27.6 per cent of the vote compared to the Tories' 42.4 per cent and the Liberal/SDP Alliance 25.4 per cent. This was the election after the Falklands war, the economy was improving and Labour was seen as being under the thumb of the 'loony left'.

I come from the mainstream Labour tradition. I have always been a person of strong and passionate commitment to equality and justice at home and abroad, but I had never been a member of any party other than the Labour Party. I was proud of the way the Attlee government had created a new settlement after the Second World War bringing full employment, the independence of India, the welfare state and growing educational opportunities. I saw these values as being most alive on the left of the Labour Party where there was still a passionate demand for change. I wanted to make our own society and the world more just and decent. But I was never tempted by revolutionary politics. I believed in elections and reform and that people knew what they wanted and should be consulted about what was to be done.

Early years in Parliament

I became active in Parliament, clashing early on with Alan Clark when he came to the Chamber with his first ministerial duty which he was highly embarrassed to find was an equal opportunities order. He had obviously had a few drinks and was reading his script for laughs. I objected and told the Speaker that I knew we weren't allowed to say another Member was drunk, but there did seem to be a problem. I learned my first lesson of press reporting from this incident. They all wrote that I wrongly accused the minister of being drunk. He had issued a rebuttal, in terms that seemed to me to amount to an admission. It said that anyone who knew him, knew he did not frequent the bars of the House of Commons. He later admitted he had been involved in some plentiful wine tasting. But of course it wasn't the wine I objected to, it was that he was making a joke of his duties in the House and making it clear by the tone that he adopted that he did not believe in the equal opportunities order he was introducing.

One advantage of coming to Parliament in such a bad year was that we could get up and speak whenever we wanted. I spoke frequently in the Chamber, worked hard in committees and like others took every possible opportunity to challenge a government that was causing great hurt among my constituents. I remember being horrified at the fawning attitude Tory MPs adopted to their ministers and particularly to the Prime Minister. I was completely astonished, after 1997, when many Labour MPs behaved in the same way. And when I returned to the back benches in 2003, I found how different it is to sit on the government side in a House with a large majority. Opportunities to speak are fewer, time is limited and the expectation is that government MPs will do the Whips' bidding and cravenly support the government.

I also worked hard in my constituency and have found my constituency work a deeply fulfilling part of being an MP. I set up regular advice bureaux in each area of the constituency and publicised my availability throughout the area. Before long, large numbers of people would come to see me. I found these sessions strangely inspiring. It used to be fashionable for MPs to say they were not there to be social workers, but over my twenty-one years in Parliament I have seen tens of thousands of people who have come to me with their problems and I have learned a lot from them. They have come from every community, men and women of all ages and ethnicities. Almost always they have tried their best to resolve their problem but come up against unhelpful or unresponsive systems. And thus I have been able to use the power of the office, which they gave to me by voting for me, to sort out many tangles and insist on my constituents being treated with respect and getting the services that were rightly theirs. Of course, you cannot win them all, some people make unreasonable demands and some people with mental health problems are strongly attracted to contacting their MP, but over the years I have learned where the problems are and what needs fixing by following the changes and shifts in the problems brought to me at my advice bureaux.

I suspect that when people think of politics and politicians, they rarely focus on the constituency work and yet this is the most human part of the job that keeps you going when the overall politics are disappointing. There is a constant string of invitations to visit schools, businesses, community groups, hospitals, colleges and the enormous range of groups and organisations that are a great strength of a society like ours. This is what the now fashionable term 'civil society' means. We did not realise what it was until we looked at the post-Communist societies and realised they had none of it. They used to live in a system where the state controlled absolutely everything. In Britain there are clubs and groupings large and small in every corner of our land, and they speak for and provide services and enjoyment for people throughout the country. Some receive public funding, most do not, but they are crucial to a healthy, democratic society and have lots to teach politicians who are willing to listen. At constituency level, being an MP is a wonderful learning experience as people invite you in and explain to you how their organisation works, what they think and how things could be done better.

Similarly, MPs get invited to visit foreign parts. There is much cynicism in media commentary about MPs 'tripping' and maybe some of the invitations do lead to self-indulgent journeying. But I remember one of my early visits in 1988 with Mo Mowlam and Maria Fyfe to the West Bank and Gaza during the first *intifada* – when the Palestinians rose up in a campaign of civil disobedience, general strikes and street protests against the continuing Israeli occupation of their lands. The Israeli army responded with considerable violence. We visited many hospitals and saw children with terrible injuries, but they were full of a sense of hope and expectation that they were going to liberate their country. I still have pictures of those children and have stayed close to the Palestinian question ever since.

So there I was in 1983, a new Member of Parliament, keen for work but with no illusions about how badly the Labour Party had done in the 1983 elections and how much work there was to do to get Labour into shape. I was determined to do all I could to ensure that we would win an election and start to repair the damage that Mrs Thatcher's governments had done to so many communities across our land.

Reforming the Labour Party

There is no doubt that Labour was in very poor shape in 1983. Urgent reform was needed, most importantly to end the infiltration of Trotskyist groups into the party, which was the major explanation of impossibilist demands, constant pressure to de-select sitting MPs and nasty attacks on any figure in a position of leadership. Looking back, it is fairly easy to diagnose the nature of the problem and the cure, but at the time, it was much more difficult to understand what had gone wrong.

The Labour Party's gut instincts are to believe deeply in social justice, a fair chance for everyone to work in decent conditions, to have access to good education and training, health care and transport. We are proud of the post-war settlement established by the Labour government which brought Britain to full employment, founded the National Health Service and created the Welfare State. And most of us believe that the Wilson and Callaghan governments made further advances and stood by our values in difficult times. Labour people also have a passionate commitment to equality of opportunity and a proud record on bringing in legislation to outlaw race and sex discrimination which was opposed by the Tories at the time.

On foreign policy, Labour negotiated the independence of India and thus began the dismantling of the Empire. The 1945 government also worked for the establishment of a strong United Nations, a World Bank and IMF that would prevent the world economy falling into a depression like the 1930s ever again, and also the establishment of Nato, an alliance committed to preventing the Soviet Union expanding by force in Europe. Labour has also, since the days of Harold Wilson, had a strong commitment to International Development, a more just world order where the poorest countries are given the chance to improve the life opportunities of their people.

All of these are core Labour values, but Labour also has a strong libertarian tradition. We were not communists. After the terrible suffering of the 1930s, many people on the left joined the Communist Party, but the Labour tradition was different. We believed in free elections and the rule of law. We wanted to create a more just society with the support of the people and not on their behalf. Similarly, we believed in a mixed economy and not in the Soviet model of public ownership. The 1945 government had nationalised the coal mines and the railways because they had been so run down and were so lacking in investment that they needed rescuing. Like other countries we thought it right that the utilities – gas, electricity, telephones and water – should be in public ownership because they were monopolies and crucial to basic wellbeing. We argued about where the line should be drawn between public and private ownership, but people committed to Labour tradition believe in a mixed economy.

Labour has, in recent years, been stereotyped as though we were a party supporting Soviet economics, the loony left, intransigent unions and pacifism. Such claims, deliberately designed to undermine and create a false impression, have tended to be reinforced by New Labour spin which constantly stresses the strength of the leader by suggesting he has whipped an impossible party into shape. In fact, Labour's record includes resistance to Franco and Hitler when many Tories were appeasing and collaborating. The core of Labour values is an ethical commitment to the equal value of every human being and a duty to organise politically to try to protect and enhance the rights of all people at home and internationally. This is what we mean by socialism and many of us had a devotion, comparable to a religious commitment, to love and work for the Labour Party in order to bring these values into being.

The job of the reformers from 1983 on was to re-establish Labour's values, update them for the present era and eject from the party those who came from a different ideological position and were misusing the democracy of the Labour Party. In 1983 there were two jobs that needed doing. One was to sort out the substance of Labour's problems, to update our policy thinking and our organisation; the other was to sort out our image. It was the Labour Party led by Kinnock and then Smith that attended to the substance and New Labour, led by Tony Blair, Gordon Brown and Peter Mandelson that sorted out the image. There is no question that our image needed improving but, as John Smith used to say, you don't ask your advertising agency what product you should sell. Your product is soap powder or beans and then you set out to make it as attractive as possible. What happened with New Labour was that appearances became more important than reality, presentational considerations dominated decision-making, and the obsession with spin led to a culture that was economical with the truth.

But back in 1983, Neil Kinnock, the newly elected leader with a deep and personal commitment to Labour's history and values, inherited a dysfunctional party. There was much on his plate. The Militant Tendency – an organised Trotskyist group with its own structure, policies and discipline – had infiltrated the party and was working with the energy of a religious sect to take over constituency after constituency. By 1983 they had two MPs in the House of Commons – Dave Nellist from Coventry and Terry Fields from Liverpool – and both were hard-working and likeable. Militant had also taken over Liverpool City Council and was determined to extend its control throughout the Labour Party. There were other Trotskyist groups in the party, the International Marxist Group which later became known as Socialist Action was strong in my own constituency party and there were other groupings elsewhere. They were difficult to deal with because they attracted committed zealots. They would take up popular causes – anti-apartheid or anti-racism or a minimum wage – and then advocate radical solutions which they saw as transitional demands, demands that sounded attractive but couldn't be met by feasible reform and thus seek to draw people into revolutionary politics by stealth.

When Neil Kinnock denounced Militant in Liverpool at the 1985 Bournemouth Conference 'hiring taxis to scuttle round a city handing out redundancy notices' he did not win praise from all sides. Other people – including David Blunkett in Sheffield and Ken Livingstone at the GLC – were also committed to resisting rate-capping and setting unattainable budgets. Action against Militant was denounced as a witch hunt and the libertarian in many of us hated the idea. But Neil was brave enough to give the lead and set up an inquiry into the shenanigans in Liverpool and over time, more and more of us began to understand that the Labour Party was and always should be a broad church but it had to have walls, and the walls were a commitment to democratic politics, reform and truthfulness.

At the same time, Neil Kinnock had the miners' strike to deal with, a bitter dispute that lasted from 1984 to 1985 where Mrs Thatcher was determined to break the miners and the miners were very badly led by the intransigent Arthur Scargill who refused to call a ballot for strike action, even though it would have been won. It was this that led to a bitter split in the union that weakened the action. For months the news was dominated by pictures of violent clashes on picket lines and Neil Kinnock, who came from a mining family himself, denounced the violence, but was called a traitor for doing so. I got myself into hot water by signing visitors' tickets for a group of miners who visited the House of Lords and then demonstrated their anger by shouting from the visitors' gallery. The then Chief Whip, Michael Cocks, denounced me in the media but we reached agreement that I would apologise if he would say he had sympathy with the miners' cause. MPs like me joined the demonstrations and were invited to speak at meetings and fundraising events in support of the miners and therefore briefed ourselves on the state of the coal industry and cause of the dispute. I understood clearly the industry was facing considerable change and that Arthur Scargill was the alter ego of Margaret Thatcher. Both of them seemed to relish the clash, but it was the miners and their families who suffered the consequences and made heroic sacrifices during the strike, winning nothing in return. I was not one of those who saw Arthur Scargill as a hero. I am afraid that he put his ego before his duty to protect the interests of his members, and I was shocked to read the Lightman report, commissioned by the NUM after the strike to investigate allegations that he and others in the leadership had used NUM funds to purchase and improve their houses during the strike. I bought a copy of the report from Kevin Barron, who had been a miner before he came to the Commons. He was disciplined by Scargill for daring to distribute it.

The miners' strike was followed by another bitter industrial dispute, between the Murdoch press and the print unions, which lasted from 1985 to 1986. I went with others to join the picket in Wapping. Print workers and journalists were very angry at the way Murdoch's papers had managed the transfer to the new technologies. We all felt so strongly about Murdoch's brutality that we encouraged Neil Kinnock to refuse to talk with representatives of the Murdoch papers, an unthinkable position for later New Labour leaders who put relations with the media above all other relationships. But we also understood that technological change cannot be boycotted. The issue in the Thatcher years was not whether or not to change, but how it was to be managed. Thatcher's methods were brutal. The job of a decent government is to assist and civilise the management of change so that people can adapt without getting hurt. Most of us felt that the Labour Party had let down the country by its inability to defeat Thatcher and protect people from the terrible levels of unemployment and cuts in public services that were experienced during her time in office.

1987 election

As the 1987 election approached, Thatcher's government had been damaged by the resignation of Michael Heseltine and Leon Brittan, and in May 1986, the *Guardian* average of five recent polls put Labour six points ahead. This was the last General Election in which local Labour parties arranged meetings where visiting politicians and the local candidate spoke and answered questions. After 1987 modern campaigning took over. It focuses on photo opportunities and diminishes discussions. I feel that this change is a big loss to democracy. The only meetings left that provide an opportunity for open discussion are those convened by the Churches, to which they invite all candidates. However, in 1987 Kinnock's reform efforts – and a slick election campaign starring a very attractive film about

Neil Kinnock made by Hugh Hudson – produced a small advance for Labour to 30.8 per cent with the Tories at 42.2 per cent and the Liberal/SDP Alliance at 22.6 per cent. This was clearly an improvement on 1983, but Labour gained only 20 seats and the conclusion for all was that elections had to be won in years not months.

I was elected to the National Executive Committee (NEC) in 1988 along with Margaret Beckett. In those days, the NEC was a major power in the party that supervised the development of policy and the administration of the Labour Party in all its aspects. I was honoured to serve for nearly ten years and to help carry through the reforms that brought Labour to power. I stood down in 1997 as we entered government, when under Tony Blair's reforms he determined who represented the government on the NEC and it ceased to be such a significant power in the party. I am proud to have been one of the team that supported Neil Kinnock and John Smith in preparing the party for power. It was the NEC that undertook a review and updating of all our policy and also had the unattractive but necessary task of expelling the Militant MPs from the Labour Party. It is worth noting here that the trade union representatives on the NEC were a major force in helping support reform and nurturing the party back to health. There has been so much spin against the trade union influence in the party, it has left a deeply misleading impression about the pragmatic and reforming role the trade unions have played over the years. There has also been a lot of rewriting of history which suggests that there was no significant reform until Tony Blair and New Labour took over. This is simply untrue.

In Parliament, I had decided, along with a number of other MPs on what became known as the soft left, to join both the Campaign Group where Tony Benn, Eric Heffer and Audrey Wise had starring roles, and the Tribune Group which had deep links back to Aneurin Bevan, Michael Foot, Neil Kinnock and the traditional left of the party. We worked to try to overcome the splitting and bitterness that had characterised the period of Trotskyist infiltration. We saw the split on the left as destructive and unnecessary and thought that by joining both groups, we could work to bring the left back together. Like many others, I was an admirer of Tony Benn, but regretted his failure to work with Michael Foot after his narrow defeat in the contest with Denis Healey for the deputy leadership in 1981. A group of us, including Jo Richardson, Margaret Beckett and Paul Boateng, left the Campaign Group in 1988 when Tony Benn and Eric Heffer decided to challenge Neil Kinnock and Roy Hattersley for the leadership. We could see no point in the challenge. There had been an increase in authoritarianism in the leadership after Kinnock had taken on Peter Mandelson as one of his most influential advisers. But a leadership challenge was not the way to deal with the problem and we were not impressed by the tiny group that had decided to create the contest, despite its inevitable effect in strengthening the image of Labour as a divided party.

In this period I was active in Parliament first as a member of the Home Affairs Select Committee, and the sub-committee on Immigration and Race Relations. The strongest memory I have of the work of the Select Committee was our report on the Chinese community in Britain. It is a large community originating from Hong Kong but because it was engaged almost exclusively in catering, it was dispersed across the country and little recognised. We visited the Chinese community across the UK and even visited Hong Kong and went to villages from which our communities originated. The strong respect for ancestors had led to the building of fine houses in ghost villages with very few inhabitants. Robin Corbett, then MP for Erdington, and I took the opportunity to visit Communist China. We took a train over the border and found lots of citizens of Hong Kong taking holidays and letting off fireworks, which was banned in densely occupied Hong Kong. Our guide was a very interesting and intelligent woman who had been, to her regret, one of the 'little red guards' who travelled around China denouncing revisionists during the Cultural Revolution. She also had two children. We had interesting discussions on the causes of the Cultural Revolution, how the one-child policy worked and on the future of China. We saw the beginnings of the economic development zone just north of Hong Kong which was to lead on to enormous change in China as it embraced Western investment and achieved unprecedented economic growth and poverty reduction.

In 1985, John Prescott asked me to join his front-bench team on employment. He made the invitation after getting his library briefing on employment issues and finding copies of various publications I had produced whilst Director of Youthaid and the Unemployment Unit. During this time I led the Labour opposition to the Wages Bill which abolished the minimum wage system that had been brought in by Winston Churchill. I was called out of the Bill committee one day in March 1986 to be told my father had died. Ian Mikardo, who was a dear friend and a very experienced parliamentarian, took over my notes and moved my amendment, and I went home to meet up with my family and mourn the loss of our father.

Page 3

A few days later, I stood up in the Commons to introduce my ten-minute rule Bill to take pornographic pictures out of newspapers. I committed to this proposal in early 1986 when Winston Churchill, the then Tory MP for Davyhulme, and the grandson of the wartime leader, introduced an Obscene Publications Bill. It was a terrible Bill. It listed a series of images that would be treated as obscene whenever and wherever they were printed, a list which included scenes of horrific violence as well as a variety of descriptions of sexual activity. Its effect would have been to endanger much war reporting, many illustrations in medical textbooks and much sex education material. I responded with an unrehearsed speech opposing the Bill, but saying that we could introduce more tightly drawn legislation, for example, to remove the degrading images of women as available sex objects that were widely circulated in the mainstream of society through the tabloid press. The speech led to an avalanche of enthusiastic letters from women and my decision to introduce a Bill to remove such pictures from newspapers. This has led to a healthy debate about the difference between sexual openness and pornographic degradation, but also to a vicious campaign of vilification of me by the *Sun*.

This campaign was renewed with great vigour after I left the government in 2003. A woman journalist asked me at a lunch whether I was still opposed to Page 3. I said I was and this led to busloads of Page 3 girls parked outside my house all day in the hope of setting up embarrassing photos, and mock-up pictures of me as a very fat Page 3 girl. They even sent half-dressed people to the house I share with my 84-year-old mother in Birmingham and had people hiding in cars and chasing me down the street in an effort to get embarrassing photographs. I deal with such attacks by not looking at the paper, but it is oppressive to have a double-decker bus plastered with *Sun* posters outside the front door from seven in the morning. In the afternoon, I rang the police to ask whether traffic restrictions applied to the *Sun*, and they were eventually moved on. It is hard not to conclude that the *Sun* sets out to frighten anyone who might dare to agree that such pictures should be removed from newspapers. It was suggested to me after the *Sun*'s 2003 campaign by a Westminster journalist of long experience that the *Sun*'s attacks should be seen as an issue of Privilege, an attempt to bully and intimidate an MP to prevent them from raising issues in the House. The Clerk of the House, whom I consulted, agreed there was an issue to raise; however, the Speaker did not agree and I did not take it further.

My own conclusion about the Page 3 phenomenon, and the subsequent proliferation of pornographic-style images across the media, together with the offensive burden of offers of pornography and Viagra that have to be cleared daily from our email systems, is that we need to push back this ugly coarsening and degradation of our society. I bow to no one in my respect for John Stuart Mill's *On Liberty*, but I do not believe that inappropriate sexually provocative imagery, plastered across society, is an example of liberty. I also find it very sad that the degraded *Sun* has been courted so strongly and shown so many favours by Tony Blair and the spin merchants at No. 10.

Labour's policy review

Following the 1987 election, we organised a comprehensive review and update of all our policies. This was led by Neil Kinnock, but in those days the democratic culture of the Labour Party was still strong and changes of policy were carefully discussed and thought through and then brought to the National Executive Committee to be finalised. The most contentious was our commitment to Unilateral Nuclear Disarmament. This had been a great passion of Michael Foot, Neil Kinnock and many Labour Party members including the young Tony Blair. It is now depicted as romantic pacifism, but the party adopted the policy when the arms race was escalating, in order to demonstrate that a medium-sized country like the UK did not need nuclear weapons in order to be safe. However, when Neil Kinnock went to see Ronald Reagan to demonstrate that he could be treated as a future Prime Minister, he was snubbed over unilateralism. The agreement we reached at the end of the policy review, for which I and Robin Cook voted but David Blunkett opposed, was that in the changed world of Gorbachev and Reagan's disarmament agreements, Britain's weapons would be part of Start II multilateral disarmament negotiations. But we also made it clear that, if agreement were not reached, we would enter bilateral negotiations with other minor nuclear powers in order to try to secure significant disarmament in return for our willingness to disarm. Thus we stayed with our commitment to nuclear disarmament but gave up the unilateralist element in order to secure disarmament from others.

Here we have another example of appearance versus reality. Appearances were that we had crossed the rubicon and given up on nuclear disarmament. In fact, we refined our policy in an intelligent way. But the new policy was never implemented. Blair was not then a member of the NEC but by the time he became Prime Minister, the threat of nuclear conflict had receded and he wished to cut a dash on the world stage and therefore retain the UK's by now untargeted Trident weapons. The policy adopted in power contradicts the policy we put in place when we moved from unilateralism. In practice we have returned to the logic that countries need nuclear weapons to be recognised as significant powers. It is this logic that has led to India and Pakistan as well as Israel deploying nuclear weapons, Iran seeking to do likewise and thus to a process of proliferation. The US is now committed to an escalation by deploying a system of National Missile Defence in space which will destabilise the current balance. Tony Blair agreed to support this when he visited Bush for the first time in February 2001. This received little attention and the issue of the usefulness of UK nuclear weapons is for the time being almost a taboo subject, but given that the US will need modification at Fylingdales in order to deploy its National Missile Defence system, these questions will return to haunt us.

Major replaces Thatcher

As we approached the 1992 election, Labour was gradually looking in better shape and the Conservatives much weaker. Mrs Thatcher had been forced out of office in 1990 after the errors of the poll tax and the resignation of Geoffrey Howe. I still remember Geoffrey Howe's resignation speech. It was an enormously powerful moment, more dramatic than any other event I have witnessed in the House of Commons. Denis Healey said that being attacked by Geoffrey Howe was like being savaged by a dead sheep, but Howe's mild-mannered criticism had a devastating effect that day.

My advice bureaux reflected the unfairness of the poll tax, with constituents coming to me desperately worried and some even crying over their inability to pay. In a low-income area like Ladywood, many small houses contain large numbers of family members and the escalating costs were, for many families, quite terrifying.

The first Gulf War

John Major became Prime Minister in November 1990 and immediately faced the challenge of Saddam Hussein's invasion of Kuwait. Labour, like most of the international community, supported the coalition to eject Saddam Hussein from Kuwait, as did I, though I ended up resigning from the front bench when Neil Kinnock insisted that I should make no comment about the war. I had given an interview about the bombing of a bunker when large numbers of women and children had died. I had said that I was willing to believe that the US were unaware that it was anything other than a military target, but couldn't understand why so much of the infrastructure of Iraq was being targeted. I was called in to see Neil, along with Joan Ruddock, MP for Lewisham, Deptford and former Chair of CND. Both of us were junior front-benchers who had expressed some reservation about the war. He asked me to be totally silent on Iraq, although the tradition was that junior front-benchers in Opposition speak and ask questions on all subjects. I refused to agree and following my resignation spoke in the Iraq debate on 21 February 1991, setting out my view that Iraq's invasion of Kuwait must be reversed but that we would not settle the endless cycle of war in the Middle East until the US ceased to support Israeli breaches of international law which caused so much suffering and anger in the region. I argued that after Saddam Hussein had been driven out of Kuwait we 'should seek the removal of all non-conventional weapons – nuclear, chemical and biological – from Israel, Syria and Iraq. We should also settle the Palestinian issue by giving the Palestinians their state based on the West Bank and Gaza.' The fact that I resigned from the front bench over the first Gulf War is used as a reference point by commentators to suggest that I was soft on Saddam or perhaps of pacifist persuasion. I was neither. I had thought about becoming a pacifist in my early twenties because all war is clearly hateful and destructive, but in the early 1970s I was much engaged in supporting the people of Mozambique, Angola and Guinea in their struggle for independence and imagined what I would do if I was visiting and Portuguese troops killed one of my friends. I knew then that I would join the fightback. I would like to have been part of a world where pacifism was possible and admired those who chose that way to challenge war, however I believed the use of force was sometimes necessary, but should always be a last resort. I was clear that Saddam Hussein must be made to withdraw from Kuwait, but very worried about the general situation in the Middle East. My resignation was not opposition to the war as such, but to an attempt to prevent me speaking. I therefore spoke in the Commons after my resignation and set out my views.

This was my second resignation from Neil Kinnock's front bench. I had resigned in December 1988 over his handling of the vote on the renewal of the Prevention of Terrorism Act which was causing enormous feeling in the Irish community in Birmingham, where the harassment of young people of Irish origin acted more as a recruiting sergeant for terrorist organisations than a preventer of terrorism. Now that the fear of terrorism is again at the top of the agenda and legislation is being strengthened, it is very important that we go back and study our handling of Northern Ireland. It was widely judged that the early, over-aggressive enforcement of the Prevention of Terrorism Act ran the risk of increasing support for the Provisional IRA. Similarly, repressive action in Northern Ireland such as the introduction of internment without trial engendered stronger support for paramilitary organisations. Britain learned slowly that action against terrorism cannot rely solely on strengthened security. There needs to be a commitment to rooting out the causes of support for terrorism which means a commitment to right injustice alongside the security response. These lessons are being forgotten in the current response to al-Qaeda.

Alex, my husband, advised me not to resign over the Prevention of Terrorism vote because it would prevent me gaining more influence and thus being able to help deliver change. But I objected to the way the change in policy was bounced through without consultation and felt I had to make a stand because the shift in policy was designed to improve Labour's image rather than attend to the merits of the case. I had been in the box of civil servants advising ministers in the House of Commons the night the Prevention of Terrorism Bill was introduced as an emergency response eight days after the Birmingham pub bombing. I was therefore well aware that its provisions had not been carefully considered.

Obviously, resigning from the front bench in Opposition is less serious than resigning from government, but I have always wanted to be able to stand by my principles and serve my party in high office. I think it is important to have a bottom line otherwise there is a danger that principles are steadily eroded and you end up wanting power for power's sake rather than to help to carry your values into practice. Looking back, it is perhaps surprising that I was allowed to return to the front bench on three occasions, but I think Neil Kinnock and John Smith knew that my resignations were sincerely meant and were generous in inviting me back.

Despite our occasional tiffs, I continued to work closely with Neil on the National Executive Committee and I still have the kind and thoughtful letter he wrote to me after my second resignation. I remained supportive of his efforts to ready the party for power and after he became an EU Commissioner and Glenys an MEP, I saw them regularly when I visited Brussels as a Minister.

1992 election

Following the Gulf War and Major's replacement of the poll tax with the community charge, he negotiated the passage of the Maastricht Treaty through the House of Commons, despite frenzied hostility from his own party, and then called an election for 9 April 1992. Opinion polls showed a slight Labour lead, leading to a hung Parliament. Labour entered the election full of confidence. The campaign was fought on taxation and healthcare. John Smith produced a Shadow budget which was later blamed for its promise to bring in 50 per cent income tax for higher earners and increases in National Insurance to pay for improved pensions. This led to the Tories' posters on Labour's tax bombshell, and caused many to conclude that it was Labour's handling of tax that caused our defeat. But there was also much argument over the veracity of Labour's party political broadcast known as Jennifer's Ear, and the unattractiveness of Kinnock's triumphalism at the Sheffield rally. I did not attend the rally. It was one of the new-style rallies where crowds of party members are bused in to adore the leader. I love working as part of a team for a cause we have in common, but am really very bad at leadership adoration. I therefore declined my place on the platform and stayed in Birmingham contacting voters. Turnout in the election was 78 per cent – the highest in eighteen years. The Conservatives received 42 per cent of the vote, Labour 35 per cent and the Liberal Democrats 18 per cent. The Tory majority was reduced to 21 and the swing to Labour was 2.2 per cent, but the result was a massive disappointment to the Labour Party and Neil Kinnock resigned as leader.

On the morning of the poll, the *Sun* produced its headline, 'If Neil Kinnock wins today, will the last person to leave Britain please turn out the lights'. Some commentators thought this might have caused the late swing to the Tories and the *Sun* headline the next day was, 'It was the *Sun* wot won it'. Tony Blair seems to have accepted this and has assiduously courted the *Sun* ever since. Other informed commentators gave the *Sun* a much less important role.

John Smith's leadership

John Smith and Margaret Beckett were quickly elected leader and deputy leader to replace Kinnock and Hattersley. John was determined to drive on with Labour's reform agenda, but also to draw the Labour family together. He was not keen on Peter Mandelson's divisive style of spinning the tough qualities of the leader at the expense of the treasured values of the party. He therefore pushed aside Peter Mandelson and his spin/focus-group approach to politics and brought in a new team to run his office. He also asked me to return to the front bench as Shadow Minister for Women.

This did not mean that John was complacent. He pushed through the reform of Labour Party conference voting and parliamentary selection from block voting to one member, one vote. The original structure of Labour's conference, which was modelled on the Methodist conference, was a federation of affiliated organisations – Co-ops, Fabians, constituencies and unions – which cast their votes after their own democratic decision-making. But as the unions steadily amalgamated, many votes were concentrated in few hands, and this reform served both to overcome the appearance and the reality of the over-concentration of power. I was a member of the NEC sub-committee that reached agreement on this reform package. As we worked through this difficult issue, I got to know and like John Smith more and more. It was also on this committee that I had my first clash with Tony Blair. He had recently joined the NEC and appeared to be advocating a break in the link between the

Labour Party and trade unions by advocating that individual membership should be the only way of being represented in the party.

Alex Lyon's illness

I was called away from the 1993 conference by the news that my husband Alex Lyon was very ill and likely to die. Alex's illness, which was a form of Alzheimer's, had got steadily worse from 1980 onwards. The original diagnosis was that he would lose mobility but never lose any mental capacity. After losing his parliamentary seat, he moved from being a senior Labour MP to running my constituency office where he gave me enormous support as well as bringing great experience to the task. Later he decided to return to the Bar, but after a time got himself into various difficulties and I began to suspect that either he was suffering a deep depression or mental deterioration. The next few years were very difficult as he engaged in strange, inexplicable behaviour. He gradually fell out with family and friends and stayed home with our St Bernard called Fred and would deal with no one but Fred and me.

All of this was distressing enough, but it was also at this time that the West Midlands Serious Crimes Squad joined up with the *News of the World* in an attempt to smear me because of the role I had played in exposing corruption in the West Midlands Serious Crimes Squad and the large number of miscarriages of justice that they had organised. I decided to inform the House of Commons what the *News of the World* was up to before they printed their story. I then made formal complaints to the Police Complaints Authority and Press Complaints Commission. Both were upheld and the *News of the World* was required to print the adjudication in a full page of the paper. Thus I was vindicated, but having the *News of the World* crawling through my life was deeply unpleasant. It is at moments like this that I understand those who say they would not come into politics because of the risk of exposing themselves and their families to the gross intrusions of the press.

After Alex was diagnosed as suffering from dementia, I did my best to make his life comfortable. Our faithful dog was a great comfort to him but it was a terrible day when I had to take away his motor car because he had become a danger to himself and others. Dementia is a dreadful thing. Alex was in his early fifties when it began, but it means that the person you love and admire gradually dies in front of your eyes although a crumbling body remains alive. When he became a danger to himself, I had to search for a place to care for him and found an enormously kind and caring place in Newport Pagnell run by Methodist Homes. Shortly after he went to Westbury, he ceased to recognise me or Fred, but we continued to visit just in case. The care he was given was second to none.

As Alex became more physically frail, the local GP who looked after patients at Westbury spoke to me about his treatment. He said he would gradually become weaker as his internal muscles deteriorated and then he would catch pneumonia. The natural course would be to send him to hospital where he would be put on a drip, revived and sent back to Westbury. I said no, I wanted him to have treatment to ease any pain, but he should not be kept alive when the quality of his life was so poor. It was only a few months later at Conference that I received the call. Alex may not have recognised me, but after I arrived, he became much calmer. I made up a bed in his room and spent the week with him as he died in his bed with dignity. We were wonderfully supported by the staff at Westbury and the local Methodist Minister, who was a very kind and caring woman.

Alex was a good man, a dedicated Methodist, lifelong Labour Party member and a brave fighter for what he thought was right. I had learned a lot from him through our joint dedication to politics as a means to make the world more just. We discussed issues constantly and influenced each other's views, but Alex was more experienced and taught me a lot. He was also generous and totally supportive even when he lost his seat in 1983 and I won mine. He had been on the right of the party – strongly pro-Europe (when this was seen as a right/left issue) – a great fighter for racial equality, decolonisation and development. I shared many of his views and passions, yet was seen as being very much on the left, which demonstrates how misleading these labels often are. His illness had been devastatingly harsh but his death and funeral were dignified and moving and restored to friends and family memories of the real Alex.

Making the Labour Party women-friendly

John Smith was dedicated to making the Labour Party more women-friendly and selecting women candidates. By 1993 I had taken over from my dear friend Jo Richardson, the then MP for Barking, as Chair of the Labour Party Women's Committee, as well as being the Shadow spokesperson for women. I also regularly attended the Socialist International Women's meetings where I got to know leading women politicians from Social Democrat and Labour parties across Europe. The Scandinavians were the leading example. They had introduced quotas throughout their parties so that equal numbers of men and women held office at every level, including in Parliament. This had helped to bring renewal and new talent into politics and also was electorally beneficial. In Scandinavia, women voted Social Democrat more than Labour. In Britain, women had consistently voted more conservatively than men.

The question of women's representation in the party had been a cause of bitter division at the Women's Conference over many years. Joyce (now Lady) Gould was the Labour Party's Women's Officer and was very committed to stronger women's representation. She and I hoped that the Scandinavian model would help us to find a way through. In making progress we were greatly helped by the reforms that had been taking place in the trade union movement as they realised they could not continue with a male-dominated organisation seeking to represent a labour force made up equally of men and women. The support for quotas gradually gained ground. In 1989 the Conference had passed a resolution committing the Labour Party to follow the example of our sister parties across the world and introduce a quota so that men and women would share power equally at all levels.

The 1989 decision also committed us to ensure that the Parliamentary Labour Party would be 50 per cent women within ten years. This was the really contentious issue. The party had tried mechanisms to improve the selection of women, such as a requirement to have at least one woman on every short list, without success. But by 1993 the Women's Committee had concluded that we should pair vacant seats and have all-women short lists in 50 per cent of winnable seats. This proposal would not have been accepted without John Smith's support and strong backing from many trade union women, particularly Maureen Rooney and Brenda Etchells of the Amalgamated Engineering Union. This change was responsible for the big increase in women's representation on the Labour benches in 1997. When Tony Blair became leader, the policy was under attack. Advancing women's equality was seen as a left-wing, feminist agenda and Tony was trying not to irritate the *Daily Mail* and those who objected to positive action. He came near to dumping the women's quota on a number of occasions but my protestations and some very firm lobbying by women from all parts of the party managed to persuade him to leave the policy in place. I have no doubt that this brought great benefits and for the first time in our history we won a majority of women's votes in the election of 1997. At my last NEC meeting, where it is traditional for the leader to say some words of tribute, Blair said he had had his doubts about my strategy on women's representation but it had been proved right and had brought the party great benefits.

The conflict over women's representation and the resistance to change from those with ambition taught me how narrow is the channel of recruitment into politics. Activists come up through local party structures. A very small number nurture political ambitions. As party membership continues to decline, the recruitment base narrows and the quality of local councillors and MPs is likely to continue to deteriorate. The commitment to recruit more women opened the doors, but the present cynicism about party politics means that very few are willing to involve themselves and this means a real danger to the future quality of political representation. My conclusion was that as we tried to build a party that was more women-friendly, it led to changes that made the whole organisation more open and enabling. Sadly Tony Blair, despite the impressive increase in membership in his own party in Sedgefield, has not followed through on the plans for building a healthy party, which we worked hard on in the NEC. We were keen to draw a much wider range of people into the party, and to offer political education and training in how to chair meetings, speak and organise. We wanted to reach those who were willing to be school governors and magistrates, as well as potential councillors and MPs. We planned to renew the party and make it a means of empowering local people to become active politically and improve their community. We organised general political education events and very successful women's conferences which were a mixture of training, holding politicians accountable, and fun. I still meet women around the country who attended some of these conferences and remember them as a high point. But sadly such an open, enabling structure does not suit the top-down, control-freakery of New Labour and thus in many parts of the country the party is crumbling, and once proud regional officials are now required simply to fix things for the No. 10 machine.

Tragically, John Smith died of a heart attack in 1994. He had spoken the night before at a glittering dinner when he said memorably 'all we ask is the opportunity to serve'. I was at a Socialist International meeting in Tokyo when the news came through. It made me desperately sad and I felt very far from home. As I travelled back I started to think through our options for the next leader. John was a terrible loss. I have no doubt that he would have made a great Prime Minister and that his Labour government would have been a government of which we could have been truly proud. Immediately after the funeral and the striking sense of loss that was expressed across the country, the party had to organise an election to select a successor.

Blair becomes leader

The likely candidates were Robin Cook, Gordon Brown, Tony Blair, John Prescott and Margaret Beckett – who had been John Smith's deputy and became acting leader when he died. Robin Cook rang around but did not have the necessary support. Margaret Beckett was determined to run and I to support her. I had been friendly with Margaret and her husband Leo for many years and knew how able and competent she was. She had also been a very good deputy to John Smith and performed admirably when she had to step in as acting leader. She also made the point that if she had been a man with her years of experience and role of deputy and then acting leader, no one would have questioned that she should run for leader. I suppose if I am honest I knew she could not win, but I could not vote for Blair. I thought he was an asset to the party, but that he did not believe in Labour's values enough to be leader. John Prescott also made clear that he would run. He had run for deputy leader in 1988 and I had supported him. I still have the award badge he gave us pinned to my notice board – 'Prescott 88, who dares loses, went down smiling'. I don't think he ever forgave me for not supporting him in 1994. But these considerations were marginal because most of the shadow Cabinet were clear that they would support Brown or Blair.

Much has been written about how it was agreed that it should be Blair rather than Brown. Brown was unlucky. He had always been the senior partner in the relationship since they had come together through sharing an office in 1983. Brown was steeped in Labour history, intellectually strong and a strategic thinker. He had also shone in the House of Commons and in his various shadow Cabinet jobs. I think that the reason he lost out to Blair was that as a loyal shadow Chancellor to John Smith as leader, he had been very tough on the shadow Cabinet in stopping them from making spending commitments, and this had bruised many egos. Blair had recently come to greater prominence as shadow Home Secretary with his famous policy of 'tough on crime, tough on the causes of crime' which it is said was coined for him by his friend Gordon Brown. The upshot of their conversations was that the decision was made that Blair rather than Brown would run. Whether or not Blair had promised to hand over to Brown, we will never know for sure, but the election went ahead. Blair won with 57 per cent of the vote, John Prescott secured 24 per cent and Margaret Beckett 19 per cent. I helped to organise Margaret's campaign. She was widely admired but we had difficulty in getting enough MPs to nominate her. It was clear from the start that we could not win the leadership, but she, like John Prescott, ran for both the leadership and the deputy leadership and we did have some hope that she would become deputy. The election result was interesting. Many Labour members who did not particularly like Blair voted for him because he was seen as the most acceptable face, and the party was absolutely determined to do whatever was necessary to win. From the very start the Labour Party elected Blair as a leader who could win, but were aware that he had little affection for the party. Many people voted for Blair with Prescott as deputy to try to ensure that Blair's attractive presentational qualities were anchored to Labour values.

There was a big shift in tone and style after Blair replaced Smith. Smith had had an inner confidence and belief in Labour's values. He was extremely able, courageous in carrying through the reforms he felt were necessary but also keen to build on our history and nurture a spirit of mutual respect in the party. Those who later invented

New Labour like to suggest that we would not have won under Smith, but the party's internal polling showed us set to win, and in the Gallup Poll of May 1994, published shortly before John died, Labour was leading the Conservatives in voting intentions by 48 per cent to 24 per cent. Forty-nine per cent of the electorate were satisfied with Smith's leadership, and 49 per cent also thought Labour would win the next election. The advice of the experts was that Labour was set to win. It has been very important to the propagandists for New Labour to pretend that we would not have won the election under John Smith. All the objective evidence is that this claim is false.

There was a small group of party 'Modernisers' who did not share Smith's perspective. They were Tony Blair, Gordon Brown, Peter Mandelson and Philip Gould – later to come to prominence as Blair's pollster. This group – perhaps with the exception of Brown – consistently exaggerated the extent to which the Labour Party before Blair was committed to excessive state intervention, expanding public ownership and a party dominated by trade unions. Theirs was a very defensive project. They wanted to win at any price and were keen to dump any policy that did not prove popular in the polls. As time was to show, Blair did not have any clear ideas apart from a determination to win and to crush any Labour traditions that he thought might detract from that objective. They had learned the technique of 'triangulation' from Bill Clinton and the New Democrats. Triangulation involves deciding which is the left and the right position and placing oneself in the middle in order to maximise support. Blair has used this approach continuously. It tends to maximise popularity, but leads to badly thought-through policy.

Rewriting Clause IV

Blair's first move was the decision to rewrite Clause IV of the party's constitution. He announced this in a speech to the Labour Party conference in 1994. He called me, Robin Cook and others into his hotel suite the night before to tell us of his intention and obviously to try to defuse any criticism. This was again more presentational than real. The old Clause IV was seen almost as a poem by most Labour Party members. It stated that we would organise a Labour Party in the country and Parliament, co-operate with the TUC and other kindred organisations, give effect as far as possible to the principles approved at the party conference and 'secure for the workers by hand or by brain the full fruits of their industry and the most equitable distribution thereof that may be possible upon the basis of the common ownership of the means of production, distribution and exchange, and the best obtainable system of popular administration and control of each industry or service'. It also committed us to promote the political, social and economic emancipation of the people and to co-operate internationally and with the UN for the promotion of peace, defence of human rights and 'the improvement of the social and economic standards and conditions of work of the people of the world'. I had no intention of engaging in public criticism of the decision to initiate a review of Clause IV, but tended to feel that it was of little significance and not worth a great deal of effort. However, as the debate rolled through the party, some of the remnants of the Trotskyist infiltration, plus those with a romantic commitment to public ownership, made a case against change, based on a commitment to ever-widening public ownership that was simply unacceptable. I therefore helped with some amendments to the redraft and argued the case for change at the NEC. I received a handwritten thank you note from Tony, which is a nice habit he has. I have received quite a few of these over the years.

The change to Clause IV was an image and positioning change and not a policy one. There had not in recent years in any positions of leadership or strength in the party been any serious advocates of a large increase in public ownership.

I should perhaps make it clear here that, despite our various differences, after Tony became leader we worked together very well.

He is easy to like and superb at presentation and I was determined to do all I could to help bring a Labour government to power. People sometimes exaggerate the personal side of political differences. Being one of seven brothers and sisters, each of whom I love dearly, I grew up in a family of passionate argument and disagreement but within an assumption of continuing love and respect. Of course, people fall out sometimes when there are political differences, but usually we come back together in what we all used to call the Labour family. Once he became leader, Tony Blair and I saw much more of each other because at that time the NEC had a significant role in the party. We got on well, in fact I can remember when the shadow Cabinet elections were coming up and I was standing again, having been a runner-up for some time, he wished me luck and said he thought I could be a very good minister if I was able to come to terms with questions of expediency that I would have to face. I have occasionally pondered since what he had in mind, and wish I had asked him.

Shadow Secretary of State for Transport

The following year brought some significant developments in my position and some turbulence that went with it. I was elected to the Shadow Cabinet in 1995 and asked by Tony Blair to take over as shadow Secretary of State for Transport from Michael Meacher. Blair said little of what he wanted me to do, but Michael Meacher had been engaged in preparing a transport policy document for presentation to Conference, as Labour had no transport policy, so I took over from where he laid off. I took on extra staff and got stuck in to consulting all those involved in transport policy. This was a considerable task; since transport takes up nearly 20 per cent of GDP, there are many groups and interests and much consulting to be done. The whole system was facing the accumulated problems of underinvestment, breakdown and worsening congestion. On top of this the disastrous proposals for rail privatisation that broke British Rail into 100 separate companies were completing their passage through Parliament.

It was not long before I had a couple of spats with the media. I never had any intention of causing a furore but simply gave a straightforward and, in my view, uncontentious answer to a question which was then played up by the media in the way they do. People rightly deplore the fact that most politicians don't answer the question. But this is largely due to the media jumping on any answer that is personal or slightly distinctive. This practice has encouraged the sound-bite culture, where phrases are honed to sound good and a little ambiguity left to allow room for manoeuvre. It has now fully matured and teams of briefers work with Blair to prepare for Prime Minister's Questions, they then provide briefing on the lines and phrases to any senior politician appearing on *Question Time*, *Any Questions*, etc. Written briefings are sent out to all MPs so that they too know the phrases to use and the line to take. The Tories under Hague, Duncan Smith and Howard have tended to denounce focus groups and sound-bites. But one has only to listen to what they say to be clear that they are engaged in the same process. It is the consequence of the media jumping on any phrase or thought that might appear distinctive. If we are to escape from it, we have to achieve a greater maturity in media reporting.

However, at this stage I was new to the shadow Cabinet and completely untutored in such ways. My first spat came on the Frost programme soon after I was elected to the shadow Cabinet. I was invited on to discuss transport but was also asked about drugs. I suggested that it might be good to appoint a Royal Commission to investigate whether we could handle the drug problem better, and consider whether cannabis should be legalised and taxed to separate its users from the suppliers of harder drugs. The second was when I said, in answer to a question, that people like me should pay a bit more tax. In both cases the media went to town because a member of the shadow Cabinet had said such things and Alastair Campbell, by then in place as Blair's press officer, strongly briefed against me as I was informed by various journalists. I think it was reasonable to criticise me for not being more careful, but I had just been elected to the shadow Cabinet and had not adapted to the heightened media interest there would be in my every word. No one took me aside to give any advice. This, I soon learned, was Tony Blair's management style, very little discussion of the expectations and duties of the shadow Cabinet job or collective discussion of policy, but nasty briefing through the media if one was thought to have stepped out of line. Following these events, I was invited to visit the Blairs at home on a couple of occasions, presumably to ensure that no offence was taken. During these visits both he and Cherie were very welcoming and friendly and it was very clear what a loving and hands-on father Tony was.

For the next year, I and my team worked our socks off preparing a considered and serious transport policy. The most complicated task was the drawing-up of a policy outlining Labour's views on the privatisation of Railtrack which was to be placed in the prospectus for the sale. I had inside help from people working at senior levels in the industry and cleared the document with Geoff Norris, who is still working for Blair in No. 10. My speech was duly inserted in the document and remains a matter of record. Under these proposals, the government would have converted its annual subsidy of £1 billion per year into shares in Railtrack up to a maximum of 50 per cent and Railtrack would have become a public–private company run by a new-style British Rail whose task would be to reintegrate the fragmented, privatised network. While it was agreed that this proposal should be placed in the prospectus for the sale, it became apparent later that there was no intention of implementing it, although in the end Railtrack was converted into a publicly owned, not-for-profit company.

There was a very strange atmosphere amongst the leadership around rail privatisation. It was deeply unpopular in the country and we agreed that we should oppose it in every way possible, but there was a great reluctance to talk about what we would do when we inherited the consequences. Then suddenly, meetings were called at short notice in Tony Blair's room which I attended together with Gordon Brown, John Prescott and various officials. John had been in discussion with friends and experts to consider whether Labour could renationalise through the issue of bonds. There were constant leaks in the newspapers and lots of tension. The meetings were short, there were few papers, and then a form of words emerged which committed us to the establishment of a Strategic Rail Authority, which was Gordon's idea. Looking back, the tension was presumably over the desire not to commit to renationalisation without upsetting those who opposed privatisation. But this very informal, media-fixated, ill-thought-through style of decision was to become familiar as Tony Blair's preferred way of doing things when he saw himself to be in a tight spot.

Then, as our transport policy document was reaching finalisation, Tony Blair called me in and asked whether I couldn't just drop it and make a series of speeches. I said this was impossible because we had consulted widely and the document was expected throughout the transport industry. We left it there and then, one night just before the summer recess when I had guests eating with me in the House of Commons, my bleep went off with an urgent summons to Blair's office. He told me he wanted me to move from Transport to Overseas Development. I was stunned and angry. There had been no warning and no discussion. I said I had no time to talk and went back to my guests and then home. I really did not know what to do. His behaviour was so unreasonable. I had, in good faith, spent masses of time consulting people throughout the transport industry and many senior people had taken the process very seriously. I had drafted a document on the basis of those consultations which was due to go to Conference and form the basis for Labour's transport policy and now all that work was to be scrapped. The media as ever got wind of the drama and came and camped outside my house. Tony rang to try and calm me down. My staff came to join me and were equally astonished at our leader's way of running things. But eventually we all agreed that if we had been offered Transport or Overseas Development in the first place, we would have chosen Overseas Development. And we shouldn't rock the boat just before an election.

It was at this time in early August 1996 that I agreed to be interviewed by Steve Richards, then political editor of the *New Statesman*. I talked about the danger of spin and the power of the spin doctors – whom I termed 'the people who live in the dark'. I also stressed the undesirability of portraying Blair as an unprincipled macho man. This caused a fuss, with the Conservatives producing posters of Tony Blair in a satanic mask. I remember talking on the phone to Peter Mandelson and saying that Blair's addiction to spin could be seriously damaging and undermine people's trust in what he said. I suggested a complaint to the Advertising Standards Authority about the satanic posters – which he did take up – then Tony went on holiday to France but he rang me to ask if I was okay, and I went to Cape Town to stay with my beloved sister Anne for my summer holiday.

It is worth noting here that as well as the shift to a totally media-dominated system of decision-making, Blair moved rapidly away from Labour's tradition of collective policy-making. I had sat on Labour NEC committees since the mid-1970s. There was a long-standing Labour tradition of the NEC setting up sub-committees, including experts with Labour sympathies, sharing draft papers, and then drawing up an agreed policy which would go on to the NEC and then to Conference. This may have been a little ponderous, but it meant that policy proposals were thoroughly considered and well-thought-through. I was surprised that I was expected to prepare a transport policy document on my own, but presumed this was because it had been left so late. I was later to learn that both before we took power and in government Blair did not favour collective decision-making. I was very comfortable with a tradition that we all engaged in agreeing a policy and then were loyal to the outcome whether or not one's own views prevailed. Under Blair we moved to policy being decided by the leader and his entourage, collective decision-making being marginalised, but an expectation of total loyalty to the line laid down.

International Development

Returning after the summer, Tony asked me to consider whether it was right that we should retain the commitment in our policy document to the establishment of a new Ministry for International Development headed by a Cabinet minister. I agreed to survey examples in other countries and consult the Permanent Secretary at the Overseas Development Administration and get back to him.

It was Harold Wilson who had first established a Ministry for Overseas Development under Barbara Castle in 1964. He had put together the remnants of the old Colonial Office with the UK aid programme with a focus on development in the poorest parts of the world. Barbara Castle had been criticised for being a 'red' because she brought into Whitehall radical economists to advise the new ministry. The Conservative Party traditionally challenged the independence of the ministry and thus folded it into the Foreign Office in 1970. It was given its independence again under Judith Hart when Harold Wilson returned to power in 1974 and then under Thatcher, again subject to the Foreign Secretary's overall command. Thus it was not surprising that Labour's policy review, chaired by Robin Cook, committed the Labour government to establishing a powerful new ministry dedicated to international development, for the first time headed by a Cabinet minister.

Reading between the lines, I am pretty certain that, when Robin Cook consulted the Foreign Office in the six months before the election, they suggested he had made a major mistake in giving away his control over the policy and budget of the Development

Department. The same message was conveyed to Tony Blair, who had previously shown no noticeable interest in foreign affairs but was now being briefed as Prime Minister-in-waiting. I dutifully looked at examples of arrangements for promoting development in other countries and consulted the Permanent Secretary at the then Overseas Development Administration. He was adamant that the department needed its independence to fulfil the commitments laid out in Labour's policy document. I wrote accordingly to Tony Blair. He left the question open until he formed the government and asked me to establish the new department.

The return of my son

Then came an absolutely wonderful development in my life. Thirty years previously I had gone to university at the age of seventeen, become pregnant and married, but we had decided that the baby should be adopted. I had regretted this ever since. It had seemed so rational – difficult husband, no income or security, shame at having become pregnant, better future for the baby – but I had missed him ceaselessly. Phillip Whitehead, who was himself adopted, had helped bring in legislation to enable parents who wanted to contact their adopted children to register and, having done so, I had been waiting for his contact ever since – expecting him at the age of eighteen, then twenty-one, but always feeling he would get in touch. And then at last it happened and the explosion of happiness and love was unstoppable. We met up frequently and were completely obsessed with each other, but then gossip started to flow about me being seen mooning over a good-looking young man and I knew we would have to make some kind of announcement. I arranged to see Tony and said it was something personal and he guessed that I was getting married, but once I told him my story he was happy for me and very supportive. My long-standing researcher, Virginia Heywood, was a friend of Suzanne Moore, whose mother had been adopted and who was working for the *Independent*, so we gave her an interview and some photos. I told the Labour Party this was my plan and both Alastair Campbell and Peter Mandelson were supportive and the party organised an event for the media to take photographs. I said at first we did not want this, but they warned us the media would follow us everywhere. It was a little daunting but we were grateful for their help, otherwise we would have had the media camped outside our houses and offices looking for pictures. My expectation was that I would be criticised and drummed out of politics as a wicked woman who had given up her baby for adoption. Instead, with one notable exception, I received a mountain of letters, cards, blue socks and messages of congratulations and good will. It was the happiest event of my life. We are very close and my son and his family are strongly integrated into the rest of the family. I am also good friends with his adoptive father. My son's return has healed a hole that had been at the centre of my life ever since he left. His existence is a source of enormous joy and happiness for me. Our story also led to a big growth in the number of adopted children seeking contact with their natural parents.

Beyond enjoying the return of my son, I got on with reading and preparing to take on the new Department for International Development. It was Richard Jolly (now Sir Richard), formerly of Unicef, who pointed me to the report of the Development Committee of the Organization for Economic Co-operation and Development (OECD), entitled 'Shaping the Twenty-First Century'. It drew together the recommendations of the great UN conferences of the 1990s – such as Copenhagen on Poverty, Cairo on Reproductive Health Care, Rio on Environment and Beijing on Women – and suggested that a great advance was possible if we focused on the systematic reduction of poverty, built on past success and drew the international system together to work in partnership to deliver clear targets in each country. The targets were to reduce income poverty, get children to school, and reduce mortality amongst children and mothers by providing better health care, clean water and sanitation. I decided that I would work to make this the framework for our development efforts and was delighted when I met John Vereker (now Sir John), the ODA Permanent Secretary, because he had been a member of the OECD committee that drew up the report. I was determined to make my new ministry an exemplary player and to use UK influence to drive the international system forward. I was clear that, in the post-Cold War world, delivering greater justice and hope and development to the poor of the world needed to become a central guiding principle of our foreign policy.

And then, at last, the 1997 election was called. One of my staff was located at Millbank and the rest came with me to Birmingham. I visited marginal constituencies across the country and also ran my election in Ladywood. Everywhere people were warm and supportive. It was hard to believe we would not win this time.

2

BLAIR'S FIRST TERM

As the votes were counted in Birmingham on the night of 1 May 1997 we had an early result in Edgbaston, a seat that had been held by the Conservatives even in 1945. Once it was won – a leafy and wealthy area of Birmingham – it was clear Labour would be overwhelmingly elected. After the Ladywood count was complete, my team consisting of my staff, agent and son popped into the local celebration, but had no wish to stay – like most people across Britain, all we wanted was to go home and join my mum and watch the results roll in as the map turned from blue to red, and enjoy the delicious moment when Portillo was defeated. I did not rush down to London to join the victory party, I cannot remember being invited, but I was deeply happy that at last we had a Labour government and a chance to make our country fairer and to play a role in making the world more just.

The next morning, we piled into a car to journey down to London. My bleep was going off repeatedly. The *Sun* had carried a story that Michael Meacher and I were to be excluded from the Cabinet, and journalists were looking for comments. I decided to ignore all the calls and go straight to my brother Michael's house where we were due to celebrate his birthday. That night, when I was in bed, my bleep went again. It was a message from No. 10

asking why I had not returned their calls. I phoned and arranged to be there next morning. I found Tony sitting in the Cabinet Room with Jonathan Powell who had been his Chief of Staff for the last few years. He said he wanted me to create the new Department for International Development. He asked who I wanted as my junior. I asked for George Foulkes, whom I didn't know well but he had been loyal to Joan Lestor when she had occupied the shadow post before me. We had an exchange about the name of the department. John Vereker, the Permanent Secretary, had pointed out we didn't want to be known as DID and thus we agreed it would be DfID. I was then whisked off to my new department where senior officials had gathered, despite it being Saturday. They handed me a hefty briefing document and we exchanged enthusiastic words about the new focus on the reduction of poverty and then I went home to read my brief and reorganise my life.

This meant a train journey back to Birmingham. I can still remember the atmosphere on the train. Everyone was smiling and greeting me and shaking my hand. One Birmingham businessman was so excited he could not stop shaking my hand and saying how pleased he was. He then said if he had realised how it would be, he would have voted Labour! This was the mood of Britain as it woke up after the 1997 election.

The scale of Labour's victory

As the country contemplated the result of the election, it seemed Labour had swept all before it. We had 419 MPs. The victory was unprecedented. We had won far beyond the target marginals in which we had expended so many resources. In fact it was notable that the swing was as good in the seats we had not expected as those where we focused central organisation, thus demonstrating that the swing was political and the enthusiasm of local party workers was more important than central intervention. In reality, the oddities of the British electoral system had exaggerated the scale of the victory. The turnout was 71 per cent, down from 78 per cent in 1992. Labour had won 13.5 million votes, 42 per cent of the electorate. The Conservatives had 9.6 million, 30.7 per cent; and the Liberal Democrats had 5.2 million, 16.8 per cent. In fact, Labour won in 1997 with the same share of the vote with which it lost in 1970. Thus, just as with Thatcher before us, we had won less than half the votes and yet had an overwhelming majority in the House of Commons. The British system sometimes has the effect of grossly exaggerating the scale of the victory or the defeat and therefore creates unrealistic expectations. More seriously it generates executive arrogance, as governments with inflated majorities in the House of Commons feel they have no need to listen to dissenting voices. This is, I believe, a significant part of the explanation of growing alienation as the public becomes increasingly angry at the failure of successive governments to respect the views of the electorate.

This is not the place for a full account of the achievements and problems of Blair's first term. My purpose is to try to explain how a Labour government could have brought the UK to support a disastrous and incompetent policy towards the Middle East which was driven by extreme right-wing neoconservative thinkers in the US. Commentators tend to suggest that Tony Blair's premiership was successful and popular until he supported Bush on Iraq, but the problem goes deeper and wider as I will try to explain. People in the UK and internationally repeatedly ask me, in a mood of total puzzlement, why Blair made these decisions. If we wish to correct what has gone wrong, we need to examine how it came about. A review of the achievements and problems of the first term helps to explain how it started to go wrong. A review of Tony Blair's approach to foreign policy also helps to explain how he ended up where he did on Iraq.

The defensiveness of New Labour

Part of the explanation of the disappointment with the new government is the extent to which New Labour was a very defensive project which was created by a small group of insiders who saw themselves as separate from the mainstream of the Labour Party. New Labour was born out of the scars of the 1992 defeat and was closely modelled on Clinton's New Democrats. Thus the New Labour project was, as I have said, focused on presentation rather than content and guided by 'triangulation'. This almost certainly increased the scale of our victory, but the result was a lack of coherent policy-thinking, a focus on spin, and a tendency to be economical with the truth. This, together with Blair's preference for very informal systems of decision-making and willingness to fly by the seat of his pants when in a tight corner, helps to explain how he got to his Iraq policy.

Blair's tragedy is that, like most of us, his strength is his weakness. He has great personal charm and great presentational skills. This is why the Labour Party elected him as leader, and gave him John Prescott as deputy to try to anchor him to Labour values. And for Labour's first term, to a considerable extent, the project worked. We had commitments to Labour policies that had been honed over many years and we had the attractiveness of the Blair style, fronting our project. But the British system puts enormous powers into the hands of its executive, an 'elective dictatorship' in Quintin Hogg's famous phrase. Because the New Labour project belonged to a small group of friends clustered around Blair and Brown, executive power was concentrated into the hands of an even smaller group of people who tended to do their thinking and planning behind closed doors with little consultation. The large majority, the Blair machine's ruthless use of its very large patronage powers, and the deep anxiety in the Labour Party not to go back to the divisions of the 1980s, concentrated power too much in a project that was led by presentational considerations. This is the fundamental explanation of the unattractive side of the government.

On policy, there is a mixed record. Some established Labour policies were being implemented successfully but because of the promise to maintain Tory spending plans for two years and of no increase in the basic or top rate of income tax, the government had boxed itself in very considerably and reduced its ability to increase investment in the public services, which was one of the urgent expectations the electorate had of a Labour government. William Keegan's very fine book *The Prudence of Mr Gordon Brown*, published in 2003, provides a 'warts and all' account of Brown's work at the Treasury and makes clear the price that was paid for the pledge to live within Tory spending plans for the first two years. This resulted in lower capital spending on public services in Labour's first term than in any comparable period in recent decades. The figures are shocking.

Net capital expenditure in the public sector was cut in successive years from £29.2 billion in 1975–76. In the four years of Kenneth Clarke's chancellorship (1993–97) it ran at £12.3 billion, £12.2 billion, £11.7 billion and £5.8 billion. Thus Labour's voluntary two-year freeze was imposed at a very low level. During the first four years of Brown's chancellorship, net capital expenditure in the public sector stood at £5.2 billion, £6.1 billion, £4.8 billion and £5.7 billion (all based on 2000–2001 prices). As a result, we continued with private affluence and public squalor, a degraded transport system and huge underinvestment in health and education. But Keegan makes clear it would not be fair to conclude that Brown has given up on Labour's long-standing commitment to reduce inequality and increase investment in the public services. Brown's upbringing as a son of the manse (he said of his father: 'He taught me to treat everyone equally, and that is something I have not forgotten') and his early allegiance to the Labour movement have ensured that his Labour values are deeply embedded.

Brown and his highly influential political assistant Ed Balls, later chief economic adviser at the Treasury, were playing a long game. They intended to expunge Labour's reputation for poor financial management – and the memory of every previous Labour government trying to spend and then being hit by financial crisis – in order to be able to pursue Labour goals with a solid economy behind them. As I have said, Brown's refusal to stray from this agenda probably cost him the party leadership, as he brutally slapped down shadow Cabinet colleagues who tried to make or to hint at future spending commitments when he was shadow Chancellor from 1992. The courageous decision to make the Bank of England independent and the wisdom of an inflation target of 2.5 per cent (in contrast with the European Central Bank's deflationary 'less than 2 per cent') have helped restore Britain to full employment and given Brown probably the best reputation of any Labour Chancellor.

There are, however, important lessons to be learned from the way the high exchange rate that has helped to secure this very reputation has squeezed manufacturing and worsened long-term balance of payments and productivity problems. There are also important conclusions to be drawn from the failure of the Private Finance Initiative to deliver the hoped-for gains of improved investment and efficiency in the public sector. But Brown's determination to reduce poverty has been sustained through his policy of redistribution by stealth and his interest in efforts to reduce global poverty.

The consequence of the pledge on taxation was that there was no significant increase in public expenditure until 2000–2001. Prior to this, there was some useful transfer of spending from interest payments and unemployment costs to poorer pensioners, but total public spending in 1996–97 was £365.8 billion, and in 1999/00 £369.3 billion. One of the consequences of this was lots of spin and constant re-announcement of new initiatives but very little substantive action. This led to a growth in cynicism. I can remember travelling to the East Midlands to a celebration of Labour's 100th anniversary and one elderly woman, who was a member of the Labour Party, saying that neither she nor any of her friends any longer believed any announcements the government made.

In addition, the delay in increased investment helped set in train an approach to public-sector reform that laid much emphasis on blaming those working in the services, 'the producer interests' as John Reid later labelled them. Thus under Chris Woodhead there were constant attacks on teachers and Tony Blair spoke in 1999 of having scars on his back from his efforts to reform public services. In my view, this has been an enormous error. As Tim Brighouse demonstrated as Chief Education Officer in Birmingham, the way to achieve improvements in services is to build the morale and pride of those who work in the public sector. On top of this, when the money did begin to flow, the proliferation of initiatives, separate funding streams, targets and bureaucracy has burdened and undermined the morale of the people we need to encourage in order to deliver the improvements in services that we promised. My experience in the Department for International Development is that, if we build clarity of objective, a pride in the service and increased resources, people will embrace change, give all they have and take enormous pride in working for the public services. I have seen the same spirit in schools and the NHS in my constituency, but sadly the Labour government set up an ethos of distrust and bureaucratic control from the centre that has undermined rather than enhanced the morale of those who work in the public sector in Britain.

Becoming a Secretary of State

However, in 1997 we were still full of hope and expectation based on the values of the Labour Party and the attractive qualities of Tony Blair as a leader, and therefore we all set about taking on our new roles in life. The first requirement was that members of the Cabinet had to become Privy Councillors and henceforth be known as Right Honourable. The Privy Council now has little meaning and PC is basically an honorary title. It used to be the group of people that advised the monarch when executive power was concentrated on the Crown. This explains the Cabinet title of Secretary of State. The Secretaries used to be the monarch's functionaries and thus it remains the top title in British politics. This causes some confusion overseas where Minister is the senior position and Secretary of State the junior, but in our eccentric British way we carry our history with us. The Privy Council lost its authority when the Cabinet grew up as an informal grouping of politicians who reached agreement on a policy, had the votes behind them in Parliament and could therefore present the monarch with an offer that could not be refused.

To join the Privy Council we were gathered together in groups and trained to kneel on the first footstool and then move up to another and kiss the Queen's hand (not too firmly, or grasp her hand too hard) after we took our oath. I was among the first group of women to take the oath and we discussed how impossible it was for people like me to consider curtseying. But we were told the Queen was quite relaxed about this and we could show our respect, as we do to the Speaker in the Commons, by bowing our heads.

As the ceremonies were being organised, I suddenly knew I must ask for the Catholic oath. When I came to the Commons I had affirmed rather than take a religious oath, but as I took on this historic title, I thought of all my ancestors who had been persecuted for being Catholics. Near Crossmaglen, my Uncle Paddy, my father's youngest brother, has a few fields where he grazes cows and if you walk across them, you come to the Mass rock in a dip on the hillside where my ancestors used to attend Mass with watchouts posted in case the troops were coming to arrest them. I felt I should represent all of them as I took my oath. Some of the rest of our group affirmed and others took the Anglican oath, but my ancestors and I inconvenienced them by requiring that the Catholic oath also be read out.

Once this was done, the Queen said a few cheerful and friendly words to each of us and then off we went to get on with our work.

Being a Secretary of State means that one is invited to various royal celebrations. I attended the occasional banquet for international visitors and always went to the annual party for the Ambassadors and High Commissioners because so many came from the countries with which I was engaged. These ended up with food, drinks and dancing either in Buckingham Palace or at Windsor and were usually enjoyable events. I also went to one Garden Party to take my daughter-in-law and got my private office to ask if I really had to wear a hat. The advice from the Lord Chamberlain's office was that it was usual, but not essential, and thus being from the generation of compulsory boaters and school hats, I went hatless and was duly attacked in the *Sun* for doing so.

I took my turn undertaking Privy Council duties. The system is that there is a rota for attendance at Privy Council meetings. The quota is about eight and you have to attend every few months. You stand in a line while the Queen reads through and agrees legislation, charters of universities and all sorts of other things she has to approve. Once, when I had been told I was essential for a quorum, I found myself very tight for time. We drove at speed to the palace and I rushed up the stairs, causing a commotion as I entered because the meeting had already started. I apologised and the Queen was very gracious and then proceeded with the business. After a couple of minutes, my bleep went off and I caused another kerfuffle as I retrieved it and turned it off. At the end of the meeting, the Queen had a word with each of us, as she does, and said to me with a twinkle in her eye, 'Well, my dear, I hope it wasn't anyone important.'

The Royal Family have had a difficult time lately, but I found the Queen witty and clever, Diana dedicated on land mines, Charles committed to a green view of the world and very concerned for the fate of the poor countries of the Commonwealth. The Queen also has a real affection for the Commonwealth which is clear at the annual reception at Marlborough House.

It is generally expected that people like me should be anti-monarchy. In fact I never have been in favour of abolishing the monarchy. Now the Queen is the symbolic Head of State, I see no point in upsetting people by trying to get rid of the Royal Family and then having to replace them with a President who would in turn have to be given all the trappings of office. I have made clear this was my position whenever asked, but have also added that I think the royals should pay tax and the younger ones go to work. It is a reflection of the general lack of respect for accuracy in our press that an article appeared in *The Times* listing me as one of several republicans in the Labour Cabinet. I wasn't much upset by this, but wrote a letter saying that this was untrue, which *The Times* refused to publish. I therefore complained to the Press Complaints Commission and the journalist concerned wrote a long defence about how such a claim had appeared in the London *Evening Standard* amongst other papers. I replied that I was a Birmingham MP and rarely read the *Evening Standard*, but in any case I had not seen these other false claims and simply wanted to correct the false claim in *The Times*. My complaint to the PCC remains unresolved and *The Times* story uncorrected. This is a relatively trivial falsity, but it does reflect the arrogance and lack of commitment to accuracy that is so common in our media.

The great change that takes place when you enter government is that you give up control over your life. The diary is controlled from your private office and your life programmed for weeks and months ahead. I had a very warm relationship with my private office and we considered it a badge of pride that I had a succession of private secretaries with small children who did get home and see them when we weren't travelling. But once I had agreed in principle to a commitment, my time ceased to be my own. I got to be very good at packing and travelling light and would sometimes realise the night before that I needed to pack and be off across the world early the next morning. I did insist, however, that I would not miss my advice bureaux in Ladywood and all my engagements had to be organised around these commitments. This both ensured I kept in touch with my voters and kept my feet on the ground.

But for six years, it was a totally different life, every minute programmed by someone else and lots of travel across the world. And then every night a red box full of papers. I took pride in reading it all, which gave me a natural authority in the department and across Whitehall because I often knew more of the detail than those I was dealing with. I enjoyed every minute of it, including my travel which took me to schools and villages and meeting real people rather than the normal political travel to hotels and conference halls, although there was some of that also. Obviously I was sad to leave my department when I did, but I have enjoyed getting a normal life back and travelling by tube and bus and chatting with people as I go. High pressure on time and chauffeur-driven cars do feed the ego, which is the most serious disease of politics.

Achievements and disappointments and the growing centralisation of power

There were various developments during the first term that caused irritation and alienation. But there were also many achievements of which Labour people could be proud, most importantly the return to full employment after the terrible damage caused by the high unemployment of the Thatcher years. When I visited Labour Party events during the course of the first term, I used to raise a smile when I remarked that the Labour aspects of the government were going well and it was the 'new' bits that were getting us into trouble. In particular, the reputation for spin rather than substance was quickly established and steadily eroded trust. This is not the place to summarise all the policy changes brought forward during the first term, but a quick review of some of the reforms shows long-standing Labour commitments being implemented and some of the negative developments flowing from the New Labour project. This also helps explain why support for Labour in the 2001 election declined considerably. There was also a growing concentration of power in No. 10 that generated the much more serious errors of the second term.

In 1997 Labour began with a bang and we committed ourselves immediately to all sorts of good things such as signing the EU social chapter; an ethical foreign policy; a ban on land mines; an aid pro gramme focused on reducing poverty; rejoining Unesco; and tight- ening controls on arms exports. We were also immediately committed to incorporating the European Convention on Human Rights into UK law; imposing a tax on the windfall profits of the utilities to fund a New Deal to get young people into jobs; legislating for Scotland and Wales to have referendums on Devolution; giving overseas gay partners the right to settle in UK; introducing legislation for the minimum wage; and making progress on peace in Northern Ireland.

But there were also some worrying developments as early as 1997. David Blunkett kept Woodhead in post as Chief Inspector of Schools; tests were also introduced for seven-, eleven- and fourteen- year-olds and league tables continued; fees were introduced for higher education; and parents invited to report bad teachers to a hotline. More damagingly, Formula One was exempted from the tobacco ban after Bernie Ecclestone's donations to the Labour Party, and even Andrew Rawnsley (of the *Observer* and Radio 4's *Westminster Hour*) concluded that 'Blair had slid into mendacity'. One-parent benefit was cut and forty-seven Labour MPs revolted. For the first time, I voted for something I strongly disapproved of because the alternative would have been to leave the government. Gordon Brown made up for this by later increasing child benefit considerably, but it was a damaging consequence of the decision to stick with Tory spending commitments and caused a lot of ill feeling. On top of this, Blair decided we must continue with the sale of Hawk jets to Indonesia, despite Robin Cook's and my unhappiness and the Portuguese Prime Minister making it clear he objected to Labour continuing with the sale.

I went to Ottawa to sign the Land Mine Treaty on behalf of the UK. The campaign for the treaty was led by charitable organisations across the world that had seen the enormous suffering caused by unexploded land mines after wars were ended. My first overseas visit after taking on the Development portfolio had been to Cambodia, focusing on land mine clearance, and on my return I had found Labour cautious on making a commitment to the proposed treaty because it would restrict the armed forces. This was one of Princess Diana's causes and she was deeply devoted to it. She came in to meet Robin Cook and me soon after the election and demonstrated that she had done her homework and was very well informed. I continued to work with her both in supporting the Treaty and to increase UK commitment to clearance. It was a cause which Diana helped to popularise in a very important way.

DfID also took the lead, and paid the cost, of rejoining Unesco. This is the UN agency based in Paris focused on sharing knowledge and working to spread a culture of peace. The US and UK withdrew in the Thatcher/Reagan years because they found the leadership flawed. When I went to Paris to sign up for our return, there were UK staff in tears at the symbolism of the UK's return. I wanted it to be a symbol of our strong support for the UN, but of a reforming, ever more effective UN, a cause that was to lead me to a strong working relationship with Secretary-General Kofi Annan and other senior UN officials.

The reshaping of our development programme on the reduction of poverty might sound obvious, but there was such a muddle of motives and programmes in the international development system that the UK clarity of focus became influential and helped to lead to significant improvement in international development efforts. It also energised the staff of the department because they were so enthusiastic about the direction our work was taking.

Some of the policies outside development were also a great reward for the work of people of my political tradition. I had campaigned with Rodney Bickerstaffe and my union the National

Union of Public Employees for a minimum wage for many years. There was a time when it was opposed by many unions because it would undermine collective bargaining, and doubts were expressed by many politicians including Roy Hattersley when he was Kinnock's deputy. Blair had also wobbled on it when he was Opposition Employment spokesperson. But now we were committed and the major beneficiaries would be low-paid women.

The Northern Ireland peace process was also a great moment for me. We had been brought up by my father to understand the injustice and bitter division that had flowed from the partition of Ireland. We also understood the pain that flowed from the IRA campaign of violence and the effects it had in Crossmaglen and in Birmingham, where we suffered the terrible pub bombings of 1974 which killed twenty-one people. I remember the night very clearly because one of my brothers used to drink in that pub and until he came home we thought we might have lost him. By the time I was elected, it was becoming clear that the wrong people had been arrested for the pub bombing, but when I said this might be so in an interview I was attacked by the tabloid press for being supposedly pro-IRA. Chris Mullin, MP for Sunderland South, who made this miscarriage of justice a personal crusade, also suffered vicious criticism. Kevin McNamara, MP for Hull North, Peter Hain, now Leader of the House, and many others were criticised for their stand on Northern Ireland, but I believe the dissenters helped to create the conditions for the peace process to move forward because, as in the Middle East, the ending of the use of violence depends on persuading those involved that it is possible to achieve justice by non-violent means.

John Hume, who is retiring from politics after more than twenty years as MP for Foyle, and who is a good friend, made an enormously important contribution throughout his political life, but particularly by engaging in talks with Gerry Adams to help put the peace process in place. He was attacked for this, but the talks helped edge Sinn Fein to the belief that they could advance through politics and give up their commitment to physical force which is a very long-standing tradition in Irish politics. Successive Dublin governments working first with John Major and then Tony Blair had taken forward the detailed thinking that made progress possible, and Mo Mowlam added her courage and enthusiasm. I felt confident that we were nearing the end of violence in Irish politics, which was deeply satisfying and made me think a lot about my father and how, no matter how long it takes, just solutions will be found.

Such considerations make me reflect on the need for parties to be able to renew themselves and be open to new thinking and policy. In our system this is achieved by some members of the party taking up unpopular and difficult causes which are often later taken into the mainstream. I fear that New Labour's party-management style allows for little such diversity of opinion and it will become more and more difficult for Labour to take on new ideas unless some of the old democracy of the party is restored.

Early in the first term there were intimations of an enormous centralisation of power and an unwillingness to encourage open discussion and collaborative decision-making. An early experience of this came at one of the first Cabinet discussions. The meeting took place in June and we discussed whether we should proceed with Tory plans for the Millennium Dome. We were all new and believed that Cabinet was supposed to proceed through a free expression of opinion summed up by the Prime Minister. One after another, members of the Cabinet said no to the Dome. A large number spoke and the view was almost universally hostile. I and everyone in Birmingham were deeply critical because we had put in a bid for a much more realistic project. I also remember Donald Dewar sitting next to me arguing that we could fund a celebration party in every town in the country and still save money. Then suddenly, Tony said he was sorry, that he hadn't expected Cabinet to go on for so long, he had to leave and John Prescott would sum up. He then went out to a pre-arranged press conference and announced that we would continue with the Dome.

This Cabinet meeting set the tone for Cabinet meetings under Tony Blair. After this, they were always short. There were no papers other than the legislative programme. The agenda was the same for almost every meeting and simply listed home affairs and foreign affairs and then Tony would bring up whatever he had in mind. Before the Budget or an announcement on public expenditure, Gordon would be asked to give an outline of his speech and would answer questions. Occasionally No. 10 would ring my private office and ask if there was anything that I wanted to raise. I presume they did this with others. I suspect they were embarrassed when meetings finished after thirty minutes and would therefore think up an issue for brief discussion at each meeting. Occasionally, people would express concern, or a little doubt about an issue raised, but only in a very mild way and others rarely took up such comments. Sometimes, if a contentious issue was current, I would be invited to see Tony before the meeting, as he did not want dissent in the Cabinet because he would say it might leak. At the side of every Cabinet meeting sat Alastair Campbell, Sally Morgan and Anji Hunter alongside the officials and Jonathan Powell always sat behind Tony. Accounts of Cabinet meetings were often given to the press. They frequently bore a limited resemblance to what had taken place and always painted a picture of a dominant Tony strongly supported by his admiring Cabinet.

I remember an extraordinary example of such briefing after the visit of the President of China, Jiang Zemin, in 1999. The visit provoked demonstrations across London over Tibet and human rights in China. We met with Jiang Zemin in the Cabinet room. The press reported that Tony had raised the issue of human rights, but I was at the meeting and he had not done so. In fact, Jiang Zemin himself had raised the question of the crackdown on the Falun Gong and said very animatedly that they were a sect, as though this made their persecution acceptable. Tony said nothing about human rights, but the press reported that he did and thus he was saved the embarrassment of having to do so in person.

Blair moved early to establish a growing band of advisers in No. 10. Many of these had no previous engagement with the Labour Party or Labour values. Whilst there is great value in a broad church, the style of the No. 10 machine was very arrogant. Unaccountable young officials would propose ideas to the Prime Minister and departments would be instructed to implement them. Consultation was seen almost as a weakness. Secretaries of State were in charge of their departments except when No. 10 gave instructions. Those who held high office had to be willing to bow to these commands.

Thus, as I said in my resignation speech, Cabinet government has become a part of the British constitution much like the Privy Council. There is some significance in who holds the offices of the various Secretaries of State, but there is no collective decision-making worth talking about. The theory of our constitutional arrangements is that leading figures in Parliament come together in Cabinet, discuss all contentious issues, thrash out agreement and then all are collectively loyal to the conclusion reached. This is the very meaning of collective responsibility, but in the Blair government, there is no discussion of this nature. I have heard David Blunkett on air chastising me for not adhering to collective Cabinet responsibility on Iraq at a time when there had been no Cabinet discussion. The term collective responsibility is now being used to demand loyalty to decisions on which Cabinet members were not consulted, let alone that were reached collectively. As the Butler Report indicated, under Blair there is no collective, there is no thrashing out of views between colleagues, and I fear the government is the worse for it. The nature of the new order was underlined at the Labour conference in September 1997 when the Cabinet was marginalised and Blair projected as the all-powerful leader. There was to be no first among equals in the Blair leadership style.

In 1998, our second year in power, the Fairness at Work White Paper promised a right for trade unions to be recognised if this was the wish of the workforce. This was one of the issues on which Blair called me to see him before the Cabinet meeting because he did not want any argument to leak. There had been much tension with the TUC about the policy. I remember saying to him then that in John Monks he had one of the most intelligent and creative General Secretaries of the TUC that any Labour leader had had and that he really should be able to work with him.

In 1998 also, the referendum on the Good Friday agreement passed with a massive majority in the Republic of Ireland and with a smaller majority in the North, despite the opposition of Ian Paisley (Leader of the Democratic Unionist Party). The Budget introduced Working Families Tax Credits, thus making work worthwhile again for low-income families. This was very important in Ladywood where, since the early 1980s, we had suffered very high unemployment and benefit dependency. The tax-credit system, which was a copy of the tax-credit system in the US, was designed to make work worthwhile again. In the longer term, there is a worry that the state is subsidising low-paid employment, but it was very important that this change and the reduction in unemployment created a new sense of hope in constituencies like mine. Legislation was also introduced to reduce the age of consent for gay couples and a Bill to reform the House of Lords by removing almost all the hereditary peers.

There were also negative developments. Lord Chancellor Derry Irvine embarrassed us all by comparing himself to Cardinal Wolsey and with his extravagant expenditure on wallpaper in his redecorated office. There was a scandal over advisers to Blair and Peter Mandelson appearing to offer access to senior figures in the government in return for cash. Welsh Secretary Ron Davies resigned after his moment of madness on Clapham Common. Peter Mandelson joined the Cabinet as Trade and Industry Secretary in July but by December he and Geoffrey Robinson, Paymaster-General in the Treasury, had to resign from the government over Mandelson's failure to disclose a personal loan given to him by Robinson.

The centralisation of power continued to grow remorselessly with No. 10 trying to control the selection of candidates to the Scottish Parliament and Welsh Assembly as well as for the London Mayor and the European Parliament. This was a major change in Labour culture, where traditionally selection worked from the bottom up and candidates were endorsed centrally unless there was something outrageously unacceptable about them.

On top of this, the proposals for the reorganisation of policy-making in the party were introduced in such a way that they would enable Tony Blair to control and dominate the Labour Party conference. Such reform had been under discussion for some time. There was a general determination to prevent the clashes between Labour Party conference and government that we had seen in the past. For example, the proposal that draft policy documents should be discussed and amended at elected forums had started to be implemented under John Smith's leadership. I can well remember John Smith and Margaret Beckett sitting in the meetings listening to what the delegates had to say. Tony Blair's leadership style was very different. He always had to be seen as a dominating figure, in control and superior to all others. An example of this increased control and manipulation of the party came when I was chairing Conference in 1996. The tradition had always been to call delegates from the floor, not knowing what they would say. This led to some delegates sending notes asking to be called, and the chair ensuring that members with an important record or contribution were guaranteed a voice, but most of the delegates were called without any knowledge of the argument they would make. However, in 1996 I was provided with a full list of who was to be called, where they were sitting and what they were wearing. I departed from it somewhat, but it has been clear since then that those who are called to speak at Conference are pre-chosen and 'helped' with their speeches and thus the conference is sanitised and manipulated. Similarly, 'clappers' are placed around the hall, to lead a storm of applause for platform speakers whom there is a wish to favour. The disorder of the 1980s had by 2003 given way to the unity of a Leninist-style rally.

The capacity of the party to use the NEC election to send a message to the leadership was also brought to an end. The 1997 elections saw Ken Livingstone defeat Peter Mandelson, but after that MPs were not allowed to stand for election by the party membership and the significance of the elections was much diminished. Thus the way in which people like me came into senior positions in the Labour Party was gradually eliminated. In power, promotion to ministerial office depends on the patronage of the leader. In Opposition, I joined the shadow Cabinet because the Parliamentary Party voted me in. Similarly, I was elected to the NEC by the votes of conference delegates. Almost all promotion now depends on supporting the leader unquestioningly.

Nineteen ninety-nine was not a good year, but there were some good developments. The budget brought the minimum income guarantee for poor pensioners, which was very popular in Ladywood because we have so many poor pensioners; elsewhere there was impatience for improvements in income for mainstream pensions. The year also brought the report on the lessons to be learned from the failure to prosecute those responsible for the murder of the black teenager Stephen Lawrence, which led to significant reform. Greg Dyke was appointed Director-General of the BBC with accusations, ironic in hindsight, of cronyism because he had made donations to the Labour Party. There was a revolt of Labour Party MPs against the Welfare Bill which reformed disability benefits. Mo Mowlam let it be known that she was being pushed out of Northern Ireland against her will. This was also the year when Tony Blair caused offence when he told a business meeting that he had scars on his back from trying to reform the public services.

By May 1999 the government was beginning to suffer from growing unpopularity in elections. Elections in Scotland and Wales led to a 34 per cent Labour vote in Scotland compared to 46 per cent in the General Election and in Wales the vote was 38 per cent in the Assembly election compared with 55 per cent in 1997. The Tories made gains in local elections and Labour's representation in the European Parliament was halved. The turnout in Leeds Central in a by-election after the sadly premature death of Derek Fatchett saw Labour hold the seat on a turnout of only 19.6 per cent.

The year 2000 was the last before the General Election. Politics was increasingly fractious. It was the year of the fuel tax protests. The House of Lords defeated proposed restrictions on jury trial. The Parliamentary Labour Party was unhappy with the proposals to withdraw financial support from the children of asylum seekers and the increase of only 75p in the state pension. Peter Kilfoyle, a junior defence minister, resigned from the government criticising its focus on Middle England and failure to listen to the regions. This was also the year when Tony Blair was heckled by the Women's Institute. Memos were leaked from Philip Gould to Tony Blair telling him the public thought him out of touch, and from Blair calling for eye-catching initiatives with which he could be associated, showing yet again that his focus was on presentation rather than substance. Mo Mowlam announced that she would not stand for Parliament at the next election; she was very low after her mother's death and the press briefings against her. I tried to persuade her to at least stay in the Commons but she was keen to work internationally. I talked to Tony about a suitable job but it was a sad ending to a sparkling and courageous political career. Mo still makes a point of ringing in solidarity whenever the leadership and/or media are having a go at me.

However, July 2000 brought a very important advance with the comprehensive spending review for 2001–4 promising a considerable increase in expenditure particularly on health and education. Health spending stood at £51.7 billion in 1998/99 and had increased to £57.6 billion by 2001/02, but under the 2000 comprehensive spending review was set to rise to £73.5 billion by 2003/04. Similarly, education spending was £42.7 billion in

1998/99, rose to £47.1 billion by 2000/01, but under the 2000 review was set to rise to £57.9 billion by 2003/04. For DfID I had some conflict with Gordon Brown in both the 1998 and 2000 spending reviews because his initial offer was inadequate. Blair was totally unsympathetic and even rang me in 1998 to say I should be satisfied with the offer. But after my complaints Gordon squeezed out some more money. It was also in the 2000 spending review that we took up the Treasury's challenge suggesting pooled funding to encourage better cross-Whitehall working. DfID proposed a pooled fund to encourage better work on conflict prevention and resolution in Africa. This caused consternation in the Foreign Office who quickly proposed a parallel global fund. Tony Blair's speech to the Labour Party conference uncharacteristically apologised for the mistakes and said he had got the message.

The year 2001 was to be election year. The foot and mouth crisis put back the election date to June. Peter Mandelson was again dismissed from the Cabinet over his involvement with the Hinduja brothers and their passport applications. And in February Blair had his first meeting with Bush when they declared their joint determination to contain the threat from Iraq.

Blair's foreign policy

Tony Blair had no record of any interest in foreign policy prior to becoming leader of the Labour Party. Given his later interest in Kosovo, it is notable that he expressed no support in Opposition for the considerable group of Labour MPs who were deeply troubled by President Milosevic's ethnic cleansing and the mass rape in Bosnia, and the failure of the UK to take a stand.

Blair's first significant foreign-policy speech was made in Manchester ten days before the election. The speech laid great emphasis upon the quality of our armed forces, it attacked the Tories for cutting defence spending, promised a defence review and said that UK defence for the twenty-first century would be based on our national nuclear deterrent and internationally competitive defence industry. It also promised a leading role in Europe; the triple lock of Cabinet, Parliament and referendum approval to join the euro; strong support for the UN; and a reversal in the decline in UK aid spending. I had been asked for a contribution to the speech. It is notable how little of it got in and how much stress there was on the armed forces. There was quite a lot of muttering in Labour Party and Non-Governmental Organisation (NGO) circles at the time, but people hoped Blair was playing to the gallery for electoral purposes and that the imbalance in the speech would be corrected in office.

Establishing the Department for International Development

The establishment of the new Department for International Development presented an enormous challenge and opportunity to shift the balance of UK foreign policy. I had a great advantage from having previously been a civil servant. I knew and respected the quality and professionalism of the British civil service, and I understood the proper roles of ministers and civil servants. I was neither intimidated by nor distrustful of my civil servants, and I got on extremely well and shared an ambition for the department with my Permanent Secretary John Vereker (later Sir John). There has been some interest, particularly in the US, about what was achieved by DfID. I take a lot of pride in this, but it is not just personal, it is also institutional. Britain became a leading player in development because we created a department with authority over the developmental aspects of all UK policy. The result was that the UK adopted more coherent and thought-through positions than most other countries. And, as I used to say at meetings of my special advisers, we could be as radical as we liked because Alastair Campbell had no interest in what we were doing!

From the beginning, the climate across Whitehall was hostile. The Foreign Office were furious that the old Overseas Development Administration (ODA) had got away from their tutelage and took every possible opportunity to brief against us and to use their private secretary in No. 10 to overrule us. We had an early battle with the Treasury to ensure that the Secretary of State for International Development held the office of UK Governor of the World Bank. The World Bank funding and policy were provided by DfID but the Treasury wanted the governorship for the Chancellor. John Vereker was a determined Whitehall player and we eventually agreed that we would retain our joint IMF/World Bank office in Washington with the Development Secretary as UK Governor of the World Bank. This is a good arrangement because it meant we could also inject a development dimension into IMF policy.

Building the new department meant taking on a series of battles in Whitehall. This hostility to DfID was institutional rather than political. One of the major problems we have in the world is that the institutional arrangements and world-view of most of those who occupy dominant positions in government were framed to run the Cold War world. Poul Nielson, who is the outgoing Development Commissioner of the European Union and was before that a highly effective Development minister in Denmark, argued many years ago that Development ministers tended to understand the challenge of globalization in a way others did not because they looked at the world through the fate of the poorer countries. They understood the need to complement the hastening integration of the world economy with international rules for trade, environment, conflict resolution and finance that make the world more equitable and enabled all countries to benefit from the changes that were occurring.

There were both institutional and mind-set battles to fight. Foreign policy, trade policy, environment policy were led by powerful, well-established departments which sought to further UK national interest. The old ODA administered the UK aid programme which had declined from its high point of 0.52 per cent of GDP under Barbara Castle to 0.26 per cent when we took over in 1997. It had high-quality officials but its views were constantly overruled by the Foreign Office which put UK contracts and arms sales before development interests. UK aid was seen through a charitable lens, a contribution to helping the poor and assisting British business after the serious work of foreign policy had been done.

The No. 10 and FCO machines expected announcements of donations to be ready for when the Prime Minister and Foreign Secretary travelled. They resented DfID interference on British business interests or arms sales. The trade policy officials in DTI were incensed that we had established a trade-policy department; Treasury officials had written off unpayable debt before and did not need new conditions which would link debt relief to the establishment of poverty-reduction strategies. Those in charge of environmental policy had little interest in the situation in developing countries. The Foreign Office wanted us to run projects and not interfere in political issues such as the ending of conflict in Africa. Africa came low down the list of Foreign Office priorities but they certainly did not want DfID poking its nose in. The old order saw the duty of British government to take forward British interests. The suggestion that poverty, inequality and environmental degradation were threats to our interests and to the future of the planet as well as major moral concerns had hardly penetrated our institutional arrangements.

Similarly, the development NGOs did not believe that the poorer countries could open themselves to trade or attract inward investment. They felt they needed protection from the globalising world economy with tariffs that would protect their dependence on subsistence agriculture. This was well meant but would inevitably mean growing poverty. Most green NGOs shared this view and were convinced the world would not be sustainable if the poorest countries set out to develop as we had done. Developing countries were unwilling to agree trade or environmental agreements that locked them into poverty, as we saw at the Seattle meeting of the World Trade Organization (WTO).

At the ministerial meeting of the WTO in Seattle in 1999, I found myself lined up alongside the developing countries against the NGOs, trade unions and President Clinton, all of whom wanted minimum labour and environmental standards in trade agreements. This sounds reasonable but in fact the worst labour standards and lowest environmental standards are in the poorest countries. If standards they could not reach were made preconditions for benefiting from trade agreements, they would be locked out of the world economy. The Seattle WTO meeting was a disaster. There were massive demonstrations organised by the US trade union movement and one of the first outbreaks of violent protest organised by the anti-globalisers. DfID and I stood very firm on the need for a trade round that gave better trading opportunities to poor countries. At first we were criticised, but by the time the WTO ministerial meeting was held at Doha in 2001 it was accepted that international trade rules were unfair to developing countries. DfID was seen as a useful player in helping to shift conventional thinking and also in having supported and funded various reforms that made the WTO more developing-country friendly.

It was a constant battle to establish the authority of the new department. Public opinion was ahead of the power structures in understanding that we had a moral duty to provide better opportunities for the poor and needy, but that it was also in our self-interest to reduce poverty and encourage sustainable development. Our White Paper, *Eliminating World Poverty – a Challenge for the Twenty-first Century*, was published in November 1997. It argued that there was a need for urgent change, otherwise by the middle of the next century, if not before, the world would become unsustainable through the combination of population growth, environmental degradation, conflict and disease.

Debt relief

Despite all our battles we continued to make progress. On debt, there was a growing campaign, strongly supported by the Churches and faith groups, to mark the year 2000 by writing off the unpayable debt of the world's poorest countries. There were a lot of inaccurate claims, for example that the UK was receiving more in payments from poor countries than we were giving in aid, but the campaign was big-hearted and reflected a very strong tide of public opinion that Britain wanted to give a better chance to the poorest countries.

We set up an early strategy meeting to discuss our options on debt relief and decide what we could achieve. I found such meetings a joy. DfID had high-quality civil servants with long memories, as well as economists, environmentalists, social development experts, health and education advisers and experts on improving governance. In all areas of the work of the department, papers would be written and we would all meet around my table – in fact I had to order a larger table – thrashing out the options before us and all focused on using any influence available to us to achieve sustainable poverty reduction. I made it clear from the start that we would not be distracted by short-term political considerations. We would think through our strategies thoroughly and carefully and then decide how to popularise them. This meant I had to disappoint many of my parliamentary colleagues who came to me with their favourite NGO and equated progress on policy with more resources for their favourite charity. All of these groups were well intentioned but the most generous possible funding for the best possible UK NGOs was not capable of bringing about the massive reductions of poverty that were needed.

There had, of course, been debt write-offs before under the Conservative government. The debt in question was foreign currency debt owed by some of the poorest countries in the world to the World Bank and IMF, aid agencies and Export Guarantee departments. Such countries had little commercial debt. The private sector tends not to lend to very poor countries and if it did, had written off the debt long ago. The debt was caused partly by corruption when governments took on large public-sector projects, for hospitals, roads, etc. that they did not necessarily need, because bribes had been paid to officials or ministers to get them to take on the contract. But debt was also caused by falls in prices of unprocessed commodities which were the bulk of the exports of the poorest countries so that many poor countries earned massively less for the same exports than they had years before. In addition, such debt was denominated in dollars so if the value of their currency fell, the debt got ever bigger and interest on unpaid debt led to massive growth in the size of the debt. Thus many poor countries were burdened with debt that was simply unpayable, yet its existence meant they could not take up their World Bank allocations and thus they remained permanently mired in poverty.

The campaigners were calling for unconditional cancellation of debt and pointing out that it had often been incurred by previous regimes and should not obstruct reforming governments. But we in DfID were clear that if debt were cancelled unconditionally, it was likely that the old problems would recur, new debt would stack up and the problem would come around time and time again. We therefore proposed that we should reach international agreement to offer more generous debt relief on condition that poor countries drew up Poverty Reduction Strategies for better economic management, a crackdown on corruption, improved management of the public finances and the delivery of basic education and healthcare for all. We decided to support the campaigners but try to ensure that more generous debt relief should generate serious economic reform and a focus on poverty reduction.

We worked hard to build an international alliance for this and through this campaign I formed a very close working relationship with the Development ministers from The Netherlands, Norway and Germany, all of whom were women. We agreed to work together in the World Bank and brought a change of tone to

Governors' meetings which were more used to the reading out of notes prepared by technocrats than to a group of women ministers talking passionately about how to reduce poverty. On top of the good work we did together, Evelyn Herfkens of the Netherlands, Hilde Johnson from Norway and Heidemarie Wieczorek-Zeul and I became very good friends. We enjoyed our battles in the international system and were strengthened by our alliance.

In proposing that debt relief should be conditional on a poverty-reduction strategy, we had difficulty at first in convincing the Treasury. Treasury officials had seen debt relief before and expected to go for more of the same. Gordon Brown's advisers were much influenced by some of the NGOs and encouraged him to favour tokenistic announcements. Gradually, however, the arguments were listened to and support for debt relief in return for commitment to poverty reduction took hold. But there were reluctant governments in Japan, Germany and elsewhere and these needed to be shifted.

A G7 meeting – a gathering of the richest countries in the world – had been held in Denver shortly after the Labour government came to power, and one year later, the G7 was to be hosted by the UK in Birmingham. The view was that the Denver meeting had been less successful than it might because the agenda was too long, so No. 10 were determined to have a tight agenda in Birmingham and were deaf to all our pleading that the richest countries should not meet and fail to discuss development when the poorest countries were mired in debt. Then Ann Pettifor of Jubilee 2000, the umbrella group organising the campaign for debt relief, came to see me to say that the campaigners and the Churches were planning to descend on the G7 in Birmingham and encircle the city, calling for debt relief. All the churches and cathedrals in the city centre were to be thrown open and a large number of bishops were planning to join the demonstration. I promised to speak at the meetings and conveyed the good news to No. 10.

On the day, the weather was beautiful and people came in their thousands from all over Britain and beyond, many wearing shorts as they gathered in the churches and cathedrals of central Birmingham to call for debt relief for the poorest countries. Then, at the last minute, the agenda of the G7 was changed and the leaders of the richest countries bowed to the wishes of the people on the street and discussed what was to be done about debt relief. Final decisions were to be made in the G7 meeting in Cologne in twelve months' time and an election was due in Germany in the meantime. The campaigners made clear that they would be in Cologne and they started a letter-writing campaign to remind the German government and Churches that they had received debt relief at the end of the war, and to ask them to support debt relief for poor countries. The Social Democrats made clear that they would do so if elected and went on to form a coalition government with the Greens and thus Germany changed its position and Japan was not willing to hold out alone.

The final piece in the puzzle was the need to get countries to pay money to the World Bank trust fund so that the World Bank could write off its share of the debt without damaging its finances. I set aside a substantial sum from DfID's budget and Gordon Brown worked hard to get other countries to do likewise.

A great advance was made and $70 billion of debt has been written off and many countries have more coherent policies focused on poverty reduction than they have had for a very long time. Tanzania, Mozambique, Rwanda, Ghana and Ethiopia, and Honduras and Guyana amongst others, have made great advances. But the task is not complete. Coffee prices continued to fall and the debt relief granted is not generous enough so that some of the poorest countries in the world like Ethiopia and Rwanda have received all the debt relief on offer but are still burdened with high levels of debt that block their development prospects. There are proposals to move from a formula of debt to export-earning ratios to decide the level of debt relief to a consideration of the development prospects of each country. This would lead to considerable improvement.

In DfID, we were determined to re-examine all policy in order to focus on the sustainable reduction of poverty. There was a buzz of excitement and enthusiasm throughout the department which spread across the international system as we brought our poverty focus to our own funding arrangements and the funds we provided to the UN and all other international agencies. The EU was particularly ineffective and unfocused on poverty but despite this the Major government had committed nearly one third of our budget for spending through the EU. Here as elsewhere we agreed how reform should be driven forward and then worked to find allies.

John Vereker and I were clear that we should decentralise the department and improve our management of staff so that good thinking, high morale and decentralised authority would improve our effectiveness. As well as using our influence to improve the working of the international system, we were determined to make the UK's own programmes exemplary. The challenge of Rwanda helped us to learn lessons and reshape our work in a way that greatly improved our thinking.

The Rwanda example

Britain had no historical relationship with Rwanda, which was colonised by Belgium and was a subject of French engagement because it was francophone. But Britain, like other members of the Security Council, shared the guilt of failing to act to prevent the genocide which led to the killing of one million people – one in eight of the population – in 100 days in 1994. Under the Genocide Convention of 1948, the world agreed that we should always act to prevent genocide and had the authority to set aside sovereignty to do so. The UN mission in Rwanda sent repeated messages to the Secretariat saying that a terrible genocide was threatened but the Security Council refused to act.

I visited in 1998 in order to decide whether the UK should engage in helping Rwanda rebuild. I was deeply moved by the visit. Rwanda is a very beautiful country with a terrible history that resulted from colonial rule creating racist myths to elevate the Tutsi over the Hutu and to divide and rule in order to exercise control. In fact the country has a long united history, with both groups speaking the same language and intermarrying, but also a tradition of some people being cattle breeders and the others tilling the land, and some of its people are tall and thin and others more thick set. On this basis divisive colonial myths were built. I visited churches where people had fled as the killing started and clothing and bones still littered the floors. There was a shed with piles of skulls beside the church and a condolence book where I wrote an apology on behalf of the people of the UK for our failure to act to prevent the genocide. Just after this, a woman came up to me with a baby on her back and through an interpreter pointed to the deep scar across her back. She said she was alive because she had had another baby. They had hacked through her baby into her back and thrown her into a pit with many other bodies, but she was not dead and had managed to crawl out.

At the time of my visit, large parts of the country were still subject to incursions and killing, emergency feeding programmes were keeping children alive, but the economy was destroyed, government institutions were hardly functioning and a very new government was deeply distrustful of the international community. We decided the UK should step forward to help Rwanda. The government was completely distrustful of Belgium and France because of their past behaviour and without external support, they would not be able to restore the country, and continuing instability and ethnic hatred would be inevitable.

The first step was to try to get the government to trust us enough to allow us to help. We invited representatives of the government including Patrick Mazimhaka, who was an influential Rwandan minister, to dinner in Brussels where we were all present at an international meeting. We talked well into the night about what was to be done and built a little trust between us. We then approached the World Bank and IMF to discuss Rwanda's prospects. The answer was grim. There was no possibility of economic growth. The Bank and Fund could not responsibly recommend such a programme. So Rwanda was stuck, the economy was devastated, population growth was inevitable because devastated populations always increase their birth rate, and no country would move beyond humanitarian aid without a World Bank/IMF programme. We decided to host an international meeting, make a ten-year UK pledge and invite others to do the same. Vice-President (now President) Kagame attended the meeting and answered donors' questions and enough pledges were made to expand the ambition of the programme. The UK became a central player in helping Rwanda rebuild.

We went on to sign a long-term partnership agreement with the government which included commitments to steadily improve human rights and we agreed we would ask an independent arbiter to assess the performance of both parties. We received a great deal of criticism over our support for Rwanda. Obviously a country with such recent bitter history had many problems but without international support had no hope of progress. My view is that we can only make progress if we are willing to engage with imperfect countries and it is right to do so as long as we can agree a serious programme of reform and ensure it is maintained.

But there are always critics and in parts of Africa there is a deep prejudice against Tutsis. President Chirac was also deeply hostile to the Rwandan government and constantly trying to persuade Blair to shift the UK position. On top of this, there was an unwritten rule in the UN Security Council that the UK leads on anglophone African countries and the French on francophone, so we had difficulty in persuading our delegation to take an active position. In 1998, President Laurent Kabila of the Democratic Republic of Congo (DRC) turned against his former Rwandan allies and started to support the forces of the genocide in their attempts to reinvade

Rwanda, and the Rwandan and Ugandan armies re-entered the Congo. There were immediate demands for us to halt all aid to Rwanda and Uganda without any consideration of what this would mean for the poor of these countries. But we continued to support reform in both Uganda and Rwanda and worked for a peace process and the troops' withdrawal. South Africa played a very useful role in brokering a peace deal and withdrawal of all foreign forces. Rwanda is now seen as one of the leading African reformers. It remains very poor and traumatised, but ten years after the genocide its progress is remarkable. Our involvement with Rwanda led me to become engaged in trying to help end the civil war in Congo and to understand how conflict resolution, the rebuilding of weak states and development were intimately linked.

The effect of this is that we became more engaged in working to end conflict and help African countries rebuild. We also changed our model of development from short-term support to long-term partnerships focused on poverty reduction. We supported programmes which governments drew up and discussed with their people, rather than structural adjustment programmes imposed by the World Bank and IMF. This change from funding a proliferation of projects, each carrying the flag or banner of the funding agency, to strengthening the institutions, financial-management systems and competence of government institutions is now widely accepted to be a more effective and respectful model of development, and is increasingly being adopted throughout the international system. The UK was a leading player in driving the new model and the challenge of Rwanda taught us important lessons that we applied elsewhere.

The millennium development goals

Our other major campaign was to win international support for the International Development targets. These were, as I have said, derived from the agreements reached at the UN conferences of the 1990s and had been carefully selected to measure progress on the range of issues crucial to achieving sustainable development. They are to halve the proportion of people in the world living in extreme poverty, to get all children to primary school, slash infant and maternal mortality, and provide water and sanitation. The targets described the changes people need to be able to lift themselves out of poverty – progress is needed on income, education and health to be sustainable. We believed that the targets could move the world to start to implement the grand declarations it agreed on through the UN. They could also provide a focus for collaborative work and would provide an agenda agreed by all countries through the UN, rather than development objectives imposed on poor countries by rich donors. We joined with others to try to get the targets agreed by all international institutions. The group of women ministers – known as the Uttstein Group from the place of our first meeting – led the campaign. Gradually the targets were adopted by the World Bank, IMF and EU, and then, as the agreed objective of the Millennium Conference of the UN General Assembly, were renamed the Millennium Development Goals. Jeremy Greenstock, the UK Ambassador to the UN, played a very helpful role in pushing the targets forward and thus we entered the new millennium with an agreed determination to work together to massively reduce poverty in the world.

Making globalisation work for the poor

In December 2000, we published our second White Paper: *Making Globalisation Work for the Poor*. This was partly our response to the chaos at the Seattle meeting of the World Trade Organization where NGOs, trade unions and industrialised countries pushed for agreements on labour and environmental standards which would, as I have said, exclude the poorest countries from the benefits of trade. The White Paper suggests that the wealth and potential of globalisation could be shaped to bring benefits to the poor. In my introduction I argued that we are living at a time of profound historical change. Great wealth and squalor exist side by side. We could move forward to a period of massive progress and the removal of abject poverty from the human condition; or we could see growing poverty, marginalisation, conflict and environmental degradation. Neither prospect is inevitable. The future is a matter of political will and choice.

The White Paper helped move forward the demand for a new trade round focused on making trade rules fair for developing countries. It also helped provide a positive agenda to manage this era of change as an alternative to the negative campaigns of the globophobe movement. It enhanced the reputation of the department and support for our work from the Treasury and the Prime Minister. At the time, we seemed to be making considerable progress with the UK adopting a very progressive stance on the world stage, but the logic of this approach clashes with the position Tony Blair has adopted since 11 September 2001. If we are to make our relationship with the US the most important focus of our international policy then we cannot be a leading player in working for agreements and strengthened institutions to shape globalisation to benefit the poor and to manage the world sustainably. The UK needs an urgent debate on the role we wish to adopt as the central focus of our international policy.

In the early years DfID had to fight a lot of battles, but as time went on the department won increasing respect for its effectiveness, international influence and the quality of its thinking. Gordon Brown always had sympathy for development, but he was initially briefed by officials close to NGOs and did not understand the ambition of the DfID agenda. It was after the publication of our second White Paper on globalisation and the rise in DfID's reputation in the World Bank that a close working relationship developed. Thus I had unpleasant battles over the very small initial offers made to DfID in the first two spending reviews, but by the time we had reached the 2001/02 settlement, the relationship with Gordon Brown and his senior officials had been consolidated and we achieved the commitment to increase our spend from the £2.2 billion we inherited in 1997 to £4.6 billion by 2005/06. This was a rise from 0.26 per cent of GDP to 0.4 per cent. I was pleased that this commitment was increased to £6.5 billion or 0.47 per cent of GDP by 2007/08 in the 2004 Comprehensive Spending Review. However, there is still a way to go to get the UK to fulfill its promise to spend 0.7 per cent of GDP on aid.

Tony Blair's interest in development started to rise as he travelled and heard compliments for DfID's work. He and Cherie made a point of telling me this on more than one occasion. It was not, however, until the Labour Party conference in 2001, after the General Election, that he said Africa was 'a scar on the conscience of the world' and pledged to take a strong interest in Africa in his second term.

'Blair's wars'

During Blair's first term UK troops were deployed in Iraq, Kosovo, Sierra Leone and East Timor. I do not think it would be fair to argue that the pride in the UK military that Blair expressed in his speech ten days before the 1997 election led him to deploy troops when others would not have done so. But if we examine the record of these actions, it helps explain how Blair came to enjoy the drama and glory that goes with military action. It also shows how he failed to learn lessons that could have enabled him to handle the 2002/03 Iraq crisis with much more wisdom and international support.

In December 1998, we had the first of what have been termed 'Blair's wars'. Operation Desert Fox saw the UK supporting President Clinton's decision to unleash a seventy-hour missile blitz aimed, we were informed, at Saddam Hussein's capacity to produce chemical, biological and nuclear weapons. The crisis had come to a head after the Chief Weapons Inspector, Richard Butler, delivered to the Security Council a detailed litany of Iraqi obstruction. President Clinton, who was well aware that he was being accused of timing the air strikes in order to distract attention from the Lewinsky affair, stressed the assault had been launched on the unanimous recommendation of his national security advisers. Tony Blair insisted that there was no alternative to force, saying: 'We are taking military action with real regret but also with real determination. We have exhausted all other avenues.'

Clinton made clear that US policy would now be focused on toppling Saddam's regime and working towards the day when Iraq had a government worthy of its people. He said the US would pursue a policy of containment and would strike if Saddam attempted to rebuild weapons of mass destruction. Washington also intended to increase aid to Iraqi opposition forces. A few hours before the attack began, 125 UN personnel were hurriedly evacuated from Baghdad, including inspectors from the UN Special Commission on Iraq and the International Atomic Energy Agency.

In the light of subsequent developments, it is worth noting that a US right-wing think-tank, Project for the New American Century, had written to President Clinton in January 1998 to say that current policy towards Iraq was not succeeding and demanding military action to overthrow the regime. They were very critical of Clinton's policy of containment. The letter was signed by Elliot Abrams, Richard L. Armitage, Richard Perle, Donald Rumsfeld, Paul Wolfowitz and Robert B. Zoellick, all of whom were to be appointed to the Bush administration which took office in January 2001.

It is absolutely clear from the letter and other documents like 'Rebuilding America's Defences', which was written in September 2000 and drawn up by the same think-tank backed by Dick Cheney, Donald Rumsfeld, Paul Wolfowitz and Jeb Bush, that the Bush administration was planning to take military control of the Gulf region. The document states that 'while the unresolved conflict with Iraq provides the immediate justification, the need for a substantial

American force presence in the Gulf transcends the issue of the regime of Saddam Hussein'. There were no doubt officials in the Foreign Office who were following this debate and well aware long before 11 September 2001 of the Bush administration's determination to attack Iraq. It is a serious failure of UK policy that more detailed thinking was not put in place to decide how to respond to these plans before the administration came to power. The Foreign Office should be asked to account for this, though, to be fair, it was almost completely sidelined in the run-up to the 2003 war, with Tony Blair taking all power to himself and his entourage in Downing Street, and Jack Straw doing his bidding.

Kosovo

March 1999 brought the second of Blair's wars. It was during the war in Kosovo, which lasted to June 1999, that Blair and Campbell honed their PR machine and Blair's image as a humanitarian war leader. Most memorable was his visit to a refugee tent with shirt sleeves rolled up. The DfID representative on the trip described how an advance party had chosen the family and the tent and arranged the Prime Minister's clothing to create the most effective image, which was duly relayed around the world. A few weeks later Blair sported a red top and black trousers when he visited refugees in Albania. This is the only occasion on which I've known him to wear red, but these were the colours of the Albanian flag and helped endear Tony to the Albanians and Kosovars. Many Kosovan babies were named Tony thereafter.

There is no doubt that Blair milked his image as a war leader, but the Kosovo policy was led by the Foreign Office and supported by all Nato governments. Blair became highly engaged after war was inevitable. I was one of those who had believed when we were in Opposition that we should have acted more firmly against ethnic cleansing in the Balkans. I was on a train on my way to Macclesfield to spend Easter with my son's adoptive family when Tony Blair rang and asked me to go to Macedonia to see what could be done to help the Kosovan refugees. They were being pushed out of their homes as a consequence of the 1996–99 civil war – which the Kosovars termed a war of liberation and the Serbs as terrorism. The refugees were trapped in no-man's-land because the Macedonian government would not allow them to cross the border.

I travelled with David Manning, who was later to be Tony Blair's foreign policy adviser in No. 10. I had to cajole and threaten the Macedonian government with promises of international support and/or isolation if the refugees were not allowed across the border. The basic problem was that there was a large Albanian-speaking minority in Macedonia who were discriminated against by the majority community. The government did not want to let in more Albanian-speakers and feared that the instability in Kosovo might spread to Macedonia. I promised that we would arrange for the immediate provision of camps and supplies if the refugees were let in. My breakthrough came when I met up with Brigadier (later Major General) Tim Cross, who was Commander of the Logistic Brigade in Macedonia as part of the Nato forces – in place to act as peacekeepers if an agreement were reached at the Rambouillet peace talks. He and his unit were much distressed at the suffering on the border, and had been supplying food. They had also provided body bags for the elderly and babies who had died whilst waiting in no-man's-land. I asked him how quickly a camp could be erected and promised DfID funding. We then made a deal with the government of Macedonia, the United Nations High Commission for Refugees (UNHCR) and the Nato forces that the troops would erect the camps and get them running, then hand over to UNHCR. On this basis, the borders were opened and the refugees allowed in.

I went on to Albania where very poor families were volunteering to host refugees from Kosovo, but where there was also an enormous strain on local resources from the sheer burden of numbers of refugees in a very poor country. I made arrangements to establish a DfID office and improve the supply of resources. On the way home I phoned Sadako Ogata, United Nations High Commissioner for Refugees, and Catherine Bertini, Executive Director of the World Food Programme, to say we must urgently improve support for the refugees. It was in Tirana, on this visit, that I saw posters extolling Nato and groups of refugees chanting 'Nato, Nato' in the style of enthusiastic football supporters.

During this trip, I also visited Nato headquarters in Macedonia and had a briefing from General Mike Jackson, who was there as the Nato commander. There was speculation over the likelihood of a bombing campaign and talk of where the partition of Kosovo might be allowed to fall, based on the soldiers' experience of the ineffectual response to ethnic cleansing in Bosnia. On my return, I stressed to Blair that such widespread expectations that Nato would compromise over Kosovo would only strengthen Milosevic's intransigence, and that it was very important that we were much firmer and clearer about our unwillingness to allow ethnic cleansing to succeed.

The talks aimed at reaching a peace agreement in Kosovo, hosted by the French at Rambouillet, opened on 5 February. The Kosovars demanded a referendum to enable them to choose whether to establish an independent state and the Serbs refused to allow Nato peacekeepers to be deployed to prevent a continuation of ethnic cleansing. When the talks broke down after five weeks, a Nato bombing campaign became inevitable. The Nato decision to intervene was based on the experience of Bosnia, where failure to intervene led to public opinion demanding action in the face of images of concentration camps and ethnic cleansing. As President Clinton said, 'We learned that if you don't stand up to brutality and the killing of innocent people, you invite the people who do it to do more of it. We learned that firmness can save lives and stop armies. Now we have a chance to take the lessons we learned in Bosnia and put them to work in Kosovo.' But Kosovo was a considerable challenge. It was the first time in its history that Nato had gone to war, and the campaign was aimed at preventing a humanitarian tragedy rather than a military threat.

The military action was controversial, Russia was hostile and early commitment not to use ground troops probably encouraged Milosevic's intransigence. There was also a danger of loss of public support as mistakes were made and the air campaign ran out of targets. Blair and Campbell moved to shore up the Nato PR machine and to start to hint publicly that there might be a commitment to the use of ground troops after all. This caused tension with Clinton who felt that Blair was grandstanding, but I suspect the threat of ground troops may have helped to make Milosevic more willing to negotiate a settlement. The French and Russians took the lead in negotiating a peace agreement which led to Serbian troops withdrawing from Kosovo and the refugees returning under UN supervision.

It is notable, in the light of later developments in Iraq, that the decision was made to halt military action and to leave Milosevic in place rather than seek to invade Serbia. He was later brought to trial at The Hague for genocide and war crimes with the support of the Serbian people because they wanted to bring sanctions to an end and win international support for economic development. There were many calls for Saddam Hussein to be indicted as a war criminal, but a strategy for helping the people of Iraq to overthrow Saddam Hussein and send him for trial was never seriously considered.

There are many lessons to learn from the war in Kosovo, one of the most important being that the failure to settle the final status of Kosovo after the war has left it in limbo, with high levels of unemployment which exacerbate ethnic tension and have led to a terrible outbreak of ethnic violence and destruction of ancient Serb churches during 2004. The underlying problem was that the decision to intervene in Kosovo was not clearly thought through, and demonstrates the new challenge to the international system posed by the post–Cold War world. For some, Nato's action, without a UN mandate, was illegal. Others argued there was a precedent in the interpretation of international law to allow action to prevent a humanitarian disaster.

Responsibility to protect

It was against this backdrop of confusion in international policy that Kofi Annan made a speech making clear that he too thought there was a strong case for Nato action to prevent a humanitarian disaster in Kosovo, and it was after Kosovo that he requested the General Assembly to review international law and to forge a new agreement on how to deal with humanitarian threats when the only remedy might be an assault on sovereignty. He posed the central question starkly and directly: 'If humanitarian intervention is, indeed, an unacceptable assault on sovereignty, how should we respond to a Rwanda, to a Srebrenica – to gross and systematic violations of human rights that affect every precept of our common humanity?' For several years Kofi Annan has worked to shift the terms of the debate about humanitarian intervention in order to build a consensus in favour of agreed principles for intervention; principles that would enhance the authority of the Security Council and improve the prospects for effective, unified action.

The International Commission on Intervention and State Sovereignty was established by the government of Canada in response to the request from Kofi Annan. His challenge to the international community was to reach agreement on the question which has been one of the most controversial foreign-policy issues of the last decade. The Commission was asked to consider when, if ever, it is appropriate for states to take coercive, and in particular military, action against another state for the purpose of protecting people at risk in that other state. They were asked to consult across the world and consider the moral, political and operational questions and to bring back a report which would help the Secretary-General and everyone else find new common ground.

The report is very impressive. Its central theme is 'The Responsibility to Protect', the idea that the concept of sovereignty includes a responsibility to protect citizens from avoidable catastrophe and that when governments are unwilling or unable to do so, the responsibility must be borne by the international community. The report makes clear that the Responsibility to Protect means a responsibility to prevent and react, and that all means short of military action must be exhausted before military action is taken. It also insists that the interests of the people in need of protection must be the only justification for such action. It lays down strict principles for military intervention based on just war principles: that there must be just cause, the primary purpose must be to halt human suffering, and it must be a last resort, pro-portionate and have a reasonable chance of success.

Sadly, the report was published in December 2001 and thus overshadowed by the events of 11 September. It has therefore hardly come to public attention and has not been taken forward given the weakening of a commitment to unified action and diminution of the authority of the UN brought about by the war in Iraq. It is a tragedy that our Prime Minister, who had discussed these questions following the Kosovo conflict during his speech in Chicago in 1999, appears not to be aware of this highly significant report. He put himself forward in his Sedgefield speech in 2004 as a lone voice determined to take military action for humanitarian reasons and appeared to be unaware of the agreement that had already been reached about how best to do this. This is a tragedy, because he could have fulfilled his commitment to take action on Iraq through the UN, and secured a proud legacy if he had invoked the thinking behind 'The Responsibility to Protect' as the way to approach Iraq.

East Timor

The end of 1999 saw the UK deploy Gurkhas in East Timor, as part of the multinational force authorised by the UN to protect the people from attacks by the militias after Indonesia's withdrawal in September 1999 after twenty-four years of occupation. The preparation of East Timor for independence was led by Sergio Vierra de Mello – who was later killed in Iraq – under a UN mandate. DfID contributed to the international effort to help East Timor reconstruct and prepare for independence and it was through this work and his previous duties at UNHCR that I got to know Sergio quite well. I also worked with Xanana Gusmao and Jose Ramos-Horta who were to be President and Foreign Secretary of the new, independent East Timor. An old friend, Ian Martin, bravely led the UN mission that conducted the self-determination ballot. The mission was driven out for a time by the outbreak of violence orchestrated from Indonesia in response to the Timorese daring to vote for independence. I have a photo of Ian retrieving a hidden bottle of whisky when they returned. The UK was a significant but relatively small player in East Timor where the lead was taken by Australia. East Timor is now in dispute with Australia about oil and gas deposits off its coast which could secure a good future for these brave and much-abused people.

Sierra Leone

In Sierra Leone the UK was the leading player – although it is wrong to suggest that this was one of 'Blair's wars' as there was no 'war' involving UK forces. Sierra Leone is a beautiful country in West Africa that was colonised by Britain and became independent in 1961. Its rich diamond and other mineral deposits fed corruption in government, and the population of Freetown, which included a significant number of people descended from returning slaves, tended to look down on the rural African population. These conditions led to an outbreak of a very brutal civil war in the early 1990s. In 1997 large parts of the army joined the rebels and there was a coup against the elected government of President Kabbah which led to the withdrawal of the government to neighbouring Guinea.

Britain's military engagement in Sierra Leone came about almost by accident. After various attempts by West African governments to defend the legitimate government and broker peace, a deal was eventually signed at Lomé in July 1999. The agreement provided for the disarmament, demobilisation and resettlement of rebel forces and the establishment of a government of national unity with the leader of the rebels, Foday Sankoh, installed as Vice President and a total amnesty for the rebels' use of child soldiers, amputations and abuse of human rights. The UN Special Representative signed the accord but made it clear that the UN could not be bound by an amnesty for gross violations of human rights. We in DfID had our doubts about the peace agreement, but saw it as the only route to peace for the long-suffering people of Sierra Leone and therefore became heavily involved in trying to move forward the process of demobilisation and resettlement of rebel soldiers. I became very involved personally and travelled to Sierra Leone many times to try to get the demobilisation process going.

Despite their installation in government, the rebels' co-operation with the peace agreement was very limited, and the security situation remained precarious with humanitarian agencies unable to access much of the country. In October 1997 a resolution was passed at the Security Council to establish a UN peacekeeping force and UN peacekeepers began to arrive in dribs and drabs. It had been difficult to reach agreement in the Security Council and there was no support for a peace-enforcement force, so a peacekeeping force was deployed when there was not yet a peace to keep. This inadequate commitment to the means necessary to end the conflicts of the post-Cold War era is a great weakness in the international system.

Shortly after the UN deployed, the rebels began to attack UN units and to seize their equipment and in May 2000 took large numbers hostage and then Freetown was threatened once again. Kofi Annan appealed for support from the international community and a UK force was sent in to evacuate UK and European nationals. It was at this point that I and others insisted, and Tony Blair agreed, that we should leave some of our forces securing the airport so that the UN authority was strengthened and the rebels unable to take Freetown. Then in August, eleven British soldiers were taken hostage by a rebel group known as the West Side Boys. In September an SAS unit went in to rescue the hostages. This led to the death of a British soldier and broke the strength of the West Side Boys. It is widely seen in Sierra Leone as one of the important developments that helped end the rebellion.

Beyond this, UK forces did no fighting but they provided a training team to establish and advise a new Sierra Leonean army. DfID funded and organised police advisers to help establish a police force and the long, painful task of rebuilding ministries, resettling rebel fighters and putting in place structures to challenge the endemic corruption began. There was no UK war in Sierra Leone, but UK troops played a very important role in backing up the authority of the UN and helping a country devastated by civil war to re-establish legitimate armed forces and enough order and security so that the long-term task of rebuilding the country would be taken forward. DfID remains heavily involved in Sierra Leone, alongside the UN and other international agencies. The excitement of military action draws media attention but the rebuilding of nations takes very many years of patient work and effort and the public hears little of it.

Tony Blair was not much engaged in the detailed discussion of Sierra Leone, but after a cross-Whitehall committee chaired by the Foreign Secretary was established, John Sawers, who was the No. 10 foreign policy Private Secretary, would represent the Prime Minister and usually supported the more robust DfID arguments about what was needed to establish a viable future for Sierra Leone. In the case of Sierra Leone, I saw once again how when soldiers are deployed, the media engage and the issue moves up the Whitehall agenda, but interest soon fades once the spotlight moves. However, some of the UK officers deployed in Sierra Leone shared DfID's view of the need to keep pressure on the UN to disarm the rebels and to engage long term to rebuild the country. I still meet Sierra Leoneans in Britain and elsewhere in the world who seek me out to thank the UK for what we have done to help Sierra Leone. Thus, without going to war the UK made a very important contribution in Sierra Leone. Sadly the hugely important lessons of Sierra Leone seem not to have been learned by the No. 10 machine.

2001 election

At the end of its first period in government after eighteen years, Labour went into the election in June 2001, with substantial achievements, facing a country that did not want to return the Conservatives to power but had been disappointed by the Labour government.

I wrote in my diary at the time that the election campaign was very centrally controlled, media obsessed and very 'boysey' – this is an aspect of the Blair leadership style that many women comment on. It is strange, because there are more women in senior positions than ever before, and yet there is a feel of a group of boys who have taken over and find it exciting to exercise power over others through their own little gang. I have reflected on this and concluded that women were represented in bigger numbers in Parliament and Cabinet, but under New Labour power moved to a small group around Tony Blair which focused on media manipulation. None of the new women was at the centre of power. During the election campaign, I made a speech about Tony Blair's leadership at the request of Alastair Campbell. He said they would provide a draft and an audience and guide the media there. I agreed, but modified the text. I was wheeled into a meeting with an audience of Labour members assembled and read my speech to a camera, there was applause and no questions and then I was wheeled out again. The speech got some references in the press but not as much as Alastair had in mind, because I was unwilling to be sufficiently sycophantic. This, however, is the style of modern campaigning and the media have a significant responsibility for being willing to take seriously such manipulation. I also visited many marginal seats and found hard-working, popular MPs and a generally supportive public, but everyone turned off by the media coverage of the campaign.

Labour won the election with a loss of only six seats on a much-reduced turnout. But someone astutely labelled it the 'yes, but' election. The figures are very interesting. The turnout was only 59 per cent, an all-time post-war low. Labour won 10,724,953 votes, 41 per cent of votes cast, the Conservatives 8,357,615 – 32 per cent – and the Liberal Democrats 4,814,321 – 18 per cent. The commentators frequently suggest that Tony Blair is the most successful Labour Prime Minister there has ever been because he has won two terms with an overwhelming Commons majority. Clearly, if success is measured by Commons majorities, this is true, but if we compare the vote with previous general elections the results are startling.

Labour General Election results (millions)

1945	11.97	47.7 % (won)
1950	13.27	46.1 % (won)
1951	13.95	48.8 % (lost to the Conservatives who had 48 %)
1955	12.41	46.4 % (lost)
1959	12.22	43.8 % (lost)
1964	12.21	44.1 % (won)

	1966	13.07	47.9 % (won)
	1970	12.18	43 % (lost)
Feb	1974	11.65	37.2 % (won)
Oct	1974	11.46	39.3 % (won)
	1979	11.51	36.9 % (lost)
	1983	8.46	27.6 % (lost)
	1987	10.03	30.8 % (lost)
	1992	11.56	34.4 % (lost)
	1997	13.52	43.2 % (won)
	2001	10.73	40.7 % (won)

The results show that the Blair 'magic' has not reached new parts and won more votes than previous Labour leaders. As I have said, the 1997 result was the same percentage of the vote as 1970 when we lost. And half a million fewer voted Blair in 1997 than Major in 1992. There was not a uniform swing. The Labour share of the vote fell in the safe seats that we held in 1992 and 1997. Tony Blair is a great election winner because of the rise of the third party and the weakness of the Tories and the distortion this leads to in seats held in the House of Commons, but in reality he has not been more successful in winning votes than Labour leaders before him.

My comment in my diary on the outcome of the election was 'the country is saying we want to return the government, we want a good economy and good public services – i.e. carry on and do it a bit more rapidly, but we don't love you and want to reprimand you, hence the reduced turnout.'

After the election, the spin was that it was the end of spin, but they span on and on about the reform of public services in a way that stressed involvement of the private sector and conflict with the unions. Again, my comments to myself in my diary were: 'This is ridiculous behaviour. The parliamentary party is fed up, the unions angry and the media says the government has started with a wobble. We need to improve public services with the help of those working in the public sector and only get into conflict if it is necessary to deliver results. But we begin with a big problem on trust purely as a result of spin.'

One month later, I wrote: 'Already there is a bad political atmosphere. This is because of briefing after briefing to the media about bringing in the private sector to take over parts of the public sector, without any specifics. This throws away goodwill and damages morale without any gains. In my view it is massively politically inept . . . Said this at Cabinet!'

This was the atmosphere in which Blair's second term began.

3

THE 'HISTORIC' SECOND TERM

There was no honeymoon after the second election victory. The Labour Party was in the same mood as the country, glad to have won but troubled over Tony Blair's leadership style and many of his proposals. Thus as early as 18 June, union general secretaries wrote to the *Guardian* opposing US plans for an anti-ballistic missile shield. Peter Kilfoyle attacked Blair's leadership style. There was anger that the promised ban on foxhunting and tobacco advertising were not included in the Queen's Speech, and a general unease about constant promises to involve the private sector in the delivery of public services.

Commentators frequently suggest that Tony Blair has a unique talent to reach parts of the electorate that Labour could never reach before. The results of the 2001 election seemed to convince Blair and his advisers that this was true and make them even more dismissive of the concerns of the Labour Party than they had been in the first term. There was a definite change of tone in Blair's behaviour from the beginning of the second term – less interest in focus groups or willingness to listen more generally, more determined to be bold, increasingly concerned about his legacy. As we have seen, both Blair and the commentators misread the results of the 2001 election. Labour was awarded 64 per cent of the seats in the House of Commons and thus seemed to have strong support in the country. The reality was that for every five people who voted Labour, seven voted for other parties and eight did not vote. As Tony Blair became convinced that he understood Britain better than anyone else and therefore had a right to drive policy through without listening or consulting, he was in fact sitting on a large majority in the House of Commons based on the support of only one quarter of the electorate.

In September, it was revealed that Labour Party membership had slumped by 50,000 and on September 11 Blair was due to address the TUC. The general expectation was that he would not be well received. I was due to travel to Brighton for the TUC dinner, when the news of the attack on the Twin Towers came through. Like many others, I cancelled everything and sat in front of the television watching those terrible pictures again and again. Tony Blair's speech was cancelled.

The events of September 11 moved the whole world. There was a deep sense of solidarity with the US and a united determination to work together against the perpetrators of the attack. The Security Council passed a resolution requiring all countries to take action to tighten their laws and co-operate in controlling money-laundering and exchanging information and intelligence, and set up a committee to monitor progress. The General Assembly also passed a resolution of support. *Le Monde* famously produced its headline: 'We are all American now'. I remember constituents, particularly Muslim constituents, asking me to pass on their regrets and condolences. The events of September 11 also seemed to electrify Blair. He had been searching for his legacy. After September 11, he seemed to have found his cause.

I wonder now just how early Blair had decided he wanted to support the Bush administration on Iraq. His first meeting with Bush took place in February, well before the election. When I was called to No. 10 after the election, I was kept waiting by the goings and comings of the move of Robin Cook from the Foreign Office and his replacement by Jack Straw. This caused considerable tension and there was a delay before Robin accepted his new post. As early as July Bush praised Blair for his willingness to think afresh about National Missile Defence. Robin was unlikely to be as helpful as Straw on this. Robin had certainly become as keen as Blair on Europe and the euro, but was likely to be more sceptical about relationships with an extremely right-wing American administration. How much briefing had Blair had on the views of the incoming US administration on Iraq and was this his real reason for moving Robin? When I eventually saw Blair he apologised for the delay and said how unpleasant he found such arguments, but was happy to tell me that he wanted me to carry on in DfID and us to work closely together on Africa. This was a surprise. Blair had shown very little interest in development or Africa in his first term, but I welcomed the prospect of Prime Ministerial muscle to back up our efforts

I have often speculated on where this new interest came from. I suspect Clinton. He showed a great flurry of interest in Africa towards the end of his presidency and continued to talk about Africa afterwards. In fact this irritated me. I used to say to myself, 'You used to be the most powerful man in the world. Why didn't you do more for Africa then?' My suspicion is that he advised Blair of his regret about not doing more for Africa. And then when I read Richard Clarke's book *Against All Enemies*, which described how, towards the end of his presidency, President Clinton became increasingly concerned about al-Qaeda and the risk of weapons of mass destruction (WMD) falling into the hands of terrorist organisations, I strongly suspected that Clinton's advice had been to do more for Africa and be concerned about al-Qaeda and WMD, and that this might help explain Blair's misjudgements on Bush and Iraq. He was looking to make his mark on history and Clinton had told him Africa and al-Qaeda were issues of historical importance. Blair frequently says when discussing Iraq, with deep conviction, that there is a danger of WMD and terrorism coming together.

There may be such a danger, though as both the US National Commission on Terrorist Attack on the US and the Butler Committee made clear, Iraq had no connection with this danger. My suspicion is that Blair misinterpreted Clinton's advice and focused his attention on Iraq rather than the broader danger from al-Qaeda. This is speculation, but certainly as late as the last week in September 2001, the Prime Minister was taking phone calls from Clinton, giving advice about the best way to handle Afghanistan, Pakistan and Iran.

On 14 September, Parliament was recalled and Blair made clear we would stand shoulder to shoulder with Bush. On 18 September, Blair flew to Washington and then to Berlin and Paris. We were told through the media that he was constantly on the phone to foreign leaders. He engaged in a whirlwind of activity and seemed energised by the crisis. In my diary of 30 September 2001, I wrote: 'TB quickly bestrode the world stage – shoulder to shoulder with the US. He loves such a role and is good at it. All of us were horrified by the events of September 11 but most decent people are very worried by the bellicose statements from Bush and fearful of the US lashing out and killing lots of innocent Afghans and making things worse.'

I said something similar in an interview which caused a press flurry about splits in the Cabinet, and inevitably meant I was briefed against by No. 10 as 'not long to stay in government'. I received phone calls of concern from Jack Straw and John Prescott – Blair being in the US. Then I received a letter from Blair on 17 September saying that he had read the transcript of my interview and could see that they had unfairly made mischief out of what I said. He went on to say nonetheless that 'it is crucially important at this sensitive stage that all bids for interviews are cleared with No. 10 and that we stick to a very tight line in such interviews. Otherwise we risk putting the whole operation at risk with serious consequences.'

I made a note in my diary that the atmospherics at the emergency Cabinet were fine. I stressed the need to deal with Osama bin Laden and the Taliban but to consider the people of Afghanistan and be aware of how serious the humanitarian crisis was with 5 million people dependent on food aid and the numbers rising. My diary entry is: 'TB asked for a word afterwards – said how much he admired me and my work. He said it was one of the proudest things in his government and if I was ever unhappy I should talk to him. I commented to myself "not exactly a ticking off!"'

We then went off to the truncated Labour conference. Tony Blair made his impressive speech insisting that 'out of the shadow of evil should come lasting good'. He argued that we must deal with Afghanistan where Osama bin Laden was organising, the Taliban oppressed the Afghans and drugs were grown that provided 90 per cent of the heroin on British streets. But he claimed that the threat of chaos was bringing the world together and that the power of community was asserting itself. People were realising our inter-dependence. He asserted that if Rwanda happened again we would act and went on to say that Africa was a scar on the conscience of the world and we must do more to create a partnership with Africa.

The atmosphere of drama distracted attention from the importance of the debates criticising the humiliating voucher system for asylum seekers and demanding more discussion of the proposed role for the private sector in the provision of public services. Blair went on to travel to Pakistan and Russia, and to host a dinner at No. 10 for the leaders of France, Germany, Italy, Spain, Belgium and the Netherlands to discuss Afghanistan.

Afghanistan and Pakistan

I, and my department, were increasingly involved in Afghanistan. A severe drought had exacerbated the poverty resulting from twenty years of resistance to Soviet occupation. Osama bin Laden and many other Islamic fighters had been funded and supported by the US and

Saudi Arabia when they were fighting Soviet occupation. But after the Soviet withdrawal in 1989, the international community turned away from Afghanistan and the militias continued to organise and fund themselves through drug production. The continuous violence and lack of government authority led to growing poverty and suffering across Afghanistan. It was in these circumstances that the Taliban came to power. They were village-educated, with a very primitive understanding of Islamic teaching, but they brought order which the people so desperately wanted. They went on to ban women from teaching, girls from going to school, television or cassette music, and to impose brutal punishments. They also allowed Osama bin Laden to return to Afghanistan after his withdrawal from Sudan. This was the situation in Afghanistan before the attack on the Twin Towers.

After years of neglect, all eyes switched to Afghanistan. There was general agreement on the need to bring Osama bin Laden to justice. Tony Blair produced his first dossier which was put in the House of Commons library on 4 October. It outlined the history of bin Laden, his relations with the Taliban and what was known of his support for terrorism and the events of September 11. The Prime Minister warned – in a way that was to become familiar – that much of the evidence was based on intelligence, was highly sensitive and all details could not be revealed without compromising people. In his statement to the recalled House of Commons on 4 October, he made clear that the Taliban must hand over bin Laden or face military action.

The humanitarian crisis in Afghanistan was very serious before September 11. Two decades of conflict and three years of drought had inflicted terrible suffering on Afghanistan's 20 million people. Afghanistan has some of the worst child and maternal mortality rates, lowest literacy rates and a life expectancy estimated at forty-four years. Disability was common as a consequence of land mines and other unexploded ordnance. Health and education services had largely disappeared as had the essential infrastructure of water supply, roads and communications. Conflict and drought had created over 4 million refugees, 2 million in Pakistan, 1.5 million in Iran and 500,000 elsewhere in the region and beyond. Since the Soviet withdrawal very little support had been provided for the camps and refugees in Pakistan and Iran.

DfID had been involved in providing humanitarian relief through NGOs and the UN system before September 11. No UK personnel were allowed to work in Afghanistan because the security assessment was that US and UK citizens were particular targets. I insisted that the agencies we funded honoured this advice. This caused some conflict with the NGOs but I was clear that I had to take such advice seriously, and in any case it was good to employ Afghan nationals. Then, following the attack on the Twin Towers, all international staff were withdrawn for their own safety, and the Taliban threatened local staff with death if they used telephones to communicate with outside agencies. Some World Food Programme (WFP) warehouses were also looted.

This led to the risk of a massive humanitarian disaster. One in four of the population was dependent on food aid and the WFP convoys had halted. On top of this, the threat of war had led to hundreds of thousands of Afghans moving within the country. I became intensely involved in trying to mobilise international support for the refugees in neighbouring countries and to get food convoys moving again. This meant that we needed more help from Pakistan, which shares a long border with Afghanistan and whose tribal areas see a constant movement of population between the two countries.

On 17–19 October I visited Pakistan and UN agencies and refugee camps in the North West Frontier which borders Afghanistan. I also met with President Musharaff and other Pakistani ministers to discuss our support for Pakistan's development. The Chief of the Defence Staff, Musharaff had taken over from the regime of Nawaz Sharif in a coup in 1999. Many people argued that we should not engage with any military government but I took a different view. Pakistan had been grossly misgoverned for most of the years since the state was created. The previous governments of Benazir Bhutto and Nawaz Sharif were supposedly democratic but deeply corrupt, and life was getting ever more difficult for the people of Pakistan. Islamist protest movements were growing in strength. General Musharaff had appointed a team of talented technocrats to his Cabinet including the impressive Finance Minister Shaukat Aziz, a former senior executive at City Bank who later became Prime Minister. Musharaff said he was determined to crack down on corruption, drive forward reform and hand over to a better democratic system. I liked both Musharaff and Shaukat Aziz and found them genuine in their commitment to reform.

We agreed to establish a significant DfID programme to support the reform effort. This inevitably led to criticism, but, as I have said, in my view this is what development is about. The poorest countries tend to be badly governed and open to criticism of all kinds. Aid should not be provided to oppressive governments to do as they wish, but DfID aid was used to improve financial management, get children to school, and improve healthcare systems and help drive reform. The Musharaff takeover was popular in Pakistan and my view was that we needed to engage with Pakistan and Afghanistan and ideally other countries in the region, otherwise there was a danger of growing poverty and instability throughout the area. The nightmare scenario was a Taliban-type takeover in nuclear-armed Pakistan. The mistakes made in the so-called war on terror have made Musharaff's position much more difficult and the region much more unstable.

My visit to Pakistan helped to lay the groundwork for our work for reform there but on this trip I focused on the situation in Afghanistan. We needed to offer more support to the communities that were hosting Afghan refugees, in order to persuade Pakistan to open its borders to Afghans in need. I also met with the UN officials responsible for the humanitarian programme who were based in Pakistan. They had large stocks of food in warehouses on the border and more coming across the seas. A massive effort was being made, led by Catherine Bertini, the impressive Executive Director of the World Food Programme, to speed up food delivery and make up for the break in supplies. People needed immediate help but we also needed to deliver a surplus in order to lay down stockpiles for the winter months. The food was taken into Afghanistan by Afghan lorry drivers in their decorated lorries. Each time they returned, they would report on the situation they had found at their destination. Afghan employees of NGOs distributed the food at the delivery points. The World Food Programme, Afghan lorry drivers and Afghan NGOs worked very hard together and prevented what might have been a massive humanitarian tragedy.

On this occasion I travelled with a team of armed close-protection officers. I refused special protection whenever I could because I feared it would mean I could not meet with people in a normal way. But these were dangerous places, and they were a great bunch who checked everything carefully but also managed to keep out of the way, and we were moving around in areas where the carrying of arms was quite normal. In the evenings we would share a drink and analysis of the state of the world. One of them was enormously well read and after the serious discussion they entertained us with a fund of funny stories about some of the situations their work had taken them to. There was also a crowd of journalists up in the mountains, on the border with Afghanistan. Even in these circumstances, Radio 5 Live was able to connect me into a live discussion in London. This massive improvement in communications technology is a welcome aspect of globalisation: it is drawing the people of the world ever closer together and making the Universal Declaration of Human Rights become an emotional reality.

Once it became clear that the Taliban would not hand over Osama bin Laden, US military action became inevitable. On 8 October, bombing raids involving US and UK forces began, causing tension and concern across the world. The general view was that action was necessary in Afghanistan, but all decent people hate the idea of civilian lives being put at risk, especially a people which had suffered as much as the Afghans. Shortly after I got back from my visit to the borders, there were calls for a halt to the bombing so that humanitarian supplies could get through. I resisted these strongly because, although well meant, they would have encouraged Taliban forces to harass food convoys in order to prevent bombing and thus extend the war. The bombing campaign was in fact a back-up to the fighting capacity of the Northern Alliance – a group of warlords traditionally hostile to the Taliban – who were the proxies fighting for the US. The US had inserted special forces on the ground, alongside the Northern Alliance, to help with money and supplies and to target the bombing.

As with all such military campaigns against weak states, the military action was soon over and international attention withdrawn. But the effort to create a new government, order and stability in the country was a long-term task. The UN, in the person of the Secretary-General's special representative Ambassador Lakdar Brahimi, was asked to establish an interim government and then a process of consultation, leading to a more legitimate interim government and the drawing up of a constitution followed by elections. Brahimi undertook this balancing act very well and agreement was reached in Bonn on 5 December. Osama bin Laden and the Taliban leadership had melted away but there was great sensitivity in the balance of the new government. The Northern Alliance expected rewards but if it was allowed to dominate, the Pushtun area of the country would be alienated. An interim government with considerable Northern Alliance representation but led by the Pushtun Hamid Karzai was put in place and a UN-approved international force was provided to stabilise Kabul. A donors' conference was convened in Tokyo, where Hamid Karzai made his first appearance on the world stage in his green cloak and made an impassioned plea for help. Colin Powell made an impressive speech telling us he had arrived with the dust of

Afghanistan on his boots. The UN, World Bank, IMF and Asian development bank and international donors came together to pledge $4.4 billion to help rebuild Afghanistan. I pledged £200 million over five years from the DfID budget and promised in my speech that the UK would work with others to help rebuild Afghan institutions and would not set up separate UK projects.

I visited Afghanistan some months later. We established a DfID office so that we could be close to developments and could insert money and expertise where it would be most effective. The UN in Afghanistan were determined to keep their humanitarian work going across the country, but to hand over to Afghan authorities as soon as possible. Yet every single institution and the infrastructure of this vast country needed building from scratch. I visited schools and slums in Kabul. The people were full of hope for a better future. I flew with the RAF to Kandahar, which had been the centre of Taliban power. We were helping rehabilitate a raisin factory – Afghanistan had previously provided 40 per cent of the world's raisins. Women, mostly widows, were employed in significant numbers, which would have been unheard of under the Taliban. We were also supporting a project to train midwives to contact women at home and build up enough confidence so that they could receive medical help and advice and thus help to reduce the terrible toll of women dying or becoming disabled in childbirth for want of simple interventions. The main street in Kandahar, as in Kabul, was bustling as businesses and markets re-established themselves. But the Governor was a warlord, with a big showy sign opposing drugs. We had a long discussion about the reforms that were needed to improve the lives of the people.

In Kabul women could be seen walking along the streets, in black or white scarves, and some still with blue burkas. But the burka is a terrible restriction on vision and often women would lift off the burka and simply drape the blue cloth over their heads and shoulders. This somehow symbolised the changing atmosphere. I went to a school we were supporting, where girls were catching up on a missed schooling. I asked them what they wanted to do when they left school. There were aspirations to be teachers and doctors and two girls even wanted to be airline pilots so that they could travel the world and see how other people lived. The International Security Assistance Force (ISAF), which was initially led by British forces, had done a good job in creating a sense of stability and security in Kabul. British troops are good peacekeepers, partly because they have learned through early mistakes in Northern Ireland that the key is to treat local people with respect. We had given them a modest allocation from the DfID budget as we did in Bosnia, Kosovo and East Timor so that they could help people with immediate patch-up jobs and set up football teams and generally establish good relations with the locals. I was hopeful at this stage that working with the international community we could really help the people of Afghanistan to rebuild their country and look forward to a better future

But then major errors were made. The US would not agree that the international force should be extended to all the major cities of Afghanistan because US forces wanted freedom to act against al-Qaeda. They remained desperate to catch Osama bin Laden and wanted maximum freedom of manoeuvre. We in DfID, with our experience of post-conflict reconstruction elsewhere, stressed that there must be an immediate effort to disarm and demobilise the warlords' militias and build a new Afghan army. Without security it would be impossible to extend the authority of the Afghan government across its territory and create the conditions for the economic and social development necessary to improve the lives of the people. DfID had an increasingly close relationship with the Ministry of Defence (MoD) having worked together in Bosnia, Kosovo, Sierra Leone and East Timor and in the MoD our message was taken seriously. Whilst I was in Afghanistan I visited the massive base the US had established in Bagram and discussed the future with the US Commander who was sympathetic to the case I was making, but it was a long way from Bagram to his bosses in the Pentagon.

Similarly in the UK in times of military action when press attention is high and the Prime Minister strongly engaged, the Foreign Office tend to wish to marginalise DfID, and the net result was that the Prime Minister was unwilling or unable to convey our advice to the US and instead made headline-grabbing announcements volunteering that the UK would take the lead in eliminating drug production in Afghanistan. We had advised that this would not be achieved quickly and was absolutely dependent on demobilising the warlords' fighters and extending security across the country, but this advice was not heeded because it got in the way of the Prime Minister's determination to make an announcement on the UK's commitment to take rapid action against drugs.

As a result of the failure to demobilise the militias, the current situation in Afghanistan is disappointing and deeply worrying. The warlords remain strong, drug production has increased, the lives of the people have improved little and the Taliban are regrouping. This is a tragedy for the people of Afghanistan and an example – which is a precursor to events in Iraq – of incompetent US policy-making and of Tony Blair's unwillingness to stand up firmly to the US. The international community supported military action in Afghanistan and came together to support reconstruction. But President Bush, who famously made clear during his presidential election campaign that the US 'does not do nation building', wanted no limits on the freedom of US troops to pursue al-Qaeda, and thus the reconstruction of Afghanistan has been held back.

The result is that we have an impoverished Afghanistan next to Pakistan, Uzbekistan, Tajikistan, Turkmenistan and Iran – all Muslim countries under strain. There is a serious danger that the region will remain unstable and impoverished despite a massive military effort by the most powerful and well-equipped country in the world. My view is that the action against the Taliban was justified but that the reconstruction has been handled in a way that leaves the country poor and unstable and a danger to its people and neighbours. Osama bin Laden remains at large and has seen his al-Qaeda movement grow in strength and support as a result of the mismanaged response to the attack on the Twin Towers. The situation in Afghanistan and the surrounding region demonstrates clearly that the notion of a 'war on terror' is completely misconceived. The way to minimise support for extremist movements is to support development and justice. Criminal sanctions must be employed, and force needs to be used as a last resort to overthrow regimes like the Taliban, but if there is not a strong commitment to development and improvement in the lives of the people, the problem and instability will remain.

Battles over arms sales

By December 2001 I was involved in a separate battle over the application by British Aerospace for an arms export licence to export a £28 million military radar system to Tanzania. Tanzania is one of the poorest countries in the world and had recently qualified for debt relief. It had no need of a military radar system and the £28 million project was only half of a two-stage proposal of twice this value. It was very difficult to believe that the contract had been agreed without corruption and it was causing great concern to the World Bank. The terms of the deal breached the conditions agreed for Tanzania's debt relief, which required any new debt to be concessional. The project was to be funded by a loan from Barclays that claimed it was concessional, but by definition it could not be. The proposal was in clear breach of a revised EU code for arms sales negotiated by Robin Cook to honour a 1997 manifesto promise to tighten controls on arms exports.

When I was first asked for my view on the proposed licence, I objected strongly but was told it was already under construction in the Isle of Wight and more than 100 jobs were at stake. This was very surprising given that no licence had been agreed, but it emerged that there was a procedure for the MoD to give a green light to a project if they thought there would be no objection. The whole project was dubious and damaging and I was determined to try to refuse the issue of an export licence on the grounds that it breached the new criteria. I gained support from Gordon Brown and Robin Cook and Patricia Hewitt, but No. 10 were not supportive. Then Robin Cook was replaced by Jack Straw and I could not persuade the Prime Minister, even in a case like this, to take a stand against British Aerospace.

Arms sales were one of Tony Blair's blind spots and in this he was strongly supported by Jack Straw. They considered it their duty to promote British arms sales whenever possible and repeatedly pressed India to buy £1 billion worth of Hawks, even when there were men mobilised on the border between India and Pakistan and a real risk of war between the two nuclear-armed countries. Blair overruled our objections to the sale of Hawks to Zimbabwe when they were engaged in war in the Congo, though this decision was later rescinded. And in July 2002 Straw even backed the sale of navigation and targeting equipment for F16 fighters being assembled in the US for Israel, despite a long-standing arms embargo and clear evidence that F16s had been used for attacks on the West Bank and Gaza.

In this, as in so many things, Blair simply did not understand the objections of Labour members. I remember him expressing extreme annoyance after a shadow Cabinet meeting about Audrey Wise, the then MP for Preston, and other Labour MPs objecting to the export of Hawks to Indonesia and asking what possible reason could there be that they should take such a stand. Jack Straw joined in and said there were jobs at stake in the region they represented. In fact, the economics as well as the morality of this promotion of British arms sales is deeply dubious. There is no reason why the British arms industry should be subsidised and promoted by British ministers any more than any other sector of the economy. We should work for fair rules and transparent procurement procedures and then leave business to its own devices. In fact, as Samuel Brittan argues regularly in the *Financial Times*, the net result of this feather-bedding of the British arms industry is that British troops are frequently provided with inferior equipment, and many high-quality British engineers are tied up in an industry that is less productive than others that would otherwise employ their talents.

Blair and Straw had a similar attitude to promoting British firms abroad. I remember when I was visiting Angola, shortly after the end of forty years of warfare, Jack Straw said to me that the most important thing about Angola was getting British Airways in. In fact in Luanda I saw some of the worst poverty I have ever seen. My view is that we should favour rules to allow all airlines to compete fairly and not pursue nationalist economics with inappropriate pressure to support British firms, which in any event in today's world often end up not being really British. The letter to the Prime Minister of Romania from Tony Blair supporting Mittal's investment in steel in Romania is another example of this attitude. We in DfID were supporting the European Bank for Reconstruction and Development (EBRD) in helping restructure the Romanian steel industry. There were only two bidders for the contract, one was French but bid only to manage the restructuring and not invest in the company, so it was obvious that Mittal would get the contract. I presume it was the Ambassador who suggested a Prime Ministerial letter. This got Blair into enormous trouble because Lakshmi Mittal had made a large donation to the Labour Party one month before Blair wrote. In fact, the policy decision lay in DfID. We knew nothing of such donations. The Prime Minister embarrassed himself to no effect because of a Foreign Office commitment to mercantilist economics.

Similarly, on the question of the Tanzania contract Blair was immovable, despite my strong support from the World Bank and the Treasury. John Prescott stepped in to try to broker an agreement, but I could not win the argument once Jack Straw and Patricia Hewitt were aware of Tony Blair's views. I had to content myself with persuading President Mkapa of Tanzania, who had inherited the contract from a previous administration, to give an undertaking not to agree a second phase of the project. The Tanzanian press took a lot of interest in the argument and the arrival of 'Mama Radar' made front page news. But President Mkapa and I managed to find a way through and have remained good friends. The result was that Tanzania wasted £28 million on a useless military radar system, but I agreed with President Mkapa that we would continue our support for his reform efforts provided there were no more such deals. Tanzania has since then made considerable progress, but the £28 million that could have been spent getting children to school was wasted. The whole episode left a very nasty taste about the behaviour of British Aerospace and the unbalanced attitude of the Prime Minister towards arms sales.

Blair's visit to West Africa

In February 2002 Blair made his first real visit to Africa, to demonstrate his commitment to the continent. I was invited to accompany him on a visit which was to take in Nigeria, Ghana, Senegal and Sierra Leone. We travelled in the first-class section of a British Airways plane, which was funded by a large troop of political journalists who travelled in the rear. Travelling with such a large group of journalists meant that everything had to be orchestrated and there was very little chance to stop and talk informally and learn as we went. Every single activity was pre-scripted and planned. An official from No. 10 had undertaken the journey in advance so that there would be no hitches and all the correct clothing was prepared for each part of the journey. The rest of us carried on all day in the clothes we started off in, but when, for example, we visited cocoa growers in a village in Ghana and a photo opportunity was provided, the Prime Minister and Alastair Campbell had changed from suits into casual clothing and then changed back again.

The Prime Minister is, of course, enormously good at presentation. He always looks good and smart and appropriately clothed. But travelling with him reveals how much effort goes into this. As we approached landing, his staff gathered around. He donned make-up and hairspray. His jacket was put on and brushed, Lady Morgan scrutinised the outcome and then stooped down to remove a little mud from the heel of his shoe. The journalists had to leave the plane first. We must wait, and then the Prime Minister exits so that the pictures will come out as planned. Probably this kind of behaviour is necessary in a modern political leader, but it is the enemy of spontaneity, and such pressure generates politicians with the characteristics of actors rather than political thinkers.

Nonetheless, the trip went well. There were gun salutes and troops to inspect in Nigeria, talks with President Obasanjo and a speech to the Nigerian Parliament that we had helped craft, but Tony presented in his inimitable way. His presence and style deeply impressed the Parliament. We went on to Ghana where we visited a village and cocoa research station and Blair got on very well with President Kufour. By popular demand Blair delivered another parliamentary speech. In Sierra Leone there was enormous warmth because, as I know from my own visits, the people are truly grateful to Britain for helping end the rebellion and then bring stability to the country. The news came through just before we landed that Princess Margaret had died. Black ties were brought out and plans made to provide a condolence interview to be relayed home. Later we went on to a village meeting where condolences were offered in that touching way that people in Africa speak about members of the royal family, as though they were our relatives. We then moved on to the speeches and entertainment. I was sitting next to Tony and after half an hour or so one of his staff approached from behind and said he could lighten up. His smile instantly reappeared; clearly it had been decided that the need to look sad at the death of the Princess had been properly acted out and it was now time to return to normal. In Senegal, Tony impressed the diners by making an informal speech in French and agreeing to be interviewed in French by a local radio station.

It was clear when we talked that he had read his briefing carefully and taken in the information provided, but I said to him how odd I found it to travel and not be able to learn anything because he was always expected to perform and be surrounded by journalists. He shrugged with regret but said that was how his travel always was. I also noticed, as Tony engaged in Africa, how he has to talk as if he knows everything. He was new to Africa, he appointed Liz Lloyd as his special adviser on Africa because she had worked for him for years, but she had no background on Africa. There are constant demands for briefing but little open-minded discussion. I think it is a form of insecurity that Tony Blair always has to talk and behave as though he knows more than anyone else on any subject and is therefore very poor at drawing on the knowledge and experience of those who know more.

Gordon and the third term

It was on this trip that Tony asked me to eat with him on the plane, and initiated an interesting conversation. He was very relaxed, and showed his preoccupation with his legacy by musing about what he was most proud of. He suggested it might be peace in Northern Ireland or our contribution to development. I was astonished by the latter because he had taken so little interest in development in his first term and the achievements of the department had often been made despite, rather than because of, the position of No. 10. He then went on to say that he knew I always preferred it when he and Gordon were working together (this was a reference to previous conversations) but he really needed Gordon to help him more. He then went on to say, in a confidential manner, that he really did not want a third term but he wished Gordon would work more closely with him so that he could make progress on the euro and if he did so he would then be happy to hand over to Gordon. The conversation then moved on to Africa and other things. I remember how he kept referring to 'my people', meaning people who worked with him in No. 10. I was struck by this and found it odd, given that Tony was so dominant across the government. It is another indication of his need to work with his own inner group. I said at the end of the meal that if he ever wanted me to say anything to Gordon, he should say so. He then made it quite clear that he wanted me to tell Gordon what he had said.

After Senegal, I left the Prime Minister's party and flew across to Kenya because I was going on to visit Uganda, Rwanda and the Democratic Republic of Congo to try to help drive forward the peace process. I telephoned Gordon Brown from my hotel and said that I needed to meet him. The two of us met for lunch early the next week in his dining room in No. 11 Downing Street. I conveyed my message and Gordon then said I was not the first to be asked to bring this message: two other members of the Cabinet had been asked to bring the same offer. Gordon's answer was that, first, such deals were not worth talking about because previous agreements had not been kept; and second, he would not contemplate recommending that we join the euro in order to advance his own position rather than advance the economic interest of the country.

Blair's attack on wreckers and conservatives

In February 2002 Tony Blair made a speech at Labour's spring conference – which is focused on those working in local government. He branded the union critics of his public-service reform as wreckers and 'small-c conservatives' akin to those who had been unwilling to abandon Clause IV or reject the ultra-left in the 1980s. He also suggested that he had won two election landslides by challenging political orthodoxy and 'an unholy alliance of the right and far left'.

It was later reported that No. 10 had apologised to the TUC General Secretary John Monks for this speech after some very critical remarks from union representatives calling the speech 'juvenile' and the GMB publishing an advertisement in the *Guardian* showing a picture of a nurse holding a baby with the message: 'Is this one of the wreckers, Mr Blair?' On 21 February in an open letter the Metropolitan Police Commissioner and a group of senior public-sector managers warned of a collapse in morale amongst public servants, and called for a championing of the value of public-sector workers struggling with criticism from politicians and the media. They called for better pay, and for less red tape and inspection.

On 23 February Blair softened his rhetoric when speaking to the Scottish party conference, but he attacked his critics saying they were twenty years out of date, supporters of old-fashioned tax and spend, and policies that didn't add up. He held out the prospect of a third term and told them such policies were no way to win elections.

I find all these references to the winning of elections notable. Blair clearly sees himself as the source of election victory and therefore entitled to reject those who criticise from within the Labour coalition. My earlier analysis of the reasons for electoral success demonstrates the weakness of this argument, but clearly Blair believes in his personal election-winning powers and feels entitled to take a more adversarial and strident attitude to his critics because he won a historic second term. Only eight months after the 2001 victory, he was using the prospects of a third term to try to silence his critics within the party.

Mutterings in the party and worry about Iraq

As the country approached the May elections in 2002 there was increasing muttering against the leadership. There was a fall in attendance at party meetings and a lack of party workers to help with electioneering. Gwyneth Dunwoody spoke in the Commons of the need for MPs to stand up for their constituents against an 'over-mighty executive'. The Prime Minister's apparent support for Bush's approach to Iraq was extending this demoralisation across the party.

In the early part of 2002, there was talk of revolt over proposals for a largely appointed House of Lords. And the pictures of detainees from Afghanistan, including British citizens, chained in Guantanamo Bay, caused widespread consternation. Alan Milburn, the then Secretary of State for Health, caused further upset when he put forward proposals for the best hospitals to break away from the National Health Service and be given freedom to borrow and increase their fees from private medicine. And President Bush sent a shiver across the world with his belligerent tone when he made his speech describing Iraq, Iran and North Korea as an 'axis of evil'.

Worries about the possibility of war in Iraq began to grow. President Bush was talking tough, European leaders were distancing themselves from the Bush rhetoric, but Blair was maintaining his shoulder to shoulder position. Interviewed at a Commonwealth Conference in Australia on 3 March 2002, Blair insisted that Saddam Hussein was developing weapons of mass destruction and was capable of using them. Blair indicated that there was a case for dealing with Iraq as a matter of urgency. Asked if this meant war was imminent Blair replied, 'Let us wait and see exactly what happens, but it's clear we need to deal with the issue.' There was widespread concern on the Labour benches about Bush's belligerence and Blair's ambiguity.

I shared this concern but I was also deeply conscious of the effects on the people of Iraq of Saddam Hussein's defiance of the UN, the cruelty of the regime, and more than twelve years of sanctions. DfID had been involved over many years in supporting efforts to ease Iraqi suffering. It was easier to work in the north but we had some projects in central Iraq and were well aware of how bad things were. It was clear that Saddam Hussein was manipulating sanctions for propaganda purposes because under the same sanctions regime life was better in the Kurdish area than in Baghdad-controlled Iraq. But there is no doubt that the people of Iraq were suffering terribly under UN-imposed sanctions. We had been engaged with the Foreign Office in trying to ease and simplify the sanctions regime and improve the Oil for Food programme, but the situation for the Iraqis remained grim.

For all these reasons, I did not agree with those who argued that containment was working in Iraq. But I was also conscious of the justified anger in the Middle East over the failure to enforce UN resolutions on Israel. My hope was that the UK could join with others to insist that the US acted through the UN, and make a precondition for co-operation on Iraq that the US support progress towards the establishment of a Palestinian state alongside Israel by implementing the 'Road Map' to Palestinian statehood that had already been negotiated by the UN, EU, Russia and US. This would transform the atmosphere in the Middle East and enable us to work with the Arab world to solve the problem of Saddam Hussein. My view was that our aims should be the return of the weapons inspectors, the lifting of sanctions and support for the people of Iraq to get rid of Saddam Hussein – just as we had with Milosevic in Serbia. Blair did say in the Commons, in answer to an intervention from Ann Clwyd MP, that he was considering indictment of Saddam Hussein, but nothing came of this. The final element in a package that would bring prospects of progress to the Middle East would be an agreement that all WMD, nuclear, chemical and biological – including Israel's nuclear weapons – should be withdrawn from the Middle East. This would all be achievable with US support and would secure an era of peace and advance in the Middle East.

My hope was that the UK would work with the rest of the international community to try to hold the US to this agenda. We were all aware that America was shocked and angry after the attack on the Twin Towers and determined to take action, but it was clear on calm reflection that if they failed to attend to the deep sense of injustice in the Middle East, there was a real danger that they would make things worse. The UK's role as a friend of the US was to get them to understand this. As I used to put it, we have to hold Tony Blair's ankles whilst he held on to George Bush. My hope was that the weight of Labour Party opinion, British public opinion and European public opinion was heavy enough to achieve this aim. This was another example where the Labour Party was in tune with public opinion and Tony Blair out of tune. It is also notable that Blair, with his usual device of creating false alternatives, claims that all he did on Iraq was justified because Saddam Hussein has gone, as though there was no other way of proceeding. The tragedy of what happened is that he failed to use his leverage to hold the US to an alternative strategy for the Middle East, which could have led to real progress for the Palestinian people and the people of Iraq and transformed the situation in the region.

I was from the start very clear about my role. I should follow events closely, read the intelligence, argue the case in Cabinet and indicate my views in public if necessary. I understood how much was at stake and clear that I couldn't remain a member of the government if we simply supported Bush's aggression against Iraq without the support of the UN. At this stage, I was concerned but hopeful that the Labour Party would be able to keep Tony Blair on the straight and narrow.

Asylum

In April 2002, the French Socialist Prime Minister Lionel Jospin narrowly lost to Jean-Marie Le Pen in the first round of the French presidential elections. This was an enormous shock. It meant that the second stage of the contest would be between Chirac and Le Pen and produced the memorable poster: 'Vote for the crook, not for the fascist'. The outcome shook Social Democratic parties across

Europe. Tony Blair said in an interview that Jospin had lost because he had failed to address electoral fears on crime and immigration and that he would not make the same mistake.

The handling of the question of asylum has been a major problem for the Blair government. Tony Blair has taken a close interest in the issue since Jack Straw was Home Secretary, but numbers continued to grow against a backdrop of mounting tabloid agitation and increasing concern amongst voters. By May 2002 there was panic at No. 10; numbers of applications had risen from 32,500 in 1997 to 84,130 in 2002, despite the passage of the 1999 Immigration and Asylum Act which brought in voucher payments and a system of dispersal of asylum seekers across the UK.

In May 2002, the Home Office drew up proposals for a new action plan designed to produce a radical reduction in numbers. One of the proposals was that development aid should be conditional on a commitment to take back asylum seekers. I was adamant that we should not do this. Asylum seekers tend to flow from countries in turmoil. Afghanistan, Iraq, Somalia, Zimbabwe and Iran are currently the source of most applications. It would be ridiculous if this condition led us to withdraw help to Afghanistan in its rebuilding, refuse support for humanitarian programmes in Iraq, withdraw food aid to prevent starvation in Zimbabwe and refuse assistance to Iran, to support the large numbers of asylum seekers they were hosting from Afghanistan. Similarly Somalia is in turmoil and has no government or stability. I was trying to develop a new approach, instead of relying on endless talks amongst warlords in Nairobi, to invite communities in Somalia to create areas of peace, as they had in Somaliland, with the promise that we would bring in support for schools, water and health and thus try to rebuild the country from the bottom up. Making aid dependent on accepting the return of asylum seekers would undercut all of this. But even if we consider countries that were not major sources of asylum seekers like China, India and Sri Lanka, it would surely be wrong to withdraw programmes focused on the reduction of poverty to try to blackmail governments into facilitating the early return of failed asylum seekers. It was notable that there was no proposal to use the leverage of trade missions or arms sales but only the relatively small sums we spend to try to improve the living conditions of the poorest in the world. On top of this, under the legislation our government had passed, it was illegal to use aid for any purpose other than the reduction of poverty, so such a conditionality would be a breach of UK law.

I therefore went to a newly established Cabinet committee meeting, which was chaired by Tony Blair with all senior officials and ministers in attendance, to try to prevent the misuse of UK or EU aid for this purpose and to make my suggestions on how asylum could be better handled. I had been involved in immigration and asylum work since the mid-1970s and regularly saw asylum seekers and those tangled up in the immigration system in my advice bureaux in Ladywood. The position before 1997 had been a mess; people who had come for a visit and wanted to stay on or new arrivals from Punjab, Jamaica, and other countries where there was no case for large asylum movements, had been advised by dubious agents to apply for asylum. It then took the Home Office so long to process their cases that they had often obtained jobs, married and had children before the system got around to saying that they should leave, and by then it was often inhuman to enforce the ruling. It is notable that from 1986–88 the number of applicants was about 4,000 each year and then started to rise rapidly to nearly 50,000 in 1991 and stood at 32,000 in 1997. I used to argue then that what Labour needed to do was get a grip on the system, refuse those with no case much more quickly and welcome the genuine. The inefficiency of the system was its undoing. A large backlog of cases meant that no one was turned away quickly, so dubious advisers, and the growing gangs of people-smugglers advertised the UK as a desirable destination.

But after 1997, despite new legislation and the humiliation of the voucher system, the Home Office could not get a grip on the system. The number of arrivals built up quickly to 80,000 per year and the backlog of undecided cases kept growing to as many as 120,000 by January 2000. The backlog was somewhat contained by the fact that asylum seekers who had not had an initial decision on their case were allowed to apply to work after six months. But the fear that many asylum seekers were economic migrants led to the withdrawal of the right to work in 2002. This in turn led to large numbers of young men being housed and maintained at public expense, hanging around doing nothing. This caused increasing resentment across the country, including in my deeply multicultural constituency. It also caused great distress amongst most asylum seekers who did not want to be a burden on the state.

By 2002 I had reached the conclusion that it was essential to renegotiate the UN Convention on Refugees. It had been negotiated in 1951 and envisaged people – such as Jews from Germany – fleeing to neighbouring countries or by ship from gross persecution. It required the first country they arrived in to offer asylum if they were in genuine fear of persecution. By 2000, in the post-Cold War world of growing disorder, weakening national borders and easier travel, there were 12 million refugees and 8 million displaced people known to the United Nations High Commission for Refugees (UNHCR). They were overwhelmingly being hosted by poor neighbouring countries – Pakistan had 2 million Afghans, Tanzania 300,000 Burundians, etc. Funding was provided by development agencies like DfID to enable UNHCR to care for the refugees. But increasing numbers of the more enterprising, who were usually the more educated, hoped to get to a developed country in order to work. Under the terms of the Refugee Convention, they were unable to apply for asylum with-out first arriving in the UK and when they arrived housing and benefits were provided so they came in increasing numbers determined to settle and improve the lives of their families.

Most of the asylum seekers came from countries destabilised by war and oppression. Some had been individually persecuted, others had their lives wrecked by the disorder. Each had to provide details of their story to prove that they had been individually persecuted to British officials with a limited knowledge of the country concerned. Some were accepted, others refused, but if you came from a country in turmoil, Iraq, Afghanistan, Somalia, etc., you could not safely be removed to your country. In these circumstances an industry of criminalised people-smugglers grew up that would offer desperate people the chance to come to the UK where they were entitled to apply for asylum. I used to ask those who came to my advice bureaux how much it cost to get here. The answer was $12–20,000 from Afghanistan, $7–10,000 from Iraq, $2–3,000 from Somalia. The journey often consisted of months of travel across Europe by various means and usually brought people into the UK in the backs of lorries. Thus the poor refugees of the world lived in UNHCR camps and the more educated would pool family resources to pay the people-smugglers to get them to the UK or France, Germany or any other OECD country so that they could work and build up the chance of a better future.

Jack Straw had floated the idea, when he was Home Secretary, that the Geneva Convention needed re-negotiation. The Convention imposed an obligation to accept all those fleeing persecution who arrived in the UK. This bound our courts and led to David Blunkett's battles with the judges who interpreted the Convention to overturn new restrictions that he had put in place. My view was that we needed a new approach in a globalising, disorderly world. A new Convention should oblige us to support UNHCR in caring for all refugees fleeing persecution and require countries to contribute resources to the costs of such care. It should also oblige us to work with the UN to restore order in the countries concerned and each country should commit to host an appropriate number of asylum seekers who should be recruited near to their homeland and not have to become entangled with people-smugglers and travel across the world in order to apply for asylum. In addition, all countries that are recruiting skilled workers from developing countries should be encouraged to prioritise the recruitment of trained and educated refugees rather than those who were trained at great expense in developing countries that needed their skills.

When I arrived at the Cabinet committee meeting hoping to argue the case for a re-negotiation of the Refugee Convention, David Blunkett was in a very agitated state. I got the impression that he was under pressure from Tony Blair to get a grip on the system. He was attacking Derry Irvine over the judiciary and jumped down my throat when I tried to put my case. It soon became clear that neither Tony Blair nor he was listening and thus couldn't help put in place a long-term, thought-through approach to asylum. This is again typical of the Blair regime; they tend to draw together a small group, particularly if a problem is getting coverage in the media, and work together in a secretive, often frenzied way. Normal government decision-making structures are by-passed and advice from those with real knowledge is often marginalised. This leads to frequent policy mistakes. I concluded I should focus on protecting aid money, looking after individuals in my advice bureaux as well as I could and providing support to UNHCR and the rebuilding of collapsing states through our development efforts.

The 2002 Asylum Act removed the right to financial support from asylum seekers who did not apply for asylum immediately on arrival and from those who had been refused. It also speeded up the appeals system. This, together with action to screen lorries, closure of the Sangatte Camp near Calais, and co-operation with the French led to a drop in numbers to 50,000 in 2003 and a further drop to 9,000 in the first quarter of 2004. There had also been a speeding up in decision-making and a rise in the percentages of applicants refused asylum. But there are still significant arrivals and the system continues to find it very difficult to remove asylum seekers who have been refused. The numbers removed in 2003 reached a record high of 12,500. But with 50,000-plus being refused each year, there are growing numbers of destitute asylum seekers sleeping rough, going hungry and suffering great strains to their physical and mental health. When I went to help out at the Hodge Hill by-election in July 2004 I was shocked to be given leaflets to hand out attacking the Liberal Democrat candidate for favouring benefits for failed asylum seekers. I refused to give them out and was very sad to find that the Labour Party could stoop so low.

The asylum issue is stirring up racial division in countries across Europe and helped lead to changes of government in Austria, the Netherlands and Denmark. Sadly, the Labour government has been led by its fear of tabloid headlines and public criticism to impose more and more hardship on applicants. There is no doubt that the system has been out of control for years and lax in refusing those without entitlement and thus the numbers have grown. My own assessment of public opinion is that it is the sense that the system is out of control and that large numbers of young men are being supported by public funds that is causing anger. This hostility exists across all communities and ethnicities. But the answers require a thorough re-examination of the system and the courage to seek out a just solution which provides for the large numbers of displaced people across the world. Sadly Tony Blair's determination not to make the mistakes of Lionel Jospin has led to an approach to the problem which has been a mixture of incompetence and cruelty. Spending on the processing of asylum seekers is £2 billion per annum. This could fund enormous improvements in care for refugees across the world.

An entry in my diary recorded:

> Over the weekend of 21 June [2002], there were constant reports from the Seville Summit on the efforts of Spain, the UK and Denmark to link cuts in aid to co-operation on illegal immigration. France and Sweden were adamantly opposed and the final report was that the UK did not get its way. I am very pleased and had discussed these issues with my Swedish colleague repeatedly. He in turn had liaised with the French.

My diary went on: 'The front page of the *Independent on Sunday* (23 June) had "knives out for Short" – [I suspect] this is Blunkett briefing.'

It was also at the Seville Summit that EU systems were supposedly slimmed down. This meant the Development Council was abolished. EU development ministers had been driving reform in the EU's very unsatisfactory development programmes. DfID had taken a leading role in this, but as in the UK, foreign ministers did not like development ministers bringing a different perspective to foreign policy. And thus both the Foreign Office and the Prime Minister were very happy to abolish the Development Council, in the name of EU reform.

In July, I wrote in my diary:

> TB said in '97, no one must think 'we are the masters now'. We must focus on our duty to serve – or something similar. The reality of his behaviour is 'I am the master now'. There is a complete arrogance in the way he runs the government and No. 10. My experience of it recently in his effort to press us to misuse and to get asylum seekers returned to their countries is a minor example but very much the style of his government.

Crime

Towards the end of 2002 Tony Blair also launched another major initiative on crime. There had been the promise of action through a sequence of leaks and briefings to the press in the period leading up to the Queen's Speech. Blair insisted that people did not feel secure and knew the system was not working as it should and therefore reform was needed. But Labour had already introduced thirteen Criminal Justice Acts since we took power in 1997. And 2002 brought three more. This is a reflection of Tony Blair and David Blunkett's attitude to reform, constant announcements, headlines and eye-catching initiatives. They call it modernisation but it is a mania for change which keeps the whole system in a constant state of flux. This does not allow those working within it to agree the direction that reform must take and then work together to improve performance. The direction of reform was also deeply illiberal, restrictions on jury trial, dilution of the double-jeopardy principle and wider use of previous convictions. Labour's tradition as a party of liberal conscience has been eroded and undermined during the Blair premiership. The prison population has grown, crime levels have fallen as they have all over Western Europe, but the fear of crime has also grown. 'Tough on crime, tough on the causes of crime', the mantra that served Tony Blair so well as Shadow Home Secretary, has led to a succession of initiatives designed to please the tabloid newspapers. A lot of money has been spent, more people are locked up, but people in Britain do not feel safer.

Of course, some of the reform has been beneficial. My experience as a constituency MP is that anti-social behaviour by some households in a tower block or street can cause untold misery. There was a need for housing authorities and the police to get together and take tougher action. Over the years I have written many letters and arranged many meetings to achieve such action. But such reform cannot be driven by constant initiatives – once the diagnosis is made and suitable powers and resources put in place, local authorities must be allowed to get on with it, and work for improvement with local people. Similarly, it is obvious that much of our crime is drug-related. Estimates vary, but between 50 and 65 per cent of theft and burglary is thought to be generated by drug addicts stealing to acquire money to feed their habit. And the growth of gun crime in our inner cities is a result of conflict between drug-dealing gangs. The move to drug testing and the offer of treatment is a step forward, but headline-grabbing policy-making does not allow for serious and honest discussion of how we might better handle the drug problem. I have discussed with successive Chief Constables in the West Midlands the desirability of providing clean drugs to addicts so that they stabilise their lives and disconnect from drug dealers and criminality, but this is a conversation that cannot take place in the political arena because the tabloids would make much of it and it might open the government to the accusation that it was being soft on crime.

The underlying problem here is Blair's understanding of leadership. He so much wants to be a leader that he thinks he has to dominate and control everything from the centre. The exaggerated majority in Parliament convinces him that he can drive through any reform without much consultation and consensus-building. Thus we have a growing demoralisation in our public services as this mania for change imposed from on high undermines the sense of service and achievement that is an essential part of the reward that keeps so many dedicated people taking a pride in working in the public services.

This also explains the shameful illiberality of the Blair approach to crime and asylum. In the case of asylum, we have another example of manic activity, constant reform and legislation but a failure to analyse the nature of the problem and develop a long-term policy solution. Tony Blair has been deeply involved with both Jack Straw and David Blunkett's handling of asylum, but Blunkett more than Straw was addicted to spin and this has constantly pushed crime and asylum into the forefront of public debate. I think this is a mistake. What we need is well-thought-through policy to address these difficult issues, and then we should work to generate coverage of our success in reducing unemployment and of our improvements in public services rather than seeking to call attention to an issue on which the right constantly thrives by generating an atmosphere of fear rather than hope.

More resources for development, and instability in Africa

In June, Gordon Brown announced the new spending commitments up to 2005/06. The increases in spending in the Health Service which had been announced in the budget were accompanied by a big increase in education spending and a very big increase in the DfID budget. We were therefore in a position to have Blair announce at the G8 summit in Kananaskis that the UK would increase its spending in Africa to £1 billion a year by 2005/06. It had been just over a third of this when we took power in 1997. This budget and comprehensive spending review made the party feel very good and helped diminish worry over the growing shadow of Iraq.

Just before the summer break, I went off on another visit to the Democratic Republic of Congo (DRC), Uganda, Rwanda and South Africa. I considered the end of the war in Angola, the possibility of peace in DRC and progress on peace in Sudan as a possible big advance for Africa. There were a number of countries engaging in significant reform; Uganda, Mozambique, Rwanda, Tanzania and Ghana were all improving economic management, reforming public finances and improving health and education. But we needed to end conflicts in Africa and support reform in the bigger states if the poorest continent was not to get poorer.

One of the tragedies of the response to the attack on the Twin Towers is that neither Tony Blair nor George Bush seems to understand that there is an overlap between a commitment to a more just world order, support for development and a reduction in poverty, and the prevention of the spread of terrorism. This has been clear to me and DfID for a long time. For example, when I visited Kenya and Tanzania in 1998 – two very poor countries where we have significant development programmes – bombs had just exploded outside the American embassies which led to the deaths of more than 250 Kenyans and Tanzanians. I laid a wreath on behalf of the people of the UK outside the Co-op in Nairobi, which was next to the American Embassy where hundreds of Kenyans died. It was these bombs that led to President Clinton authorising a cruise-missile attack against a pharmaceutical company in Sudan because it was alleged that it was producing chemical weapons (it was widely accepted afterwards that there was no such activity at this site).

Osama bin Laden had moved from Afghanistan to Sudan after the defeat of the Soviets and at the invitation of the government in Khartoum. Sudan was engaged in a civil war between the Arabic-speaking Muslim north and black Christian and traditionalist south, that had gone on for all but ten years since independence in 1956. This had led to the death of more than 2 million people, terrible impoverishment and displacement and the imposition of UN sanctions.

There are weak states, poverty and disorder extending across the horn of Africa from Sudan to Somalia into northern Uganda and across the Congo (the former Zaire). Ethiopia and Eritrea had emerged from years of civil war and then turned on each other in a destructive border war in 1998 which led to the deaths of 70,000 young men and held back the prospects of development in these desperately poor, famine-stricken countries. Rwanda was stabilising and recovering from the 1994 genocide but still threatened by militias in Congo. Burundi was suffering prolonged civil war. Angola had come to peace after nearly forty years of war but was desperately poor and ruled by a corrupt elite. And in West Africa Sierra Leone was recovering but frail, Liberia mired in conflict, and Côte d'Ivoire, once the star performer in francophone Africa, has now collapsed into a civil conflict. Nigeria had restored democracy but was desperately poor and deeply corrupt and subject to outbreaks of ethnic and religious conflict.

Post-Cold War Africa has half of its people living in deep poverty with very weak state institutions and thus prone to conflict. In such circumstances, small arms circulate freely across the continent, political conflicts merge into criminal conspiracy with diamonds helping to drive the wars in Sierra Leone and Angola, rich minerals feeding corruption and disorder in Congo and oil riches feeding deeply corrupt state institutions in Angola and Nigeria. As a result, the people of Africa suffer great poverty and disorder and the continent is a perfect hiding-place for money launderers and drug smugglers. The answer is to work to end the conflicts and support the building of effective modern states that encourage economic and social development. Instead, the inadequate post-conflict management in Afghanistan and the attack on Iraq are spreading bitter division and disorder across the world, have distracted attention from Africa and led to a growth in the strength of the al-Qaeda network.

Rumblings on Iraq

When I got back from my Africa visit I found the press full of speculation about whether the US would attack Iraq. But as I noted in my diary, 'TB just keeps saying nothing decided.' The worry rumbled on, but in August Parliament and Cabinet closed down and Blair and family went off to Mexico for their summer holiday. I went to Galway and then Achill Island, the home of Captain Boycott, and did lots of walking and swimming. I then met up with my son and we drove across Ireland to visit Crossmaglen. I had not been for four years and my father's remaining brother and sister were getting older. There were many complaints about the noise from helicopters and disappointment that the military base in the centre of town had not been closed down, despite the peace process. I resolved to have a word with John Reid, who was then Secretary of State for Northern Ireland, on whether we couldn't do a little better.

4

THE DRUMS OF WAR

In early September, I travelled with Tony Blair on his visit to Mozambique before we went to the World Summit on Sustainable Development (WSSD) in Johannesburg. In July I had asked for a Cabinet discussion on Iraq and Tony had invited me to see him before the meeting. He said he feared that a Cabinet discussion would get hyped. I recorded in my diary that:

> He said nothing decided and would not be over the summer. I said it would be better to settle the Palestinian State and then get Arab world to help with Saddam Hussein. He said he agreed. Said what kind of military action, whether there is a threat of him using weapons of mass destruction, what regime follows, etc., etc. – all have to be settled. I said I respect staying close to US to influence them but not to follow if they make reckless mistakes. He said sure, etc., etc.

and he then 'promised to discuss with me before any decision made.'

He arranged for the two of us to meet in his hotel room in Maputo. He had been catching up on sleep and was in bare feet and casual clothes. He opened the complimentary bottle of champagne that was provided and assured me that it was his intention to work through the UN and get progress on Palestine first. But at our meeting with Kofi Annan a few days later, during the Johannesburg meeting, he talked tough about North Korea. After that he flew to his constituency to give one of his televised press conferences and was very belligerent. My diary recorded these events:

> He said his aim was to get the US to seek Security Council support for the return of weapons inspectors. I asked what were the military options and he said he hadn't had a presentation yet. I said best to settle Palestine and deal with Saddam Hussein with help of Arab world – he said sympathetic, etc., etc.
>
> At meeting with Kofi at WSSD he preferred to deal with N Korea via South Korea but if not there must be action (not clear, but implied military action).
>
> Then press conference in Sedgefield, he was very bellicose. Trip to US and press briefing makes clear UK go with US – no Cabinet or Parliamentary discussion – yet he commits us.
>
> I had discussion with GB and said Iraq would divide government and party and affect world economy – inflame the Arab world. We needed a better strategy.
>
> I told him TB also said must go into euro before election and still meant what he said on trip to West Africa about not wanting a third term.
>
> GB said he would think and get back, but on the euro it would take time to converge the economy. He also said No. 10 had already asked Geoff Hoon to make 20,000 troops available.

It was during our very relaxed discussion in Mozambique that I realised how Tony believed his personal charm could solve all problems. Because he said he agreed with me on the need to make progress on the Palestine/Israel settlement first and to work through the UN, we did not linger long in our discussion of Iraq. He moved on to ask me my views on the euro. I said I agreed with the government policy. We must act in the interests of the British economy. I had assumed that this would lead to conditions being ripe for entry in our second term, but it was clear that the management of the euro economy was much too deflationary and there would have to be significant change in the criteria for public expenditure and the terms on which the euro was being managed. He said, enthusiastically, that this was no problem, that he had a good relationship with Chirac and Schroeder and would be able to persuade them of this. It was at this point that he said he still meant what he said in West Africa about Gordon Brown, the euro and the third term.

Relations with the Security Services

By September I was feeling increasingly sure that the US and Blair were determined to attack Iraq. By then I was starting to cancel my travel commitments and to ensure I read all the intelligence on Iraq. Because DfID was engaged in foreign policy, we had access to all the SIS briefings that were circulated in Whitehall, unlike most other Cabinet ministers. In fact, from the establishment of the department in 1997, we were strongly courted by SIS (MI6) who were feeling threatened in their role and resources by the end of the Cold War. I had regular visits from successive 'Cs' and they listened carefully to our explanations of why we did not find their Africa briefings very useful. However, as I became more focused on the need to end conflicts in Africa I became more interested in working with SIS, not least because they tended to have access and influence with African Presidents. In 2000, with Treasury help, we established a pooled funding mechanism to improve cross-Whitehall working on conflict in Africa. I chaired a new Ministerial Committee, with representation from the Foreign Office, MoD, the Treasury, DfID and SIS. This led to a closer working relationship with SIS in Africa and elsewhere.

SIS had a growing understanding of the importance of our work on poverty reduction and nation-building to create stable states. They were also sympathetic to our efforts to build more just state institutions and reduce poverty in places like India and Pakistan. The tension and public concern over the situation in Iraq meant that the real prospect of war between India and Pakistan, which could easily have led to a nuclear exchange, almost escaped public notice. We decided in the summer of 2002 that there was a real danger of war leading to nuclear fall-out and therefore withdrew our staff from India and Pakistan. This had a beneficial effect in India where our staff evacuation caused consternation and led to greater public understanding of the risks of war. It also increased the discussion within DfID on how we might extend our work to Kashmir and try to bring development and progress to both sides of the Line of Control as well as help to empower local people to demand a peaceful settlement of this long-standing dispute.

When No. 10 renewed work on the Iraq dossier which was published in September 2002 and contained the notorious claim that WMD could be deployed within forty-five minutes of an order to use them, I instructed my private secretary that I did not wish to read and comment on the drafts that were circulated. I was well aware that the production of the dossier was being closely supervised by Alastair Campbell and thought therefore that it would be a propaganda instrument. I decided that I would be unlikely to be able to have much influence on the draft and would be likely not to approve it and it was therefore best to leave Alastair to his own devices and try to use my influence in other ways. The subsequent notoriety of the dossier might make this decision shocking, but Alastair had produced dossiers before and would do so again, it was

a favoured technique. I had run my department since 1997 by trying
to concentrate on the merits of policy and keep well away from the
spin machine.

As my anxiety mounted I decided I should ask SIS for a full
briefing on the situation in Iraq. Very unusually, the message came
back that they could not do so because No. 10 would not allow it.

On 19 September my diary entry reads:

> Was feeling very, very irritated with TB and that he and US
> were determined on war at any price. Asked to see V+
> [Vauxhall Cross – the headquarters of SIS] and told not
> allowed. Even more irritated. Made a fuss then got briefing.
> V+ said SH had masses chem and biol dispersed across
> country. Nuclear not imminent but would get.
>
> Military option target elite – no repeat Gulf war + big
> humanitarian effort.

I added

> This makes a big difference. TB must say this to Parl.

As I look back, I find this effort to block my access to SIS
significant. Prior to this, I was in regular contact. I went to lunch
with 'C' and his team regularly and met people working on the
areas of the world about which I was concerned whenever I asked.
My request for a briefing from SIS was not unusual. When they told
my private secretary they couldn't respond due to No. 10's
instructions, I asked her to take it up with No. 10. Her enquiries
took her up the chain to David Manning, who said he could not
authorise a briefing without the PM's agreement. I asked her to tell
Manning how irritated I was and to ask him to talk to the PM.
Permission was then granted.

I ask myself now, why the attempt to restrict access? I think it
reflects the fact that Tony Blair and his entourage were running the

whole policy in a very informal and personal way and wanted to keep knowledge to themselves in order to keep control. I cannot emphasise strongly enough how Tony Blair's highly personalised system of decision-making is a significant part of the explanation of the lack of properly considered policy and thus of the disaster in Iraq.

There is a prestigious Cabinet committee called Defence and Overseas Policy (DOP) which is meant to supervise strategy on major foreign-policy issues. It is chaired by the Prime Minister, attended by the Chancellor, Foreign Secretary, Secretaries of State for Defence, Trade and Industry, Development (I had a fight in the early days to get DfID included), the Chief of the Defence Staff, heads of the intelligence agencies and senior officials. It is the machinery in our government system for dealing with foreign-policy crises. It brings together all the expertise across government to consider policy. For the Iraq crisis, DOP never met. There were frequent informal discussions at Cabinet after the summer of 2002 but there were never any papers or proper analysis of the underlying dangers and the political, diplomatic and military options. The whole crisis was handled by Tony Blair and his entourage with considerable informality. I believe this breakdown of proper decision-making is a serious erosion of the effectiveness of our government systems. It explains much of the badly thought-through policy and is in need of urgent correction. I did charge Andrew Turnbull, who is Cabinet Secretary and head of the Civil Service, with this failure in a discussion before a Cabinet committee meeting. He obviously felt stung and dismissed my claim that he had allowed proper government decision-making to break down by saying that Blair had given his commitment to be totally with the US in August 2002 or before.

The other important issue that follows from briefing I received from senior figures in the intelligence services, both when I met them and through the written intelligence, is that it was clear that they were convinced that Saddam Hussein was dedicated to the possession of chemical and biological weapons and would acquire nuclear weapons if he could, though they made clear this would take at least five years. They also believed that he had hidden programmes and probably materials across Iraq. But they *never* suggested that something new had happened that created a risk that had to be dealt with urgently. It is a matter of record that Saddam Hussein had a nuclear programme and had had chemical and biological programmes, some of which were dismantled by the UN weapons inspectors prior to their withdrawal in 1998. Hans Blix also dismantled 70 ballistic missiles with a range greater than that allowed in the Security Council resolutions passed at the end of the first Gulf war. Our agencies, who told me they had much better information from Iraq than did the US, were clear that Saddam Hussein was dedicated to having WMD and was hiding material from the UN, but the exaggeration of the immediacy of the threat came from the political spin put on the intelligence and not from the intelligence itself.

Iraq claimed repeatedly that it had got rid of all its WMD in 1991. The UN review that established the United Nations Monitoring, Verification and Inspection Commission (UNMOVIC) in December 1999, following the withdrawal of the previous inspectors in 1998, recognised that this might be true but needed to be verified. Blix also recognised that this could be true but Iraq's resistance to inspection made people suspect otherwise. However, it was also acknowledged that the UN inspectors had been widely infiltrated with spies, which would explain Iraq's attitude. UNMOVIC was therefore set up from January 2000 in a way that excluded spies by ensuring that all the staff were employed by the UN and paid by a charge made on the Oil for Food programme, which was funded by Iraqi oil. Iraq had an interest in the return of inspectors if it really would lead to the lifting of sanctions. All who were expert on Iraq understood this reality. They suspected Saddam Hussein still had hidden programmes but there was no suggestion that the problem had escalated or that he had significant programmes that were weaponised and therefore posed an immediate danger. It was absolutely clear that he had no nuclear capacity and experts understand that chemical and biological programmes can produce unpleasant results but are not in reality weapons of mass destruction. The intelligence agencies shared the US view that the situation in Iraq needed to be resolved, but they did not suggest that there was an emergency that needed instant attention. Perhaps the CIA succumbed to political pressure to this effect, but British intelligence never suggested there was any immediate danger. This suggestion came from political spin.

The right policy would have been to assure the US that the problem of Iraq needed action but, as there was no immediate threat, make it a condition that there must be progress on implementing the Road Map to a Palestinian State, before the UK and the international community were willing to support the US in taking action on Iraq. This was Tony Blair's big failure. He could have built an international coalition to use US determination to act in Iraq as a lever to get progress on Israel/Palestine. Instead, he seems to have convinced himself that the US was determined to act and that it would be a disaster if the US acted alone and thus lost all leverage.

Cabinet discussion and the Labour Conference

In September 2002 we had a long and full discussion on Iraq at Cabinet. Tony Blair asked to see me before the meeting. He asked if I had seen SIS and said, as my diary records:

> He said he didn't want to lose me, but couldn't give me a veto.
>
> I had done an interview for GMTV on Sunday stressing UN, no repeat of Gulf war and hurt to Iraqi people. Need for progress on Palestine and Kashmir. Big stress on keeping to UN route. No complaint from TB. I briefly reiterated my points.

The Cabinet discussion was full and open. Once again my diary entry summarised:

> Cabinet discussion good. Big beasts lined up to support –
> JP – GB – JS – DB [John Prescott, Gordon Brown,
> Jack Straw, David Blunkett]. JP said something like must
> all stick together but didn't disagree with me. GB stressed
> UN but brief. DB a muddled contribution.
>
> M Beckett came in with, not against. Then I did
> teaching on the just war etc. Alan Milburn and Estelle
> Morris and others then spoke v openly re why now? Why
> him? What about the Palestinians? Palestinians came up
> repeatedly and UN.
>
> V good discussion. I think it influenced TB statement to
> Parliament, less belligerent and more UN.

I have made clear, as did the Butler Report, that there was not a collective Cabinet strategy for Iraq and the answer is always given that the Cabinet discussed Iraq twenty-four times. This is true and I sometimes initiated and always participated in those discussions. But there is a great difference between the Cabinet being updated each week on the events they are reading about in the press and any serious discussion of the risks and the political, diplomatic and military options and the hammering out of an agreed strategy to handle the crisis. There was no such discussion and we now know from the Butler Report that papers were prepared for Cabinet but never circulated, and that there was a review of UK strategy towards Iraq in March 2002 which was not shared. This is Blair's style. He wishes to keep information to himself in order to keep control to himself. It is worth remembering that most Cabinet members were not seeing the intelligence or SIS except for the one set of briefings arranged for groups of Cabinet members. The discussion in September was, however, very full. Cabinet does not meet in the recess and the press had been full of Iraq over the summer. There obviously had to be a discussion. Everyone was allowed to say what was on their minds and there were many voices stressing the need to reach agreement through the UN and to make progress on Palestine. It was clear that Blair had taken the precaution of ensuring the senior members of the Cabinet were lined up to support him. At the time I was encouraged by this discussion, as I was by various private conversations I had with Blair, but the reality was that he was managing us, reassuring us and keeping us on side whilst he and his entourage decided what to do. No decisions were made in Cabinet.

We then went off to the Labour Party conference with threats of defeat for the leadership as they indicated that they would reject the call from the unions, which was widely supported, for an enquiry into the benefits and disadvantages of the Private Finance Initiative (PFI). And, of course, there was the looming threat of war in Iraq. I was sitting on the platform with Jack Straw and Geoff Hoon during the Iraq debate. We were all due to speak. There was a tense and heated atmosphere in the hall. As had become usual, the Chair called a series of speakers sympathetic to the government's position. Then people started shouting from the gallery and the hall. Jack Straw and I pressed the Chair to call some of the opponents and suggested Alice Mahon, the MP for Halifax, who had opposed the Kosovo and Afghan wars and was deeply hostile to military action in Iraq. As the pressure mounted, the Chair gave in and the debate became more balanced, with passionate and eloquent contributions from all parts of the argument.

My diary entry was:

> Very good debate at Conference. NEC statement withdrawn. 40 % vote for Composite ruling out any war. 52 % + support war, only if explicitly authorised by the UN. Clinton speech – which I missed – also greatly stressed UN.

I strongly think Conference did its job and TB much more firmly tied to UN and because US opinion doesn't want to go alone, ties the US more.

Also at Conference, I asked Jack Straw if he trusted TB not to go with the US outside the UN – he said no, but he was working on it.

I had a chat with GB – he stressed UN and Palestinians.

My entry went on:

Since then, things have gone quieter, public opinion less fraught. I think this is because of stress on UN route . . .

Various people have said don't resign. I am clear my best leverage is not to want to resign but to go if TB adopts impossibly bad position ie US alone with UK.

Blair's speech at Conference stressed that globalisation made the world more interdependent. His theme was that Labour was at its best when at its boldest. He argued that we must take firm action against dictators as well as care for Africa and reduce poverty. He said that 'sometimes in dealing with a dictator, the only chance of peace is a readiness for war'. But he also warmed the Conference heart by promising to host 'final status negotiations' and 'they must have explicitly as their aim an Israeli state free from terror, recognised by the Arab world and a viable Palestinian state based on the boundaries of 1967'. He said these talks would take place before the end of the year.

John Kampfner's book *Blair's Wars*, published in 2003, tells us that Foreign Office officials were astonished by this, as there were no such proposals and says Blair and Jonathan Powell inserted this promise into the speech at the last minute without consultation. Blair covered his back by calling a conference on the Middle East at Lancaster House in December. Jack Straw opened it and I attended and spoke briefly. I also hosted dinner for the delegation from the Palestinian Authority. DfID were closely involved in helping the Palestinian Authority build the institutions of their proposed state. We also provided regular funding for the United Nations Relief Works Agency (UNRWA) which was the UN agency charged with responsibility for supporting Palestinian refugees. We had to keep increasing our contributions as the situation of the Palestinians got ever worse. Unicef had reported that in the West Bank and Gaza malnutrition was worse than in Zimbabwe and the Democratic Republic of Congo. I put to the Palestinian ministers that we might get progress on Palestine as a quid pro quo for action on Iraq. They were not convinced and said this would not be fair on the people of Iraq. They were not optimistic about prospects in the Middle East. We ended up swapping jokes from our respective countries as a way to try to cheer ourselves up.

I still find it completely shocking that Blair would irresponsibly promise such a massively important thing as final-status talks for the establishment of a Palestinian state by the end of the year when there was no substance in the promise. When a British Prime Minister makes such a promise, one believes it is a real promise. But again it seems Blair was flying by the seat of his pants. Perhaps he thought he could somehow achieve this, and he certainly pleased the Conference, but there were no responsible plans capable of fulfilling the promise.

Foundation hospitals and Estelle's resignation

In October 2002, the rows over Alan Milburn's plans for foundation hospitals were causing growing concern. All serious people were agreed that Labour's approach to public-sector reform was too control-freaky, with too many targets, and far too centralised. There was an urgent need to slim down the targets and de-centralise the system, but the NHS certainly did not need yet another re-organisation with some ill-thought-out proposals designed to bring market forces into the management of hospitals. Also in October, Estelle Morris resigned as Secretary of State for Education because targets of improved achievement promised by David Blunkett, when he was in her job, had not been met. She said later that she could not stand the press barrage and intrusions into her private life that came with the controversy. A little later, when Tony Blair floated the possibility of bringing in top-up fees for higher education, in another policy announcement bounced out of No. 10, it was suggested that Estelle had been hostile to top-up fees and it was one of the reasons for her going.

Estelle is a genuine, very lovely and straightforward person. Her seat is Birmingham Yardley, which is always targeted by the Lib Dems, so in every General Election we take workers over from Ladywood to help in her campaign and this has helped to bond us as friends. When she resigned she issued a statement to the effect that she had been a good Minister of State but was not really capable of being a Secretary of State. I was shocked by this. Estelle was a widely admired and respected Secretary of State within her department and across the world of education. Her problem was that she often had to play second fiddle to Andrew Adonis, Blair's policy adviser in No. 10, who came up with reactionary policy proposals that Blair backed and Estelle had to implement. I rang her from my car, on the way to Birmingham, and found her through the No. 10 switchboard. I said how sorry I was and that I didn't think she should have gone and she was certainly capable of being Secretary of State for Education, her problem was advisers in No. 10. She said that she had drafted a statement but Alastair Campbell had 'helped' with the final version. I do find this astonishing. Even Robin Cook makes clear in his book that Alastair helped him draft his resignation letter. The spin goes on, even when people are leaving the government and efforts are made to influence ex-ministers and build on their instinct for loyalty with promises of patronage yet to come. Estelle was promised a return to government. The press was used to hint that Robin might become a European Commissioner.

Progress in the Security Council

Bush had been persuaded to go to the UN in early September. Claims were made in the press that this was Blair's achievement. There is no doubt that Blair pressed for this, but so did many others, including Colin Powell and a variety of senior Americans who had been members of Bush's father's administration. Bush going to the UN brought much relief to those of us who were dedicated to resolving the crisis through the UN, but his tone was to challenge the UN, suggesting that, if it did not take on Iraq, it was as useless as the League of Nations. Following this, the Security Council started work on preparing the resolution that was to become 1441. The usual practice in preparing a Security Council resolution is for drafts to be prepared and circulated and amended over and over again until agreement is reached. At every stage of the process telegrams are sent back to London by our mission in New York recording progress. I and my officials followed the process closely.

My diary entry towards the end of October says:

> Slow wrangling in Security Council. I am v. pleased at Chirac position (2 resolutions). US want to go before March because of chemical suits [ie fear that troops may have to wear such suits in very hot weather]. I think must get through March and go slow and get progress on Palestinian state. TB said at Conference, final status talks before the end of the year.
>
> Asked him at recent Cabinet as part of discussion on Bali [where a terrible bomb had killed 202 young tourists, mostly from Australia, but including 26 Britons], what progress had been made in planning final status talks on

Palestine. He said he'd talked to Bush who had promised, but we will see.

Also stressed no security answer to Bali and similar events – real danger of 'war of civilisations'. If civilians seem as legitimate targets, means major moral deterioration and no people could be safe. Must have progress on Palestine . . .

Overall – I feel more hopeful that UN will prevail and disrespectful of TB for getting so far out with US – not good judgement.

V+ view UN route now more likely. [They say] TB did push Bush to UN but he was going there anyway because US public opinion doesn't want to go alone – issue now whether inspectors find anything – know it's there – if they don't, what? That was why wanted P5 [representatives of the Permanent Five countries in the Security Council] on inspection teams – to pass over intelligence coming from inside Iraq on where it is. They repeated point re not another Gulf war – more refined military action – regime crumble quickly.

I commented:

But this would be wrong, my conclusion is still, weapons inspectors in – take time they need – move forward on Israel.

In November Security Council Resolution 1441 was passed. This was achieved by the usual process of repeatedly amended drafts in order to build consensus. The resolution is not formally tabled until agreement has been built up. In the light of later claims that 1441 gave authority for war, it is worth noting the formal speech setting out the UK position that our Ambassador Sir Jeremy Greenstock read out to the Security Council. He said that the fact that the Resolution had unanimous support sent a powerful signal to Iraq and created a chance that Iraq would finally comply with its obligations and that military action could be averted. He went on to say

> We heard loud and clear during the negotiations the concerns about 'automaticity' and 'hidden triggers' – the concern that on a decision so crucial we should not rush into military action; that on a decision so crucial any Iraqi violations should be discussed by the Council. Let me be equally clear in response, as a co-sponsor with the United States of the text we have adopted. There is no 'automaticity' in this Resolution. If there is a further Iraqi breach of its disarmament obligations, the matter will return to the Council for discussion as required in Operational Paragraph 12.

This speech is very important and was an on-the-record statement of the UK government position. There had been tension in the drafting of the resolution over whether it would give Iraq a last chance to disarm and if it failed the issue would come back to the Security Council, or whether the resolution would give the US authority to declare war if they judged Iraq had not complied. This is what automaticity meant. The US had wanted a resolution giving them authority to declare war if they saw fit. The rest of the Security Council did not want this. This is why it took nearly two months to reach agreement on the resolution. Jeremy Greenstock's statement was therefore very important. He made a promise on behalf of the UK in that statement which was later broken when Blair decided that he had legal authority for war without another resolution. The point was later fudged by the claim that the issue went back to the Security Council for discussion, but that is not a fulfilment of the promise 'there is no "automaticity" in this resolution'.

My diary entry for 10 November is:

I have failed to [make a] note [of] various developments. I asked for assurance – we would not go alone with US v Iraq, outside UN and if not Cabinet discussion before decision made. TB spoke in friendly tone, said didn't want to be tied to an assurance as such but promised constant discussion. Said we are on tightrope trying to keep with UN . . . if we were likely to fall off 'you' (pointing at me) will be first to know.

Next Cabinet – I asked what exactly our bottom line for Security Council was. TB said if inspectors blocked, would go back to Security Council. Problem was if need force to back up UN but likely veto. (Can't always be sure TB doesn't say what one wants to hear but this is full Cab with a note taken and tone is friendly and careful).

Blair repeatedly qualified his promise that we would return to the UN if inspection failed with the proviso that this would happen unless there was an unreasonable veto. He said this in Parliament as well as in Cabinet. This was clearly designed to give him what has come to be known as 'wriggle room'. In the run-up to war, Blair repeatedly promised his party, Cabinet and country that we would go back to the UN for a second resolution if it was to come to war. He did not keep this promise and he used his wriggle room to blame the French in a way that was deeply misleading, as we shall see.

On 22 November I wrote:

Had startling discussion with GB this week. Said not too worried re economy but sick of fighting against bad proposals

– removing child benefit from parents whose children truant
– foundation hospitals
– top-up fees

No. 10 briefing against him would get worse and nasty. He wouldn't take any other job. Was in a hurry to move forward on extra $50 billion oda [i.e. increase in international aid] because he did not know how long he would have.

TB doesn't listen to him anymore and was listening only to non-Labour voices and thinking about his reputation in history.

In December the attacks on Cherie over the purchase of two flats in Bristol broke out. I was in no way connected to it and was therefore very surprised to receive a call from Alastair Campbell to ask me if I would defend her. Alastair very rarely spoke with me so I knew they were desperate. I thought about it and felt sorry for Cherie. I knew she had been worried that, after they sold their house in Islington, they had no stake in the property market. All she had done was buy two flats and use an unreliable man as her agent and say he was not her financial adviser. I agreed to do so and made my point that she hadn't done anything wrong. I received a note of thanks from Cherie and a thank-you from Tony.

In January 2003, the Foreign Office called all our Ambassadors and High Commissioners back to London for an unprecedented gathering. Such recalls of Ambassadors to discuss foreign policy are common in other countries but are not usual in the UK. Tony Blair addressed them, as did Jack Straw. I was asked to join a question-and-answer session which Jonathan Dimbleby had been asked to chair. I was warmly received and a range of Ambassadors made clear in the session and in various other ways whilst they were in London that many of them were pressing to pull back from a war against Iraq. They were warning that a war would strengthen al-Qaeda. There were hardly any who supported war and they were concerned at Bush's extremist advisers. They also stressed that it was clear that Bush needed the UK because US opinion polls showed that the American people would not support war alone. Our military contribution was insignificant. It was our political support that was needed. This gave us leverage and created the possibility of Blair playing a very important role in history.

Sadly, Foreign Office advice was marginalised throughout the crisis. All the wisdom and experience of the Middle East, and of what it takes to get a Security Council resolution, was pushed to one side. Blair handled the whole crisis personally with his entourage. David Manning was an experienced diplomat and was part of the entourage, but otherwise it was Alastair Campbell, Jonathan Powell, Sally Morgan and constant telephone contact with the White House. Our own professionals and proper decision-making structures were cast aside. Jack Straw was closely involved throughout but he became Blair's agent rather than the representative of the Foreign Office. Jack is an extremely nice man, always smiling and jokey and polite, but he appeared to do anything Tony asked him to. Loyal to a fault, perhaps. His job was to keep in constant contact with Colin Powell by phone and in person. Colin Powell was the dove in the Bush camp. Interestingly, the one man with experience of war had doubts about war, but as the crisis accumulated, he appeared to give in and simply support the Bush strategy. Some said it was the soldier in him, who in the end has to obey the Commander in Chief. Jack Straw took his orders from Blair and his job was to be in constant touch with Powell. Even statements were co-ordinated across the Atlantic. They echoed each other – Bush and Blair, Powell and Straw. I feel sorry about the way Straw diminished himself.

Also in January, there was great agitation in the PLP. Tony Blair came to address a meeting of the full PLP. The spin in the press was 'Blair wins time with bravura performance'. What he did in fact was stress his respect for progress through the UN which was the view of the overwhelming majority of the PLP. The Tory party were gung-ho for war – with a few honourable exceptions; the bulk of the country, the membership of the Labour Party and the PLP well understood that Saddam Hussein was an evil tyrant, that the people of Iraq were suffering as a result of sanctions and that the authority of the UN was being undermined. The majority were willing to threaten and indeed use force, if all other means had been exhausted, and if it was authorised by the UN. Tony Blair used, as he does, deliberate ambiguity that made many of us believe that we could persuade him to stick with the UN route, but after it was all over, it became clear that he was determined that the US would not act alone and therefore gave up any significant influence. But by adopting this deliberately ambiguous position, he imposed a considerable strain on himself and began to look quite gaunt and ill. Tony Blair as a strongly presentational politician takes great care with what he eats, he works out regularly and has his clothes chosen carefully, but the pictures of him dating from about that time show the strain he was suffering from making one set of promises to his country, party and Cabinet and another promise to President Bush.

Top-up fees and House of Lords reform

In the midst of all this, Blair produced the White Paper on top-up fees. Its origins, like the tragic mishandling of Iraq and the unthought-out proposals for foundation hospitals, came out of his second-term determination to be bold, alongside his reliance on what he called when we talked in West Africa 'my people' in No. 10. This became a pattern. Once the policy has been announced, despite inadequate consultation, the authority of the Prime Minister and constant arm twisting and calls to loyalty are used to get the PLP to vote for things that they do not really support or believe in. It was Frank Field, MP for Birkenhead, who said during the debate over foundation hospitals that if it were a free vote there would be about fifty Labour MPs in favour. The same was true of the Iraq vote and policy on top-up fees. Loyalty is a good thing, but alongside threats and bullying and the ruthless use of patronage, it corrodes democracy and leads to bad policy.

At the end of January, Blair also enraged Robin Cook by committing himself to a wholly appointed Second Chamber with no elected members in the Lords. My view on this is that heredity is obviously an unacceptable way of constituting the second chamber of our Parliament, but as one sees the consequences of patronage, it becomes even more unattractive; at least there are some accidents in heredity! Blair has appointed 125 Labour peers to the House of Lords. This is massive patronage power and a disgracefully undemocratic way of constructing the second chamber of our Parliament. There are of course good and talented people appointed to the Lords, but when you see the process at work and know some of the people involved, it feels tainted. There are constant scandals over people being appointed to the Lords because they have made large donations to the appointing party. Under Blair there has been a pattern of older Labour MPs being persuaded to retire at the last minute by the promise of appointment to the House of Lords so that the regional offices can bounce Blairite candidates into safe Labour seats. People who have never stood for election are put into the Lords by Blair, made ministers by Blair and of course do his bidding absolutely. They have no independent base and little political experience. They are his creatures and act accordingly. Some of them are able, some less so, some nice, some less so, but 22 ministers and whips are in the Lords of whom 17 were nominated by Blair. Many of them have never been elected or had any account-ability to the public. Similarly, in the present Parliament some MPs have started to act out of character. Former ministers appear on the media to defend the indefensible, using briefings that can only have come from the No. 10 machine. Others produce craven speeches, former rebels do not rebel, and MPs who have expressed one view in conversation, vote with the government against their true opinions. Of course, this could be pure loyalty, but the muttering in the PLP is about yet another one who wants to be nominated to the House of Lords.

The preference of Robin Cook and the radicals was for a 50–60 per cent elected element in the Lords. I didn't think either option satisfactory. We need a second chamber because in our system the power of the executive is so enormous and the House of Commons is dominated by Whips. But if it were a wholly elected chamber, say on a regional PR system, we would have two houses with clashing legitimacy. Also, as we've learned from the new system of electing MEPs on a regional list, such a system gives the party hierarchy the power to insert whom they like with little connection to the locality that they are supposed to represent. My own conclusion is that we should have an indirectly elected second chamber, as in Ireland. We could allocate seats to the Scottish Parliament, Welsh Assembly, regional councillors and all the major faiths and other important interests, trade unions, business, etc., but it is essential that they and not the Prime Minister should choose their representatives. I think it is probably beneficial to keep the Law Lords and to appoint senior politicians and Chiefs of the Defence staff for the experience they bring, but all such appointments should arise from the office held and not rely on Prime Ministerial whim. There may be other interests that should be represented, but indirect election would give us an authoritative and legitimate revising chamber without either patronage or heredity. This option started to gain favour just before the vote but was not specifically put before the Commons. I ended up voting in the same lobby as Blair, for different reasons, and felt bad about it when the Whips grabbed me and wanted me to stand near the door because they wanted others to see me in that lobby. This was meant to be a free vote. The outcome was inconclusive, despite Blair using his influence to get MPs to vote for an appointed House. Robin was very upset and disappointed by the outcome of the vote. There was talk of him considering resignation.

Blair visits Washington, February 2003

In February, Blair visited Washington again. The spin was that they agreed the weapons inspectors would be given as long as six weeks to complete their task in order to persuade a sceptical France and the Arab countries to come on board for military action. Bush let it be known he was willing to wait weeks not months and that he considered that Security Council Resolution 1441 gave him authority to act.

I had regular discussions with Gordon Brown at that time. He said they planned a short war and a reshuffle. He felt very much under pressure and believed that they wanted to move him from being Chancellor.

On 28 February, I wrote in my diary:

> I went to Canterbury for Rowan Williams' enthronement and then to Watford to [speak at] a public then Labour Party meeting for Claire Ward, the local MP. People were very worried and astonished. The Labour people kept suggesting that Tony must know something they didn't know.
>
> At Cabinet – mood serious. Need for second resolution the theme. Jack Straw reported on the countries whose votes were needed and on Valerie Amos's trip to Africa.

Baroness Amos was one of the first black women to be appointed by Blair to the House of Lords. She was appointed a Whip and I asked her to speak on DfID business. She did well and was then promoted to be a junior minister in the Foreign Office and represented Blair in the G8 committee on Africa. Her visit to Africa was undertaken with SIS representatives to provide briefings on the intelligence. The purpose of her visit was to press the African members of the Security Council to vote with the US and UK. I had to ensure that her briefing made it clear that it would be illegal to offer any aid inducements. The Americans and French also sent representatives to visit Angola, Guinea and Cameroon. Thabo Mbeki put them under pressure to stand by the African Union position, which was opposed to war. Never have three poor countries been courted so strongly. Mexico and Chile were strongly leaned on by the US but their people were overwhelmingly hostile to war and they did not give in.

Here we begin to see the distortion of the promise on the second resolution. People wanted this promise to ensure that war was a last resort, if all other means of resolving the problem in Iraq were exhausted. It now becomes clearer and clearer that the US, with Blair's support, was working for its own timetable for war, which was mid-February and then was put back to March because Turkey refused US access to Iraq across their border, and in order to try to help Blair get his second resolution. And then an effort was made to pressurise and bully Security Council members to agree the resolution to fit in with the American timetable for war.

DfID preparations for war

By now I was deeply embroiled in detailed preparations for the possible humanitarian consequences of war. Back in September I had visited Geneva and had lunch with all the UN humanitarian agencies which have their headquarters in Geneva, together with the International Committee of the Red Cross (ICRC). The lunch had been arranged to discuss humanitarian issues across the world, but we ended up talking about the threat of war and what the humanitarian agencies should do. There was a general concern not to make war more likely by preparing for it and the UN agencies were very aware they had to respect the views of member states. On the other hand, humanitarians must be prepared if people are likely to suffer. Jacob Kellenberger of the Red Cross was pessimistic about avoiding war and was making full preparations. Shortly after this meeting the UN and my own department decided that the right thing to do was to make preparations for all contingencies. There was a danger that full-blooded preparation for military action could make war more likely, as those who had wanted to find another way through the crisis accepted the inevitability of war. Equally, it would be irresponsible not to prepare. The UN quietly began detailed preparations, as we did in DfID.

The Tories tried to play a game over this issue. They were strongly in favour of war, but aware of my frequently expressed doubts. They therefore used their time in an Opposition Day in February to try to suggest that I was failing to make preparations for the humanitarian consequences of war. My opposite number was Caroline Spelman, the Member for Meriden who was elected to the House of Commons in 1997. My pet name for her was Sweetie-pie. She had a sweet manner but played pure Opposition politics. She met with a few NGOs in November and called for them to be provided with funds, even though many of them had never worked in Iraq, and talked as though it was all a simple matter of a quick war and then getting some NGOs and the UN in afterwards to clean up.

In the debate on 30 January, I tried to spell out how the duty of the humanitarians was to try to avoid war, but I also said:

> I am clear, and all sane people should be clear, that there should be no rush to war. We must be invincibly committed to backing up the authority of the United Nations and this time, not backing off. Saddam Hussein's regime must know that the world will remain united behind the authority of the United Nations, that he will be forced by one means or another to dismantle his weapons of mass destruction and that, if necessary, the world will be willing to use force to back up the authority of the United Nations.

During this debate I argued the case for first making progress on implementing the internationally agreed Road Map to the establishment of a Palestinian state and giving the inspectors enough time to complete their work whilst maintaining the threat of military action to back up the UN. At that time Tony Blair was still talking as though this was the strategy. All those who now claim that war in March was the only way of dealing with Saddam Hussein are not being accurate. If the US had been willing to take a little longer and Blair to use his leverage with the US, we could have had a much better outcome for Iraq and the Middle East.

When John Howard, the Australian Prime Minister, visited London shortly before I left the government, he asked to meet me. He talked dismissively of those who wanted delay and were willing to leave troops sweating in the desert. Thus we were told we had to prepare for war in order to avoid war but then could not wait because the troops were hot. Obviously it would have been possible to rotate the troops. The date for war was chosen by the US and they went to war before the possibilities of inspection backed by force had been exhausted. Hans Blix's compelling, understated book, *Disarming Iraq*, makes this extremely clear.

In the House of Commons debate on 30 January, I summarised the risks we were preparing for. The first was that order and stability were essential to avoid a humanitarian disaster. The second risk was that bombing could damage water and sanitation facilities. The third was that there would be a repeat of the last war's booby-trapping of oil installations which would cause an environmental disaster. The fourth risk was that the Oil for Food programme on which most of the people of Iraq depended for their basic supplies would be disrupted. The final risk, and the most difficult for the international humanitarian system to prepare for, was that chemical and biological weapons might be used in fighting, including fighting around Baghdad and other urban areas.

By this stage, the House of Commons was performing very badly. Blair was strongly backed by the Tories, who were even more gung-ho for war than he was. Both sneered at the Liberal Democrats, and a discussion on the humanitarian risks was used to get at me for not being sufficiently keen on war, rather than for a sober consideration of the options. Given the Tories' efforts to distort the humanitarian argument, I asked various members of the Development Select Committee to undertake an inquiry about the humanitarian risks and preparations. This did not stop the Tories and the media from making false claims about DfID's preparatory work, but it did mean that the truth was on the record in a memorandum and an evidence session, all made available in a report to anyone who was interested in the reality rather than point scoring.

As I worked through the humanitarian risks, I realised I needed to know more about how the war was to be fought in order to prepare for possible humanitarian consequences. I therefore sought presentations from the RAF team that was discussing targeting with the Americans. They said targeting would be much more careful than in the first Gulf war and there would be few civilian casualties. I met with a representative of our special forces who said the hope would be to get areas of the country to fall away from Baghdad's authority and then treat people well so that the regime crumbled with little resistance. I fully believed that this was their intent but none of this proved to be the reality, which demonstrates a point that our media constantly overlook, that UK troops were only a small part of the operation and therefore had limited influence on the strategy.

We also asked Defence Intelligence for an assessment of the risk of the use of chemical and biological weapons during the fighting. Clearly the military had to make such an assessment in order to protect the troops. We needed to understand the risk to Iraqi civilians. The paper – when it arrived – said there was not a high risk of the use of chemical and biological weapons but if there was prolonged fighting around Baghdad there would be a risk. Our medical advice was that there was no preventative action we could take and no antidote. The UN made it clear that if such weapons were used they would withdraw their staff. We in turn made it clear to our military that, if this happened, they would have to care for civilian casualties.

Thus at the same time as media spin was suggesting that there was a high risk from these weapons, our advice from the experts was that their use was unlikely. Later on, when war was inevitable, I asked my

SIS contact what was to be done if chemical and biological weapons were used and civilians harmed. He said that now Blix was back, they would be more thoroughly hidden and use was extremely unlikely.

On 15 February 2003, we had the biggest demonstration against war there has ever been in British history. Most of my friends were there and I was there in spirit. My son, his wife and daughters went with their church. I have met many people since who had not previously demonstrated who did so on that day. They made me very proud of our country.

At the Cabinet in February I stressed that we would need a UN resolution for reconstruction, as well as to authorise war. The importance of a UN resolution to authorise reconstruction had not been sufficiently addressed in public debate. Under the Geneva Convention and The Hague regulations, occupying powers in occupied territory have a duty to keep order and to provide for immediate humanitarian need. They have no authority to make political changes or reform institutions. If the US and UK wanted international support for reconstruction they needed to give the UN full authority to assist the people of Iraq to put in place an interim government and a process of constitution-building. Legality, UN help and international support for reconstruction would be dependent on a UN resolution.

My diary on 28 February records:

> TB said this week [he] would concentrate on humanitarian issues. He had told Bush this was the way to bring the world back together on Iraq. Hoon said he needed more help from my department. . . . J Reid [the then Chair of Party] and H Armstrong [Chief Whip] were inclined to minimise worry in the party and demean the PLP suggesting concern because of re-selection. I said people were genuinely troubled.

I commented:

Most commentators [say] TB brave and clear. I feel a grudging respect but think his weakness is so pro-American, won't criticise at all – don't feel he is getting all the leverage he could get from being the only one willing to contemplate military action. Without UN, rebellion would be bigger and I would join.

US Churches' last-minute peace plan

In February, I was approached by my friend Jim Wallis, a Methodist Minister in the US, who worked with Martin Luther King in his youth. He is Editor in Chief of *Sojourners Magazine* and convener of Call to Renewal, a US church federation working to overcome poverty and revitalise American politics. He was working to build a church network in the US that pulled the people of faith back from the Christian right who had organised most churchgoers to support right-wing politics, and thus ignored the gospels' constant demands to care for the poor. We had been working together to try to increase the commitment to international development in the US. He rang this time because he wanted to bring a delegation to the UK which included representatives of all the US Churches – who for the first time ever, with the sole exception of the Southern Baptists, were united in their opposition to war. (And President Carter, who is a Southern Baptist, had made it publicly clear he agreed with them.) They were also bringing the Bishop of Jerusalem and Church leaders from South Africa, Cyprus and the Gulf, Syria, Jordan and Lebanon. They wanted to avoid a war and thought the best way to achieve this was to make representations to Tony Blair. Jim Wallis asked if I could arrange for the UK delegation to see Blair. I arranged the meeting for 18 February.

I saw them first and we talked about how war could be avoided and Saddam Hussein disarmed and the people of Iraq relieved of sanctions. We had a great discussion. All were very worried, the representatives from the Middle East particularly so. They felt war would create such anger in the Middle East that life would become impossible for ancient Christian communities. The Papal Nuncio who had served in the Middle East also came to see me to make the same argument. They all argued that the way to a settlement in Baghdad led through Jerusalem. After our meeting, we all trooped over to No. 10 from my office. It was interesting to watch Blair at work. He was totally charming, appeared to listen and agree with all that was said. But he made no firm promises. They were much encouraged by the meeting and went away to draw up a last-minute plan for defeating Saddam Hussein without a war.

Jim Wallis wrote an article for the *Washington Post* setting out details of the plan and they made sure it was sent to the White House. Their plan insisted that there were

> unpredictable and potentially disastrous consequences of war against Iraq, massive civilian casualties, a precedent for pre-emptive war, further destabilisation of the Middle East and the fuelling of more terrorism. . . . Yet the failure to disarm Saddam Hussein and his brutal regime could also have catastrophic consequences. . . . The threat of military force has been decisive in building an international consensus for the disarming of Iraq. . . . The serious consequences threatened by the Security Council need not mean war. They should mean further and more decisive action against Hussein and his regime, rather than a devastating attack on the people of Iraq.

Their plan was

1. To remove Saddam Hussein from power. As urged by Human Rights Watch and others, the Security Council should establish an international tribunal to indict Hussein and his top officials for war crimes and crimes against humanity. It would then become

an internationally agreed aim to remove Hussein and the Ba'ath Party from power and to separate him from the Iraqi people.

2. To enforce coercive disarmament. Inspection should be greatly intensified. The existing US military deployment should be restructured as a multinational force with a UN mandate to support and enforce inspection.

3. To foster a democratic Iraq. The UN should plan immediately to temporarily administer a post-Hussein Iraq backed up by a UN-mandated international force, rather than US military occupation.

4. To organise an immediate and massive humanitarian effort for the people of Iraq. Rather than wait for the end of the war, there should be an immediate UN and NGO relief effort.

5. To recommit to implementing the Road Map to a Palestinian state by 2005.

An American benefactor provided $200,000 to enable the Churches to place adverts in the major UK newspapers but they appeared just after the House of Commons vote on war. No one was listening, and the US and UK had abandoned the pretence of searching for an alternative to war. If they had wanted to avoid war, they could have come up with a similar plan of their own.

By the end of February Saddam Hussein was allowing the weapons inspectors to destroy his ballistic missiles and international lawyers in the UK were saying that Resolution 1441 did not give authority for military action.

My diary entry for 7 March was:

> had a couple of days feeling gloomy and sleepless nights writing my resignation statement in my head. It seemed they were into military action whatever Blix said, we are arm-twisting Security Council non-permanent members and don't seem to care that they can't reconstruct the country without a UN mandate.

I was growing ever more concerned and decided to do something I had never done before. I rang Cherie, who agreed to see me, and gave her a copy of my letter to Blair about international law on reconstruction and the need for a UN mandate. My diary records:

> I said 'Tony should reposition, give more time for the Blix process, respect UN authority, talk to Kofi, get him to help with France, Germany and Russia, calm things down and confirm a UN mandate for rebuilding.'

Cherie gave me a cup of tea and was very friendly but firmly assured me that Tony would not contemplate breaking international law. I was left with the impression that Cherie was involved in discussion of the issues and very supportive of Tony.

Tony asked to see me before Cabinet, and said Cherie had told him about our meeting. My diary records:

> He is very friendly . . . I tell him need to reposition and must have UN mandate. He asks if I have stopped my department from preparing. I explain Geneva Convention duties on army. UN humanitarian engagement needs mandate for reconstruction. DfID are preparing for all eventualities but I won't ask department to do illegal things. He seems to be listening and friendly but that is his style.

It was at this stage that the UK, having failed to get enough support, despite all the arm-twisting for the US/UK resolution which simply said the conditions laid down in Resolution 1441 had not been met, indicated that we were willing to modify the resolution. This was Blair's last attempt to get what came to be known as the Chilean compromise. It was to be tabled by the Chileans and list six conditions Iraq must meet to avoid war and to provide a few weeks more for Iraq to meet the conditions.

After the Cabinet meeting my diary records:

> TB says trying to get UN support. R Cook says need
> more respect for UN. I say regret we couldn't use our
> leverage to get publication of Road Map. Arm twisting
> members of Security Council looks bad and diminishes
> the UN. Can't we let Blix process have integrity. Have to
> have UN mandate for reconstruction, otherwise occupied
> territory.
>
> TB says in meeting with me, he may go to see Bush. I
> say not Bush again. He says only way he can get him to
> listen. I say if you do, please go and see Kofi as well. He says
> yes, may also go to see Chilean President and Putin. I say if
> it looks like more arm twisting, won't look good.

My entry goes on

> I heard from two senior officials in DfID that it is rumoured
> that Attorney General has said 1441 may not give authority
> for war and he would resign. Also military would not go if
> legal authority not clear.

I should explain that in DfID we already knew that Foreign Office
lawyers had disagreed on the legality of war under Resolution 1441.
I told Jack Straw this at Cabinet. He appeared not to know.

Blair then called a meeting about the post-conflict situation.
Gordon said the US and UK could not afford the costs alone. I
explained the need for a UN mandate, the doubts of the
international community about getting involved; and the absolute
need to keep Oil for Food working in the short term to avoid
widespread hunger and shortage of other essentials. Blair said he
wanted work done on what to do in the immediate, medium and
longer term. He asked Gordon to sort out the position. My diary
said:

I conclude that we are creeping forward. I made clear at meeting, humanitarian preparations not ready and to TB stressing UN lead for reconstruction might help on second resolution. As one of my senior officials said, problem is TB thinks in sound bites. My view UK government system not working. Why doesn't FCO and Andrew Turnbull get a grip? I spoke to him before Cabinet and said system was being incompetent. My own view TB in his lack of attention to detail is reckless.

DfID's plans for a post-war humanitarian effort involved a UN mandate and us providing financial support, back-up and personnel to the UN, Red Cross/Crescent and bringing in the IMF and World Bank and the rest of the international community as soon as possible. This was modelled on what we had done in Kosovo and Afghanistan, where we worked to provide strong diplomatic and financial support to get the international system working and established a local DfID office with a substantial devolved budget and capacity to call in expertise, to get local systems working. We had enormously efficient staff and systems capable of working in this way and call-down lists of UK experts in all fields that we could bring in very quickly.

We were in close contact with the UN system. Louise Fréchette, the UN Deputy Secretary-General, had taken charge of preparations. The UN had a lot of knowledge of Iraq because of its obligations under the Oil for Food system and had very large numbers of Iraqi staff. They were planning to pull their international staff out in the event of war, but keep them in the region. They had stocks and organisational structures pre-positioned in the region ready to move back in as soon as possible. The International Committee of the Red Cross (ICRC) was even more prepared. They were ready to stay in Iraq during any war. They had materials and people ready to undertake emergency repairs to electricity and sanitation systems. They had stocks to provide emergency support to hospitals and plans for longer-term support to rehabilitate the system. DfID had provided funding to the UN and ICRC to help enable them to make these preparations.

But sadly, US preparations were another story. The State Department and USAID had done a considerable amount of work to prepare for the reconstruction of Iraq. I can remember Andrew Natsios, the Administrator of USAID, telling me that his greatest fear was ethnic conflict and chaos. He also stressed that they planned to remove the leading figures but leave in place the Ba'ath regime's administrative structures. The State Department and USAID shared their thinking with DfID and we with them. But then the Pentagon decided it wanted to be in the lead in post-war Iraq and was allowed to take over. All the State Department preparatory work was brushed aside and, just a few months before the target date for war, the Office for Reconstruction and Humanitarian Assistance (ORHA) was set up in the Pentagon, under retired General Jay Garner. My old friend from Kosovo, now promoted to Major General, Tim Cross was appointed as his deputy. He told me that when he arrived, just a few weeks before the US date for war, they were still moving in the office furniture.

There is no doubt that was a totally irresponsible failure on the US's part to prepare for the post-war situation, even though they were rushing to war at a date of their choosing. Looking back, it is clear to me that, although Tony Blair was spending a lot of time seeing me and attempting to charm me, he was not listening to me. And the government system was not working so that the messages my officials were conveying, as they liaised with the international system, were not being taken seriously. There were two massive failures in Iraq: the first to rush to war by a pre-ordained date rather than act together through the international system; the second an almost criminally irresponsible failure to prepare for the situation after an inevitable speedy victory. Although the US was the major player and the UK in a subsidiary role, Tony Blair's failure to listen to advice and take a stand with the US implicates him heavily in both these serious failures.

On 8 March, I spoke to Kofi Annan about the situation in Ituri in Eastern Congo. My diary entry is:

> On Iraq he said he was still trying. I said I thought there was a bit more hope. He said there was still deep division in the Security Council. He hoped US/UK would not table their resolution because the votes were not there. The consequences would go wider than Iraq. The UN was also needed for reconstruction.
>
> I said yes, it was clear we need a UN mandate. I was trying to convince TB, KA [Kofi Annan] might consider ringing him (I know they get intelligence on all KA calls so they will get this).

On 9 March, my diary simply says:

> Decided to do Rawnsley and say I would resign and whole thing on need to stick to UN and international law and not US timetable. Rang Alastair Campbell and told him.

By now I had decided war was unstoppable. I had experienced enough wars to know that it was too late to criticise when our troops were on the ground, so I made my own arrangements to be interviewed by Andrew Rawnsley for the *Westminster Hour* on Radio 4. I chose Rawnsley because it was a radio programme that could accommodate a substantial interview and I could drive to Pebble Mill from my home in Birmingham in about 15 minutes and do the interview without any fuss. They readily agreed to pre-record the interview the day before it was broadcast. I said that I thought Blair was being deeply reckless in supporting the rush to war and that I would resign if there was no second UN resolution authorising war. When I got back into my car, I phoned Alastair Campbell through the No. 10 switchboard and told him what I had said. I also sent a message to Gordon through one of his staff. I was well aware that this would cause a fuss. I intended it as my last effort to shake the system before I resigned from the government.

John Prescott rang to see what I had said, and then when I was driving up Grove Lane in Handsworth near my home to get some money from the cash machine, Tony rang. I pulled in and stopped the car. My diary entry says:

> TB rang, furious. Said I'm undermining his delicate negotiations. Should have rung him first.
>
> I said I made my position re UN clear over and over. He said never said would resign. I said clearly implied.
>
> He furious – have to see what would do (threatening). I said sorry to upset but doing what I think right, no good resigning after war started. He said 7 days yet, can't leave that man there.

5

STAYING ON

Planning to resign

My diary on 11 March:

> Phew – lots of media outside house, office, etc., etc.
>
> TB rang again. I said happy to go now or agree now to go later, whatever he wanted. He said no, need you for reconstruction.

When I got into the office, Suma Chakrabarti, my permanent secretary, and senior officials had obviously been instructed by No. 10 to try to get me in line. I had an enormously good relationship with all my officials and we worked very well together, but the atmosphere was fraught. They had been asked to find out what it would take to make me stay.

My diary records that, after our discussion, we agreed my conditions were:

1. Publish Road Map
2. Absolute requirement UN mandate for reconstruction

3.   UN mandate for military action

Suma says, what if veto. I said need legal advice.

Suma Chakrabarti then wrote a letter to Andrew Turnbull setting out my conditions.

My diary goes on to record:

> Briefing from No. 10. I had not raised these issues before. Shocking! Raised at every Cabinet and at a series of private meetings with TB. Means:
>
> (i)   First instinct of No. 10 is to lie
> (ii) TB saying he feels personally betrayed, means he wasn't listening to anything I said, most recently last Thursday
> (iii) I had said three times via media where I was and twice hinted resign.
>
> Radio says editorials against me, hanging in the wind.
>
> I feel the same, not long for government – even starting to think I'll have evenings to myself. Reality is, I don't support top-up fees, foundation hospitals, handling of asylum or TB's arrogant, centralised management style.
>
> But clear I should hang on re Iraq, go if my bottom line is broken, especially second resolution (and then campaign for TB to stand down).
>
> PS Peter Mandelson out in media saying I hadn't said these things before! How would he know? And Alan Milburn apparently said hadn't raised in Cabinet.

This really is a sad aspect of New Labour. The obsession with presentation of course leads to putting the best face on things. But it has moved beyond that, beyond being economical with the truth, to having no respect for the truth, only the danger of being caught out. Members of Cabinet would not break rank, Cabinet records would not be made available for decades, so they decided to undermine me by lying at the same time as the Prime Minister was still trying to sweet-talk me.

12 March diary:

> Spoke TB last night on [senior official's] advice about a meeting on legality of military action with Attorney-General, Chief of Defence Staff, G Hoon, J Straw [the point being DfID not invited to meeting]. It was I understand re the use of UK bases by the US in war, but the fundamental question on whether there was legal authority for military action was presumably the same. I said if department being disabled because I am seen as problem, I couldn't have that [implying I would go now]. He said no, no, no, you will see all, decided to defer base decision. Hopeful on second resolution. Attorney-General said 1441 enough. A bit later, 1441 enough if detail available to show SH had not complied. Will get UN mandate for reconstruction. Assure me won't breach international law. He said bound to be a reaction to Sunday [ie Rawnsley interview] – ignore press. I said not reading it but it demonstrates that first instinct of some people is to lie. He said we will talk etc., etc. Back on charm!

Diary, 13 March:

> . . . what a day. Cabinet met (radio saying first since I said TB reckless). Very much felt getting near end of line. Found myself feeling sad/tearful for first time. Friendly chat G Hoon and Bruce Grocott about nothing much. Then asked Paul Boateng to protect the work of the Africa

conflict prevention committee. Then Sally [Morgan] asked me to see TB. He asked how I was. Said Bush had promised UN mandate for reconstruction. I asked about publication of Road Map. He asked whether it would make a difference to me. I said it would give me 2 of my 3 conditions – give me dilemma. He said that might help him with Bush.

I said can't you at least try a process at UN that treats UN with respect not just forcing US timelines. He said he could get more time. I said if seen to really try will help the world.

At Cabinet I asked if we could have a special Cabinet with Attorney-General present. This was agreed. I said if we have UN mandate, possible progress on Palestine/Israel and try with second resolution process, it would make a big difference.

GB spoke animatedly about what France was saying – no to everything. Jack Straw also anti France. J Reid silly contribution about no members leaving the party. David Blunkett said we must stand by the PM and Chirac was reckless (silly man). Felt hopeful of progress.

Talked GB. He had had dinner with JP and TB. Said would do media . . . said he didn't want me to go but if I did make sure preparing for reconstruction so can return. I said preparing anyway.

What had happened was that John Prescott had brought Tony Blair and Gordon Brown together for dinner and Gordon had agreed to get involved and help Blair. It is also now clear that they had agreed that their best way forward was to blame the French. Later I had tabled a statement in the Commons on humanitarian preparations. There had been a request for interviews and I decided to do a few. Alastair Campbell told my press officer he was not keen for me to do interviews, so, as my diary records:

I rang TB. He said it would be good. GB thinks we should make more of commitment to UN for reconstruction. I said very pleased you and GB talking. He said I feel really boosted.

He said want to see you tomorrow. May have good news for you.

Diary, 14 March:

Telegram says Chirac never said veto any resolution, just one on the table. Intelligence says fighting in Baghdad will risk use of chemical and biological weapons. Core of Republican Guard will fight.

Saw TB 12.30 talked it through. He said Chirac had called. I said need to cool megaphone diplomacy. Get Kofi involved. . . . He said can have longer if 6 tests accepted but all have to mean it. I said yes, yes.

Told him Jim Wallis's message and plan. I said it matters how we talk about UN, not just fact we go there. Up to now gave us resolution or war, need to respect 'integrity of the process' – your own words.

I showed him intelligence on CBW [chemical and biological weapons] and likelihood some of Republican Guard would fight. I said this is your place in history, it could go wrong. He said wouldn't fight in Baghdad. I think it's [military planning is] siege and invite people out . . .

Bush, Blair, Aznar to meet and announce UN mandate for reconstruction and sanctions lift and oil money into UN account.

Also Bush would announce publication of Road Map at 3 pm (but not if it leaked).

I had gone over to see Blair at his request in his small office next to the Cabinet room. There were just the two of us. There was no antagonism in any of these meetings. He was trying to keep me on side. I was trying to get him to stand firm on the need for a second resolution. For the first meeting after my *Westminster Hour* interview, he had made notes. He said he wanted to try to persuade me to stay. He then told me Robin was going but that my position was different from Robin's. I think that this is true, Robin had not spelled out a full position in Cabinet discussions but I thought his view was that containment was working and should continue. My view was that sanctions were hurting the people of Iraq and support for sanctions was crumbling. We needed action on Iraq, but there was no immediate threat and no need to rush to war. In this discussion we rehearsed the three points set out in my permanent secretary's letter to Andrew Turnbull. It was at the end of this discussion that Tony said that the fact that publication of the Road Map was significant for me, that this might help him with Bush. I was desperately concerned about the dangers of the situation, but I also felt concerned for Tony. I thought he was making mistakes, but I understood the strain he was under. When I went to the second meeting to be told Bush would agree to the publication of the Road Map, I was asked to come in through the Cabinet office entrance in Whitehall so that the press wouldn't see me going to No. 10 so often. When Blair told me Bush would announce his agreement to the publication of the Road Map at 3.15 pm, provided it did not leak, I remember thinking, how silly, presumably he was telling me not to leak. But he was suggesting that the President of the United States would change his mind on publication of the Road Map if his announcement leaked!

Diary, 16 March:

> Rang President Museveni, Vice President Zuma and President Kagame re Ituri and risk of Uganda/Rwanda clash.
>
> Jim Wallis rang . . . He had his article in the *Washington Post* about the plan to avoid war and was getting good feed

back. Rowan Williams was being supportive. He asked if I could ring Rowan Williams to ask him to get the plan to the Vatican.

Rang TB, told him about US Churches, adverts and pressed US Churches' plan on him. Said he would look at it and it would be brilliant if we could find a way through. [Blair had seen the Churches' delegation on 18 February, but their plan for avoiding war was published just before the House of Commons vote].

Rang Kofi Annan re Congo and pressed on him American Churches' plan. He hadn't seen it, but said he would get back on it.

He said he had talked to every member of Security Council and governments across the world were ringing him saying, surely one more effort at compromise was possible. I said blaming the French here. He said, not so, all agree time too short and should not be automatic trigger to war. I said I agreed.

Later rang Gordon – pressed US Churches' plan on him. He kept on about French. I told him what Kofi said – wasn't just French and they hadn't said [veto] any resolution. I suggested he rang Kofi.

I said to GB and TB – let's at least try a resolution with respect for UN process – not vote automatic trigger for war, by our deadline or we're going anyway which has been position up to now.

TB asked my advice (!) re whether to announce UN lead on reconstruction in Azores. Sounds like war inevitable. I said if it is, it is all you've got. He said would still be open to other possibilities. I pressed US Churches' plan.

On 16 March, my family was gathered in London for Mass and then to visit my father's grave as we do every year on the anniversary of his death. My diary records:

Gordon rang 3ish – couldn't talk Jim Wallis – wife in labour. Watched Azores press conference. TB seems to have got little, even UN lead on reconstruction unclear. In Mass, thought could stay if didn't vote and could let it be known mishandled. Later thought nonsense, can't not agree with something so fundamental to Gov which shows flaws in Gov ie so centralised. PM machine in No. 10 so arrogant, Cabinet so poodle-like – explains mistakes. But I feel so sad about department and Rwanda and need to get peace and development in Congo. . . . I think it will be personal statement on Tuesday.

On Monday, 17 March, the special Cabinet with the Attorney-General was held. We were told Robin had resigned and Peter Goldsmith sat in Robin's seat. Two pieces of paper were sitting on the table before each of our places. This was later published as a parliamentary answer. The Attorney started to read the statement. We murmured that there was no need to read it aloud and he stopped. I tried to start a discussion and asked why it was so late, had he had doubts? The Cabinet was impatient with me. They didn't want such a discussion. His advice was that war was legal under 1441 and that was it.

One day we will know how the Attorney came to be persuaded that there was legal authority for war. One of the Foreign Office's long-standing legal advisers had said there was no authority for war and later resigned. A prestigious group of international lawyers had written to the *Guardian* on 7 March and said 1441 did not give authority for war. War would be a breach of the UN Charter without explicit Security Council authority. There were rumours across Whitehall that the Attorney thought there was no legal authority and was planning to resign. The military made it clear that, without the Attorney's approval, they would not go. Then we got a short opinion saying there was no problem and no discussion.

There has been pressure for his full opinion to be published but nothing longer was circulated in Whitehall. There has also been pressure for his instructions to be published. What were the assumptions about the likely use of WMD, for example? The Butler Report provided new evidence on this. It is clear that the Attorney had given Blair earlier advice which had not been shared in Whitehall. This was Blair's informal style being allowed to change the way that Whitehall works. For example, notes of phone calls with foreign leaders were always circulated. This happened with his early calls with Bush, and then notes ceased to be circulated. The tension was considerable across Whitehall on the question of legality, yet no note of the Prime Minister's meeting with the Attorney was made available. This was a considerable change in Whitehall practice. Blair controlled the Iraq policy personally and very informally and normal information-sharing systems were closed down.

For me, this was a significant moment. Up until 17 March there was no legal authority for war. The process leading up to the Attorney's opinion was fishy, but in the British system, for the civil service and military, it is the Attorney's advice that is sacrosanct. Officials in DfID had been very concerned about legality and I felt very protective of them. I was very surprised by the Attorney's advice, but then I accepted it. But looking back it is difficult not to believe he was leant on. He was appointed to the Lords and to his office by Blair and it was clear when I went to see Cherie that there had been discussion on legality. I did ask him later why he had delayed, did he have any doubt? He just said he was slow. The later rumour was that he went shopping to find the one UK international lawyer who would say 1441 gave authority for war.

Deciding to stay

And so I went on with sleepless nights; charm and pressure from the PM, John Prescott and Gordon Brown; phone calls from Africa and messages from our NGOs asking me to stay; and the Prime Minister stressing repeatedly that the Road Map was published and the UN would lead on the reconstruction of Iraq. This was an agonising time for me. I was absolutely clear that the run-up to war had been mishandled and that Blair had not used UK leverage or respected the UN process. But I was also desperately worried about the consequences for Iraq, the Middle East and the authority of the UN. I was also worried about the consequences for the Labour government. I had tried throughout to use whatever influence I had to persuade Blair to stay with the UN and move first on the Road Map. I was trying to use Blair's anxiety to keep me in the government to get a firm commitment to UN-led internationalisation of the reconstruction of Iraq and progress on Palestine. I was not calculating my own position. Obviously, it would have been easier and more popular to simply leave the government, but pacing around my living room on my own on the night before the vote, I decided I should not abandon the government. It was too late to correct the mistakes that had been made, but I would stay and really try to ensure reconstruction was done right.

I sent the following letter to every Labour MP on the morning of Tuesday, 18 March, the day of the House of Commons vote on the war:

> I am writing to all colleagues in the Parliamentary Labour Party to tell you that I have decided to support the Government in the vote tonight. Given my remarks of last week, I thought I should explain my reasoning. I hope this might be of some help to those of you who are agonising over your decision.
>
> I remain very critical of the way the Iraq crisis has been handled. I think the UK could have exerted more leverage and the approach to the Security Council should have been more respectful and less dominated by US timelines and

demands for automaticity. But we are where we are, and we must decide how we can best take things forward.

There have been a number of important developments over the last week:

Firstly, the Attorney-General has made clear that military action would be legal under international law. Other lawyers have expressed contrary opinions. But for the UK government, the civil service and the military, it is the view of the Attorney-General that matters and this is unequivocal.

Second, the Prime Minister has persuaded President Bush that there must be a new UN resolution creating a UN mandate for the reconstruction of Iraq. This is crucial. Without it, coalition forces would have been an occupying army under international law. They would have had no legal right to rebuild any Iraqi institutions. The UN, as in Afghanistan, will now have the authority to support the people of Iraq in drawing up a legitimate constitution, building new institutions, and holding elections.

The UN mandate is also essential for the engagement of the international development community in the provision of humanitarian aid, and for the engagement of the World Bank, IMF, Asian Development Bank and others in the reconstruction effort.

Third, a UN resolution is to be tabled which will give Kofi Annan charge of the Oil for Food Programme and lead to the lifting of sanctions. This will rapidly improve the condition of the people of Iraq.

Fourth, the Road Map to Palestinian statehood by 2005 is to be published. This has been achieved by UK pressure. We all know that the failure to implement the Oslo peace accords and establish a Palestinian state alongside Israel, is the underlying cause of deep anger and bitterness in the Middle East, and the sense of double standards around the world. Publication of the Road Map is important, but we have to maintain constant pressure to ensure that it is implemented. The UK government will have a special responsibility for this.

However, in the last week, we have also failed to secure a Security Council resolution authorising military action. As I have said, I do believe this issue could have been better handled, but when our Prime Minister made clear last week that he would support a Chilean proposal giving three weeks for Saddam Hussein to begin to fully comply with Dr Blix's six tests, France responded by ruling out a resolution involving an ultimatum.

This meant France had moved back from the agreement reached in 1441, and had created a situation where a second resolution was impossible.

So now we must all decide what is to be done. I have until today been clear that I should leave the government. I have now decided that this would be cowardly, because I would be offering no alternative way forward or making any contribution to resolving the problems ahead of us. I know I will be heavily criticised for this decision, but we must all do what we think is right in the circumstances we are now in. We cannot leave the situation as it is, with Saddam Hussein defying the UN and the people of Iraq continuing to suffer.

There are of course grave risks in military action, but I am confident that targeting will be as careful as possible and that our military will take very seriously their humanitarian duties under the Geneva and Hague Conventions. I am hopeful that the regime will crumble very quickly.

I believe the real test we are about to face is our commitment to care for the people of Iraq, and to mobilise the will of the international community to help them rebuild their country. The second test will be the full

implementation of the Road Map to Palestinian statehood.
This is, I think, how history will judge us.

And with a very heavy heart I voted with the government. There
was a strange atmosphere in the Commons that night – Labour MPs
were subjected to enormous pressure and arm twisting. The PM,
Cherie and the Whips all worked overtime, threatening, cajoling
and appealing to loyalty. I was stopped by Rob Marris, MP for
Wolverhampton South West, in the corridor. He asked if it was true
that Tony was considering resignation. This was the first I had heard
of such a suggestion and I said I found this ludicrous. The vote
would be won because the Tories were voting with the government
and many MPs were abstaining rather than voting against. Troops
were on the ground, the situation had been brought to this point by
the Prime Minister and now it was suggested he planned to resign
if he didn't get a big enough majority! After the war was over this
story was spun to the press to make Blair seem heroic and Straw and
Blunkett were quick to say they would have gone too. I find it
astonishing that our political journalists should be willing to swallow
such nonsense.

On 23 March, I wrote in my diary:

> . . . terrible week – decided to stay in the Gov – horrendous
> media and bitter disappointment to all who were buoyed by
> my threat to resign.

I set out my reasons in a letter I sent to the thousands who wrote
and emailed, largely critical of my decision to stay but with a
growing minority saying they were glad I did so. My letter said:

> I am sorry that my decision to remain in government
> disappointed many of you. It would have been easier to
> walk away. I had prepared my personal statement of
> resignation, but was pressed by many groups and the Prime

Minister to stay and lead the UK humanitarian aid and reconstruction effort.

I spent a night reflecting on what I should do. My conclusion was that the crisis had been mishandled. The Permanent five members of the Security Council should have worked harder to remain united and exhaust the possibility of progress through inspection backed up with the threat of force. The UK should have used its leverage more effectively and the US should be more respectful of the UN.

However, many of the criticisms set out in my interview had been met. The commitment to publish the Road Map to Palestinian statehood had been made, it was agreed that there must be a UN mandate for reconstruction, the French veto for the Chilean compromise had made a second resolution impossible and the Attorney-General had given unequivocal advice that there was a legal authority for military action under Security [Council] Resolution No. 1441 and previous resolutions.

It was clear that conflict was now inevitable and a second resolution impossible. UK armed forces were about to go into action against a cruel dictatorship that had been defying the UN on the issue of chemical and biological weapons for 12 years. The people of Iraq had suffered terribly under the Saddam Hussein regime and the UN sanctions which were meant to be short-lived had been in place for 12 years.

I concluded that I should not weaken the government in these circumstances and should stay to drive the humanitarian and reconstruction effort and work for the implementation of the Road Map. The way forward is now to end the war as soon as possible, minimise casualties, provide quick and effective humanitarian support and support the Iraqi people in reconstructing their country under a democratic government. We must also work to heal

the divisions in the international community which weaken
the UN and increase instability in the world in these fragile
times.

I knew my decision would be unpopular with many, but
decided that it would be wrong to walk away.

I left the UK immediately after the vote to visit the UN, World
Bank and IMF and the White House to try to get everyone working
together to support the reconstruction of Iraq.

The reconstruction of Iraq

Kofi Annan was very focused on how to heal the bitter division in
the Security Council. He talked about the need to get a resolution
to keep the Oil for Food programme running so that the Iraqi
people continued to be supplied with their basic needs. He hoped
this might lead on to agreement on a UN mandate for
reconstruction.

Jim Wolfenson, the President of the World Bank, was very
solicitous. He had been following the British press and knew I had
been through a battering. He said he was happy that I had stayed
and that the Bank was ready to be very active in rebuilding Iraq and
the West Bank and Gaza.

Horst Kohler, the Chief Executive of the IMF, was very critical
of international leaders, including Blair. He said he had told Chirac
and Schroeder what he thought. He said a long war would cause
grave economic problems beyond the Middle East. He said the IMF
was ready to engage in Iraq if there was a UN resolution leading to
a legitimate government.

At the White House I had lunch with Andrew Natsios, the
Administrator of the US Agency for International Development
(USAID), whom I knew well, as well as people like Elliot Abrams
and various others. I told Abrams that they should get Negroponte,

their Ambassador to the UN, to be more subtle than he had been up to now, in order to get agreement on the Oil for Food resolution. I also said we had to have a UN resolution to appoint a special representative of the Secretary-General in order to appoint a transitional government. I went on to meet with Richard Armitage, whom I knew quite well since we had worked together to try to drive forward the Sri Lankan peace process. Both he and Abrams said the President was sincere about the Middle East Peace Process. Perhaps they meant this, but it turned out to be untrue.

On 19 March, special forces started moving into Iraq and the US got an intelligence report that Saddam Hussein and his sons were together in a restaurant and an effort was made to bomb them. I came back from the UN to attend the daily special Cabinet – which was known in the press as the War Cabinet. The early preoccupation was whether or not Saddam Hussein had been killed or injured in the bombing. John Scarlett, the Chair of the Joint Intelligence Committee, summarised the intelligence each day. For quite some time they did not know whether or not Saddam Hussein was alive.

My own preoccupation was to prepare for reconstruction. I knew the war would last no more than a few weeks. I went to the War Cabinet every morning at 8.30 am and had a meeting with my staff beforehand so that I was fully briefed on the humanitarian situation. We were closely in touch with ICRC who were in Iraq and feeding out reports of the situation for the people. Their major concern was repairing damage to water supplies and keeping the hospitals functioning. When I fed in my reports, they would often be contradicted by Michael Boyce, the Chief of the Defence Staff, who kept reporting that water and electricity were being patched and holding up. ICRC reports were more worrying. After a few days, I noticed Michael Boyce and John Scarlett coming out of Blair's study before the meeting. Even with a very small group like the War Cabinet, Blair liked to have an informal pre-meeting. He simply cannot work collectively. My concern was focused on the situation of the people in Iraq and preparations for reconstruction.

I was determined to get the UN lead Blair had promised. Work began on a draft resolution and instead of doing the usual drafting by continuous consultation between Security Council members, the UK worked with the US to prepare a draft. It put the UN in a subservient position and would definitely mean the US was seen to be leading the reconstruction, which would make an international effort impossible. I made clear that the US draft UN resolution would not do. I wrote in my diary:

> Manning must stop talking to Condi Rice on the phone and state our position on paper and say no. . . . TB seems clear. This is crucial to legality, international healing and the funding of reconstruction.
>
> Day 6 of conflict – targeting is careful – seems to be going fast.

I was at this stage feeling very sad and low that we had failed to prevent war. My son was angry with me, I had disappointed many people and the battering I had had from the media was very unpleasant. But I was clear that my job was to try to bring the international development system back together so that we could all help Iraq rebuild and the people have a better future.

20 March was the first full day of the war. On 9 April, US troops entered Baghdad and 'helped' a small group of Iraqis to topple a statue of Saddam Hussein. War lasted only 20 days, but the aftermath was to last very much longer. I was still focused on reconstruction.

On 26 March, I recorded in my diary my meeting with the French Ambassador the day before. I said:

> Please can we all work together on the humanitarian situation and reconstruction.
>
> He said France very hurt by UK attacks, believed we should have got another resolution as we did 1441 and exhausted inspection backed by force. I asked if they had

said there could be no ultimatum and therefore opposed the Chilean compromise. He said the Chilean compromise was always a non-starter, there was such division in the Security Council, the US had denounced it but it was true the French would have no automaticity.

We talked of what kind of Europe we wanted to build. I said I hope the model is not an alternative great power. We agreed that we needed a Europe that was a countervailing force to American power but based on a commitment to justice, multilateralism, rule of law, development for the poor etc.

I said the only way now was to stand by the Iraqi people and drive the Middle East Peace Process forward and that at least we had agreement in the Security Council on continuing the Oil for Food Programme.

He said we should work for a UN lead on reconstruction and would get agreement if could agree:

(i)   to bring into being a transitional Iraqi government
(ii) have UNMOVIC involved in searching for WMD
(iii) assemble a coalition of forces to keep order

I asked if it should be Nato. He said no, a coalition of the willing.

He said France and the UK could be strong, in face even of Washington if they stood together.

I asked how we could move things forward. He said as TB was going to see Bush, it would be good if he talked to Chirac first. I said I would try.

The Ambassador was a very experienced and senior French diplomat. I concluded that there was still a chance of healing the divisions and internationalising reconstruction. This meeting made me hopeful.

At the War Cabinet on 26 March, the Attorney-General gave his advice on reconstruction, as I had requested. He said that there must be a UN Security Council resolution for the transitional government to legitimise any significant reform of Iraqi institutions. Later I met with my officials for a debrief on the Special Cabinet, they were very worried that the legal advice was being fudged and everything was focused on what could be renegotiated with Washington.

I then arranged to see Blair about the UN resolution. I told him about my meeting with the French Ambassador and asked him to ring Chirac. He said he would do so after his visit to see Bush. I pressed that it would be much better if he rang before.

The German Development Minister, Heidemarie Wieczorek-Zeul, rang. She was very upset by the war and worried that the bombing would be continuing when we were due to meet for the World Bank spring meeting. She thought this would create a disastrous atmosphere. I said I thought the bombing would be over and that I really hoped we could all unite at the meeting to say that, if the UN resolution is right, the world will come together to support the reconstruction of Iraq.

My note in my diary is:

> Hm, TB seems clear but can't be trusted to be firm with US (but might be on this). UK Civil Service working very badly because all power has been sucked into No. 10.

John Prescott chaired the Special Cabinet on 27 March because Blair was in the US. The Attorney-General had produced his written advice saying a UN mandate was required for reconstruction. He then went on to say that we must not make public the fact that the opinion had been requested or provided. I challenged this and said the government were quick to publish his advice on 1441 when it was helpful to the PM's position. Now that the advice created difficulties over how reconstruction was to be organised, it was to be kept secret. I said that I thought his advice was useful and it was the same understanding of international law that the UN held. John Prescott said we would have to await Blair's return.

This was a crucial issue for me. International law was clear, whether or not 1441 gave legal authority for war, the US and UK were occupying powers in occupied territory. If we could agree a UN mandate, similar to the one passed for Afghanistan, the UN would help the Iraqis put in place a transitional government and the international community would come together to help Iraq rebuild. It was worrying that the Attorney-General suggested that his advice to this effect had to be kept secret.

My senior officials told me that they and MoD officials were both worried that the government might be contemplating asking them to take on a role that was not legitimate in international law. I rang John Prescott to tell him how important the point was. He said I had made this clear at the Special Cabinet. I stressed that that was the question of publication of the Attorney's advice. This was about officials being asked to act in breach of international law.

On 28 March, I recorded in my diary:

> Pushed boat out really hard at 8.30 am [Special Cabinet] meeting on need for UN resolution for legality. TB said got agreement, no problem but agreed with Kofi, need to keep subterranean to get agreed.
>
> I came back time and time again. Jack very irritated. Says don't need another row about a UN resolution . . .
>
> I said agreed need careful tactics but need to agree bottom line is legality. FCO been fudging for ages – now got Attorney-General's advice.
>
> TB says can be sure no breach of legality.
>
> Jim Wallis then rang, said American NGOs were in conflict with the Pentagon, had been told to take orders

from military – had withdrawn from meetings. Wanted to know where things stood. I explained the law and need for UN resolution to create transitional Iraqi government. I explained to him that ORHA [Office of Reconstruction and Humanitarian Assistance] was an instrument of the Pentagon and was not effective. I said there was a real danger that the US would become isolated and get bogged down in Iraq and this would be dangerous for US and the world.

He agreed and said we must work together. All the noise in the US was that the Pentagon was in charge. There was no UN [role] and even Colin Powell was saying it.

I said TB said he had agreement with Bush but it mustn't become a public issue or Bush wouldn't be able to do it.

SIS said afterwards that they thought the atmosphere in the White House had changed, they were chastened, Condi Rice subdued, clear on Road Map, perhaps UN resolution gettable.

I also made clear at meeting seriousness of humanitarian situation in West Bank and Gaza.

The same day our Executive Director at the World Bank came to see me. The World Bank spring meeting, which would be attended by ministers from all countries in the world, was looming. The outcome would be crucial to whether we could get the international community to work together on the reconstruction of Iraq. He said the Bank were terribly worried that the divisions in the Security Council would spread to the Bank. They were taking legal advice on the Bank's position in relation to Iraq, but it was difficult because the situation was unprecedented. They were looking at the Japanese case because that was a war that ended with US occupation, but didn't think the Bank went in until after General McArthur left. They expected to come under pressure from the US to start work in Iraq, but were fearful that this would split the membership and could damage the Bank in the same way that the split on Iraq had damaged the UN.

My Special Adviser told me at this time that she had been to a meeting with Philip Gould on the current polling. This is worthy of note because it indicates how Blair had turned away from focus groups in his second term. Gould had said that if there was an election today, the Liberals would beat us. The Tories were nowhere, a lot of people said they would abstain or turn to the Liberals. He said that our only hope was to deliver on public services. Asylum, crime and terrorism were the top issues. He also made lots of comments about Blair not listening to focus groups any more. I remember commenting to my Special Adviser that it almost makes you nostalgic for focus groups. If Blair had continued to be guided by focus groups we would not have got into this situation in Iraq. I also commented then that I suspected the second-term spin was Blair, the conviction politician.

Sir Philip Watts of Shell came to see me that day about the work they were engaged in following the UN meeting on environment in Johannesburg, promoting sustainable development in Ethiopia. I suggested he get his people to contact the DfID office we were building up in Addis Ababa. We then got on to talking about Iraq. He said the worry in Iraq was not so much the war but the aftermath. We could end up with the sort of long-term trouble we had had in Ireland or in Malaysia in his youth.

On 29 March, I commented in my diary:

> Not at all clear that TB visit to US achieved anything.
> I gave out copies of Afghanistan resolution 1378 at Special Cabinet to demonstrate how short resolution could be and where nub lay.

I reported on UN preparations and that my officials' trip to Larnaca where UN staff were headquartered showed very high levels of UN preparation to re-enter Iraq and take forward the reconstruction effort. I informed the meeting that the amount of food in the pipeline for Iraq now Oil for Food was working again was limited and that we needed to get more food onto the sea or we could end up with widespread hunger. I also reported that the ICRC and Unicef were telling us there were real strains on electricity and water supplies in Basra and Baghdad. Both organisations were working hard to keep patching the systems and keep water flowing. Military reports on water and electricity were much too optimistic and complacent.

I went on to confide in my diary:

> I fear the same mistakes being made as in run-up to war, UK not using leverage on US.

After this meeting Andrew Turnbull said that the big problem was that the intelligence failed to predict that the people were so terrorised, they would not rise up. This was the first time I heard anywhere other than in the press that this was their expectation. I said to him that my UN contacts told me that many Iraqis were fiercely nationalistic people and if the military action was seen as illegitimate and badly motivated, they would be very unlikely to rise up to support it.

On 30 March, my diary records:

> Good weekend for me, more like normal. Conversation with an old Labour Party friend. He is very upset about false claims that some dead UK soldiers had been executed by the Iraqis and effect of this on families. I say deep culture in No. 10 to say what sounds good, not on truth.
>
> He asks why I believed TB on second resolution. I said I checked what French had said and French Ambassador later confirmed but French Ambassador and public record shows US rubbished Chilean compromise.

I regret TB doesn't attend to detail. He likes the stage, charm and PR rather than detail and truth. Not a bad person – this is the man.

I still feel conflict will end in weeks but real test what post-conflict arrangements are.

In the week of 5 April I had a telephone conference with the Development ministers from the Netherlands, Norway, Canada and Sweden. We agreed to meet with French and German ministers when we are in Washington for the spring meeting of the World Bank. The German minister, my friend Heidemarie, had agreed to join the conference call but she pulled out at the last minute. She felt uncomfortable talking about business as usual when the war was still going on.

I arranged to see the Russian Ambassador. I commented to my diary:

> My plan is that if the whole world is united on what the Security Council resolution must say and UK makes a stand, US will have to give.
>
> The next development was President Bush's visit to Hillsborough. [This was a return meeting, Bush coming to see Blair and it was to be held in Northern Ireland at Hillsborough Castle.] As I read the briefing for the meeting, I became worried that it is selling-the-pass on the authority needed for the UN to reunite the international community. The briefing talks of the establishment of an interim authority and then a Security Council resolution to 'endorse' these arrangements. US representatives had been in the UK working with the Foreign Office to prepare the draft declaration.
>
> Outcome does not look good. It seems that the US is determined to establish its own interim government and push the Security Council to approve these arrangements.

This would inevitably prolong the division in the Security Council – who might let such a resolution through but it would not give the UN a sufficient role to reunite the international community to support the reconstruction of Iraq.

By 7 April, I record in my diary:

Feeling terribly pessimistic re TB willingness to have bottom line with US re role of ORHA and need too for UN to create the interim authority and political process in Iraq.

Already the atmosphere was going sour. I had stayed in the government on the clear understanding that the UN would be given a proper mandate for reconstruction and that I would work to unite the international community to this end. After the Cabinet meeting when I told them I had decided not to resign Tony had asked me to come to his study. He said that he would never forget and would make sure he helped me. I said I hadn't done it for him but for the future of Iraq. He said he knew, but he was really grateful. Less than three weeks later, it was clear Tony's promises would not be kept. He intended to support the US in marginalising the UN once again. This meant there would not be an internationalisation of reconstruction. The Iraqis would suffer the consequences and the bitter division in the world would continue. I had not yet given up but was feeling increasingly pessimistic. I wrote a sharp, clear letter setting out the bottom line and said this should be a UK red line on both the legality and politics of getting the international community involved. This was crucial to engage IMF, World Bank, France, Germany and most other countries.

I spoke to Gordon Brown and John Prescott about how crucial this was but could feel them both pulling away. I spoke to Peter

Goldsmith, the Attorney-General, who said he had not been consulted; he said he had told the FCO that asking the UN to 'endorse' coalition arrangements for the reconstruction of Iraq was not good enough to comply with international law.

I remarked in my diary on 7 April:

> Atmospherics in No. 10 hostile to me, maybe not stay long in Government after all.

And so it seemed I had been a fool to believe the promises, and all the attacks I had taken for agreeing to stay in the government had been for nothing. I had thought I was making a sacrifice for a higher purpose. It seemed that I had simply been used. I was becoming increasingly pessimistic, but had not completely given up.

I rang Louise Fréchette – Kofi Annan's deputy whom I knew quite well. She said all the talk around the UN was too general and positions were too dogmatic. France, Russia and Germany had met in Paris and made useful noises but were saying nothing in New York. I said I was pushing Blair to see that the nub of the issue which would reunite the international community was the UN leading the political process. She said she agreed and that Kofi was saying nothing so as to remain as a bridge-builder.

After the Bush–Blair meeting at Hillsborough, President Bush said at the press conference that he would work as hard for peace in the Middle East as Tony had for Northern Ireland. This sounded good. They also said they had agreed that the UN would have a 'vital' role in the reconstruction of Iraq. This made me a bit more hopeful and I thought that perhaps the fuss I had made had done some good.

On 10 April, the day after the toppling of the statue of Saddam Hussein in Baghdad, Jack Straw offended me greatly with his attitude to France at the Special Cabinet. He used cynical phrases like they had 'missed the boat' and 'backed the wrong horse'. Negotiations were still going on to agree a UN resolution for reconstruction. He criticised them for saying that the US was the 'demandeur' at the Security Council. But I agreed with the French. The reality was that the US needed a resolution to legalise its occupation of Iraq and thus was the country that needed a Security Council resolution. This attitude from Jack did not bode well for agreement on the crucial UN resolution for reconstruction. He also went on to say he thought the Middle East could be won round over Iraq. He simply did not seem to understand the feelings the Iraq war had unleashed.

We went on to a new Ministerial meeting which had been established to supervise reconstruction. It was chaired by Jack Straw who said at this meeting that, on ORHA and the legal limits of its powers, we must not let word get out that we had any difference with the US. He went on to argue that we must secure contracts for UK firms. My diary records that he said: 'We took the risks and bore the costs, we cannot let the French and Germans get their noses in the trough.' I was deeply shocked by Jack's attitude and language. It was bad principle and bad economics and reflected that he did not understand the seriousness of the situation in Iraq and had begun to see it as a business opportunity.

We then went off to the IMF and World Bank spring meetings in Washington, which Gordon Brown and I always attended, supported by teams from the Treasury and DfID. There was a deep fear that the bitter divisions in New York would spread to and contaminate the Bank and the Fund.

My diary records:

> Our Executive Director worked closely with me, the Germans and Nordics. I spoke with Trevor Manuel, the Finance Minister of South Africa who had recently taken over as Chair of the Development Committee. Jim Wolfenson was very worried about what might transpire. Our first step was to agree that we would seek agreed text on Iraq or no text at all.

> I had dinner with Ministers from the Nordic countries, France, Germany and Canada and we simply talked the whole thing through. It helped to ease the tension and hostility to the UK.

We ended up with agreed text which went into both the IMF and World Bank communiqués. The communiqué made clear that we needed to agree a Security Council resolution for the reconstruction of Iraq and that as soon as this was in place the International Financial Institutions (IFIs) should engage. We also got agreement that they should do an immediate-needs assessment (this means they should make a technical assessment of need in order to prepare to engage). This was a considerable achievement. All countries in the world had signed up to this, despite the bitter division not many miles away at the UN. After the formal meeting of the Bank Governors, there is always a lunch attended by the President of the World Bank, Managing Director of the IMF and ministers who are Governors of the Bank representing all the countries in the world (bigger countries like the UK have their own seat, smaller countries are grouped into regional constituencies). It is at this lunch that the most difficult and contentious issues are settled by ministers with no officials present. In this meeting, Trevor Manuel, who was in the chair, was able to make clear how stunned he had been by the decision to go to war, and the Governor from the Arab constituency how much upset and distress there was in the Arab world. I knew most of these ministers well, and put forward my case about the need to get a good resolution and unite to help Iraq whatever view countries had taken on the war. This was agreed by all and we broke up hopeful that we might be able to begin to work together to heal the bitter divisions, and to help the people of Iraq to rebuild their country.

I concluded after this meeting that if the UK ceased to negotiate as the second fiddle to the US but worked to get agreement across the international community, we could still bring the world together. Gordon Brown and I flew back overnight on the same plane. We had a meal together before going to sleep. I was feeling hopeful and expansive, and we talked about the happiness of his expected baby after the terrible loss of tiny Jennifer. I said teasingly that he should eat his salad to get strong for all the sleepless nights ahead and he immediately did so.

When I got back, the No. 10 machine seemed little interested in what had happened at the Washington meeting of the IMF and World Bank. It was also notable at the Special Cabinet that they again wanted to minimise the problems of disorder and looting and question reports from the ICRC that I conveyed. They wanted to believe all was well, but my reports were that Baghdad was in a terrible state, with order, water, power and health services collapsing. In Basra there had been minimal improvements.

My diary records:

> TB made a statement in the House of Commons. I went to listen. He said, noble cause, we did right thing, good that Saddam Hussein regime gone, there is disorder but getting better and will be put right.
>
> Tories' great admiration for TB's great leadership, etc., etc. They all heckle and jeer Charles Kennedy . . . very unattractive, House of Commons at its worst, no doubt not in tune with country.

I had a run-in with the *Telegraph* because I was unwilling to say that the death of an innocent civilian was a 'price worth paying' for the overthrow of Saddam Hussein. I still think this is the wrong way to talk about human life. The overthrow of Saddam Hussein's regime was of course desirable, but the death of every person is regrettable and it is wrong to talk of Iraqi lives in this way.

It is this attitude that has led to the failure to count the Iraqi dead. A voluntary group has therefore taken on this task – www.iraqbodycount.org. They are keeping a record of civilian deaths. They record that between 11,429 and 13,398 Iraqi civilians have died up to the end of July 2004. On top of this more than 6000 Iraqi soldiers were killed in the bombing – many of whom were young conscripts. Experts tell me that we should multiply this number by four for serious injuries. The question is, is this a price worth paying or was there a better way of dealing with the problem of Saddam Hussein? It is because every single human life is precious that the teaching on the just war requires that all other means be exhausted before the resort to war. There is no doubt in my mind that in the case of the Iraq war of 2003 this requirement for a just war was not fulfilled.

However, at this stage those who supported the war were feeling triumphalist. Blair started to give interviews and to suggest that he was willing to resign if he had not won the vote in the Commons, though there was never a realistic prospect of losing it. These were false heroics. I was reminded that Gordon had said that they planned a short war and that Blair, much strengthened, might even move Gordon from the Treasury. The truth is that all those who supported the war were gloating and keen to attack me because I had not been enthusiastic about it.

Within DfID there was a disagreement about whether we should install our staff into ORHA, as the Foreign Office and No. 10 were demanding, or establish a DfID office in Baghdad as we had in Kosovo and Afghanistan. There was a battle across Whitehall where all departments wanted to send people to Baghdad and expected DfID to pay. This was a recipe for chaos. ORHA was already very inefficient and if it was joined by lots of individuals from a scattering of departments, with no clarity about their role, it would make things even worse. But every department wanted to be part of the action in Iraq because it was top of the agenda.

The breaking point for me came over the draft UN resolution. I had spelled out repeatedly that under the Geneva Convention US and UK troops were occupying powers in occupied territory. The proper way forward was a UN Security Council resolution that gave the Secretary-General the authority to appoint a Special Representative who would help the Iraqis to establish an interim government and a process leading to elections, and the establishment of new constitutional arrangements. Such a resolution was also essential to reunite the international community and internationalise the reconstruction of Iraq. However, in the wake of their 'victory' in Iraq, US voices were making clear how little respect they had for the UN, their unwillingness to recognise UN authority and their determination to appoint their own interim government. Tony Blair had reported, after his visit to the US at the end of March, that Bush told him that the Department of Defense had been told that they could not create a government of Iraqi exiles, it had to be a bottom-up process. But clearly the intention was that this should be a US, rather than a UN-supervised process. If Blair had stood firm on this point, linked up with the rest of the Security Council, and demanded a UN lead in helping the Iraqis form their government, the US would have been totally isolated and might well have given in. This would have created the prospect of widespread international support and troop contingents from Muslim countries to support the rebuilding of Iraq. When asked for troops, Pakistan and Bangladesh, for example, made clear they would only send troops under proper UN authority.

Instead, Tony Blair and Jack Straw started to behave with total secrecy over the US draft Security Council resolution. Whitehall was concerned at being excluded from the drafting of a resolution which would affect their day-to-day work. And then when we saw it (and my senior staff, whose work would be governed by its provisions, shockingly got it from the BBC website after its publication) it gave a minor role to the UN, and the major role to the coalition in leading on reconstruction and the establishment of an interim Iraqi government and the process of constitution-building. This was the end of the line for me. I would not support or defend it and therefore had to leave the government. This was also the point when it was decided that the reconstruction of Iraq would not be internationalised. The Security Council decided not to resist, as there was enough bitterness in the system already, and thus they passed a resolution which gave legal authority to the coalition. But this downgrading of UN authority meant the work would be left with the US and UK with minor support from a handful of other countries.

We will never know how Iraq would be now if the UN had been given proper authority and the occupying powers had focused on securing order. But Blair did not attempt to do it right and this confirmed for many – who had increasingly been reading the publications of the neoconservatives – that the US was looking for a client state and long-term military bases in Iraq. This made a growing Iraqi resistance much more likely.

The period from late March until I resigned from the government on 12 May was a very miserable time for me. I had sacrificed a lot by responding to Tony Blair's pleadings to stay in government and had done so because I believed his promises. I had not changed my mind that the rush to war had been wrong but had thought we could limit the damage by securing a better future for Iraq and peace in the Middle East. But it seemed that these promises were made to manipulate me. The question is, does Tony Blair even realise that he so often gives promises and breaks his word and has so little respect for the truth? Paddy Ashdown said of Blair, that he means it when he says it. There does seem to be a pattern of commitments made but not kept. He uses his charm to persuade people and is deliberately ambiguous and if necessary misleading. He does not seem to believe that the word of a Prime Minister is a very special, almost sacred, thing. He allows his promises to be part of his charm and does not seem to worry if they mislead.

I have been asked many times, at meetings around the country, whether I regret staying. My truthful answer is that despite everything I am glad I tried. I still believe that even after the errors in the rush to war, we could have internationalised reconstruction, and moved forward on Palestine, and this would have brought progress to the Middle East, eased the division in the world and prevented the growth of al-Qaeda.

This was Tony Blair's big opportunity in history. He was looking for his legacy in years to come. The US needed an ally to legitimise its action in Iraq. He could have used this possibility to lever significant progress in the Middle East. Instead he simply acted as the US fig-leaf. The UK and Blair added nothing to the handling of the Iraq crisis. This really is a terrible tragedy for the reputation of the UK and of the Labour government.

6

LEAVING GOVERNMENT

I was absolutely clear I had to leave the government. Blair had failed to restrain the US rush to war and then broken his promises on internationalising reconstruction. The situation in Iraq and the Middle East was disastrous and the behaviour of the Prime Minister indefensible.

Two final jobs

There were just two jobs I thought I should complete. My first obligation was to chair the meeting of the European Bank for Reconstruction and Development (EBRD) which was to be held in Tashkent at the beginning of May. President Karimov presided over a state riddled with corruption and terrible abuse of human rights. The EBRD had been established in 1991 to support development in the former Communist countries. DfID provided funding and was responsible for UK policy towards the Bank. I had worked closely with President Jean Lemierre, who headed the Bank, in planning the Tashkent meeting. There had been criticism and calls from NGOs not to meet in Uzbekistan. But this is an old argument. If we boycott all the badly governed countries, we bring no hope and relief to some of the poorest and most oppressed of the world. The challenge is to engage in such a way that we help promote reform, and that was what we planned to try to do. Jean Lemierre had arranged that the opening session would be televised. I was to chair the meeting and we had agreed I would make a hard-hitting speech and the EBRD and not the government would provide the interpretation. Local NGOs would be invited to attend and the EBRD would offer a programme for Uzbekistan that required progress on corruption and torture. If I had left before the meeting, I really would have let Jean Lemierre down. So the meeting went ahead, though the local TV coverage of my speech was cut off when I spoke about our concerns over closed borders, lack of respect for freedom of religion, the prevalence of torture, and the failure of the judicial system to protect the rights of the citizen.

Whilst I was in Uzbekistan, our brave and outspoken Ambassador Craig Murray arranged a meeting with local families who were facing persecution because they wanted to explore their Islamic heritage. We visited the borders which had been open for centuries and then suddenly closed, destroying economic activity and dividing families and communities. A year later Uzbekistan has not met the conditions of the EBRD strategy and the Bank has continued to work in Uzbekistan but has withdrawn from working with the government. But the pressure this might have brought has been limited because Uzbekistan acted as a crucial base for US operations in Afghanistan and the US closed its eyes to the abuse of human rights there.

The second task I had to complete was to host the talks between President Museveni of Uganda and President Kagame of Rwanda. The first round of talks had taken place in 2001 after a clash between the two armies in Kisingani nearly led to war. I knew both men well and we had substantial development programmes with both countries. I had hosted talks that had brought them together where they agreed a programme of confidence-building measures which were supported by our ambassadors, SIS and defence attachés. It had been agreed that we would meet every six months to review progress. The second meeting had been held on the border between the two countries. I will never forget the happiness of the people who lived on the border when the two Presidents and I travelled together in an open-topped Land-Rover after the talks. These were people, often related to each other, on both sides of the border who would have suffered most in the event of war. The third meeting was due at Lancaster House on 8 May. The tension had been significantly defused but there were still problems and I did not want to upset the process. The talks went well and I am pretty confident that the prospect of armed conflict is now behind us.

Goodbye

On Monday, 12 May, I arranged a slot for my personal statement with the Speaker and told my staff I was going. There was an emotional atmosphere and some of the staff were in tears. We put in a request to speak with the Prime Minister by phone. I had deliberately chosen the Monday so that No. 10 could not have the weekend to pump out nasty briefings. The hours went by with no call from the PM, in contrast with the speed with which he had answered my calls in the run-up to war. Because time was running out, my permanent secretary rang Andrew Turnbull to say that I was going. The PM came on the phone shortly thereafter. I said I was going, he said he knew I had been having a hard time, but didn't realise . . . his voice trailed off. I did not take up the point. It was too late for discussion. Then he asked what would happen. I said we would exchange letters and I would make my statement in the House of Commons. He said OK then, and we said goodbye. Within minutes, the news was on Sky and No. 10 had rung DfID to say that, if I wasn't too critical, they would get me an international job.

I sent off my letter straight away. It read as follows:

Dear Tony

I have decided that I must leave the Government.

As you know, I thought the run-up to the conflict in Iraq was mishandled, but I agreed to stay in the Government to help support the reconstruction effort for the people of Iraq.

I am afraid that the assurances you gave me about the need for a UN mandate to establish a legitimate Iraqi government have been breached. The Security Council resolution that you and Jack have so secretly negotiated contradicts the assurances I have given in the House of Commons and elsewhere about the legal authority of the occupying powers, and the need for a UN-led process to establish a legitimate Iraqi government. This makes my position impossible.

It has been a great honour for me to have led the establishment and development of the Department for International Development over the past six years. I am proud of what we have achieved and much else that the Government has done.

I am sad and sorry that it has ended like this.

Yours,

Clare

Tony's reply arrived after a short time:

Dear Clare

Thank you for your letter of resignation from the Government. As you know, I believe you have done an excellent job in the Department, which has the deserved reputation as one of the best such departments anywhere in the world. That is in no small measure down to you. Our record on aid and development is one of the Government's proudest achievements, and I would like to thank you for your role in bringing that about.

I know you have had doubts about the Government's position on Iraq, but I was pleased you stayed to support the Government during this military conflict. Had you stayed on, there was clearly an important job to be done in the continuing efforts to bring about the reconstruction of Iraq. My commitment to that effort remains as strong as ever.

I am afraid I do not understand your point about the UN. We are in the process of negotiating the UN resolution at the moment. And the agreement on this resolution with our American and Spanish partners has scarcely been a secret.

As for who should lead the process of reconstruction, I have always been clear that it is not a matter of the UN leading or the coalition leading. The two should work together. That is exactly what the resolution stipulates.

Yours ever,

Tony

I then said goodbye, very sadly, to my senior staff and private office and went over to the House of Commons.

Resignation statement

An hour or so later, I was on my feet making the following statement:

With permission, Mr Speaker, I would like to make a personal statement.

'I have decided to resign from the Government. I think it is right that I should explain my reasons to the House of Commons, to which I have been accountable as Secretary of State for International Development, a post that I have been deeply honoured to hold and that I am very sad to leave.

The House will be aware that I had many criticisms of the way in which events leading up to the conflict in Iraq were handled. I offered my resignation to the Prime Minister on a number of occasions but was pressed by him and others to stay. I have been attacked from many different angles for that decision but I still think that, hard as it was, it was the right thing to do.

The reason why I agreed to remain in the Government was that it was too late to put right the mistakes that had been made. I had throughout taken the view that it was necessary to be willing to contemplate the use of force to back up the authority of the UN. The regime was brutal, the people were suffering, our Attorney-General belatedly but very firmly said there was legal authority for the use of force, and because the official Opposition were voting with the Government, the conflict was unavoidable. [Interruption.] There is no question about that. It had to carry.

I decided that I should not weaken the Government at that time and should agree to the Prime Minister's request to stay and lead the UK humanitarian and reconstruction effort. However, the problem now is that the mistakes that were made in the period leading up to the conflict are being repeated in the post-conflict situation. In particular, the UN mandate, which is necessary to bring into being a legitimate Iraqi Government, is not being supported by the UK Government. This, I believe, is damaging to Iraq's prospects, will continue to undermine the authority of the UN and directly affects my work and responsibilities.

The situation in Iraq under international law is that the coalition are occupying powers in occupied territory. Under the Geneva Convention of 1949 and the Hague regulations of 1907, the coalition has clear responsibilities and clear limits to its authority. It is obliged to attend to the humanitarian needs of the population – to keep order – and to keep civil administration operating. The coalition is legally entitled to modify the operation of the administration as much as is necessary to fulfil these obligations, but it is not entitled to make major political, economic and constitutional changes. The coalition does not have sovereign authority and has no authority to bring into being an interim Iraqi Government with such authority or to create a constitutional process leading to the election of a sovereign Government. The only body that has the legal authority to do this is the United Nations Security Council.

I believe that it is the duty of all responsible political leaders right across the world – whatever view they took on the launch of the war – to focus on reuniting the international community in order to support the people of Iraq in rebuilding their country, to re-establish the authority of the UN and to heal the bitter divisions that preceded the war. I am sorry to say that the UK Government are not doing this. They are supporting the US in trying to bully the Security Council into a resolution that gives the coalition the power to establish an Iraqi Government and control the use of oil for reconstruction, with only a minor role for the UN.

This resolution is unlikely to pass but, if it does, it will not create the best arrangements for the reconstruction of Iraq. The draft resolution risks continuing international divisions, Iraqi resentment against the occupying powers and the possibility that the coalition will get bogged down in Iraq. I believe that the UK should and could have respected the Attorney-General's advice, told the US that this was a red line for us, and worked for international agreement to a proper, UN-led process to establish an interim Iraqi Government – just as was done in Afghanistan.

I believe that this would have been an honourable and wise role for the UK and that the international community would have united around this position. It is also in the best interests of the United States. Both in the run-up to the war and now, I think the UK is making grave errors in providing cover for US mistakes rather than helping an old friend, which is understandably hurt and angry after the events of September 11, to honour international law and the authority of the UN. American power alone cannot make America safe. Of course, we must all unite to dismantle the terrorist networks, and, through the UN, the world is doing this. But undermining international law and the authority of the UN creates a risk of instability, bitterness and growing terrorism that will threaten the future for all of us.

I am ashamed that the UK Government have agreed the resolution that has been tabled in New York and shocked by the secrecy and lack of consultation with Departments with direct responsibility for the issues referred to in the resolution. I am afraid that this resolution undermines all the commitments I have made in the House and elsewhere about how the reconstruction of Iraq will be organised. Clearly this makes my position impossible and I have no alternative than to resign from the Government.

There will be time on other occasions to spell out the details of these arguments and to discuss the mistakes that were made preceding the conflict. But I hope that I have provided enough detail to indicate the seriousness of the issues at stake for the future of Iraq, the role of the UN, the unity of the international community and Britain's place in the world.

All this makes me very sad. I believe that the Government whom I have served since 1997 has a record of which all who share the values of the Labour Party can be proud. I also believe that the UK commitment to international development is crucial. The levels of poverty and inequality in a world rich in knowledge, technology and capital is the biggest moral issue the world faces and the biggest threat to the future safety and security of the world. We have achieved a lot, and taking a lead on development is a fine role for the UK. There is much left to do and I am very sorry to have been put in a position in which I am unable to continue that work.

I do think, however, that the errors that we are making over Iraq and other recent initiatives flow not from Labour's values, but from the style and organisation of our Government, which is undermining trust and straining party loyalty in a way that is completely unnecessary. In our first term, the problem was spin: endless announcements, exaggerations and manipulation of the media that undermined people's respect for the Government and trust in what we said. It was accompanied by a control-freak style that has created many of the problems of excessive bureaucracy and centralised targets that are undermining the success of our public-sector reforms.

In the second term, the problem is the centralisation of power into the hands of the Prime Minister and an increasingly small number of advisers who make decisions in private without proper discussion. It is increasingly clear, I am afraid, that the Cabinet has become, in Bagehot's phrase, a dignified part of the constitution – joining the Privy Council. There is no real collective responsibility because there is no collective; just diktats in favour of increasingly badly thought-through policy initiatives that come from on high.

The consequences of that are serious. Expertise in our system lies in Departments. Those who dictate from the centre do not have full access to that expertise and do not consult. That leads to bad policy. In addition, under our constitutional arrangements, legal, political and financial responsibility flows through Secretaries of State to Parliament. Increasingly, those who are wielding power are not accountable and not scrutinised. Thus we have the powers of a presidential-type system with the automatic majority of a parliamentary system. My conclusion is that those arrangements are leading to increasingly poor policy initiatives being rammed through Parliament, which is straining and abusing party loyalty and undermining the people's respect for our political system.

Those attitudes are also causing increasing problems with reform of the public services. I do believe that after long years of financial cuts and decline, the public services need reform to improve the quality of services and the morale of public-sector workers – the two being inextricably linked. We do not, however, need endless new initiatives, layers of bureaucratic accountability and diktats from the centre. We need clarity of purpose, decentralisation of authority and improved management of people. We need to treasure and honour the people who work in public service. As I found in my former Department, if public servants are given that framework, they work with dedication and pride and provide a service that, in the case of the Department for International Development, is known throughout the world as one of the finest development agencies in the international system. Those lessons could be applied in other parts of the public service.

I have two final points. The first is for the Labour Party and, especially, the parliamentary Labour Party. As I have said, there is much that our Government has achieved that reflects Labour's values and of which we can be very proud, but we are entering rockier times and we must work together to prevent our Government from departing from the best values of our party. To the Prime Minister, I would say that he has achieved great things since 1997 but, paradoxically, he is in danger of destroying his legacy as he becomes increasingly obsessed by his place in history.

Finally, I am desperately sad to leave the Department for International Development. I apologise to those in the developing world who told me that I had a duty to stay. I shall continue to do all that I can to support the countries and institutions with which I have been working. It has been an enormous honour to lead the Department. It is a very fine organisation of which Britain can be proud. We have achieved a lot but there is much left to do, and I am sure that others will take it forward. I hope that the House and party will protect the Department from those who wish to weaken it.'

I saw two journalists, one from the *Guardian* and one from the *Financial Times*, after my statement. I said that I thought terrible mistakes had been made and it was time to organise an elegant hand-over of the leadership so that we could put things right.

And then for the last time my very likeable and reliable driver Chris Sullivan took me home. My son came with me. We stopped off at a wine warehouse under the arches at Vauxhall and I bought Chris a bottle of champagne. This was the first time he had dropped me off without leaving any red boxes. I then went off to Birmingham on the train and then to the west of Ireland to walk and swim and stay with my dear friends, Gay and Rolph. I thought the beauty of the west of Ireland would be good for my frazzled spirit.

I did not follow the media reporting of my resignation. Since my *Westminster Hour* interview, I had been under attack from all sides.

Even when Tony was spending a lot of time treating me with respect and trying to charm me into staying, the No. 10 machine seemed to be spinning against me for having dared to call Blair reckless, and speculating that I would be dropped from the government as soon as Blair was through the crisis. A number of political journalists, and some of my colleagues in the PLP, have commented since that I fatally weakened myself politically by agreeing to stay in the government. Such comments suggest that my interest was to calculate my own position. But I was not playing a political game. I was trying to prevent my government from making a terrible mistake and to secure the best way forward after the first mistake had been made. For me, the political decisions I make are about the meaning of my life, and my contribution to society. If I was simply looking to rise in a rewarding career, I would never have gone into politics. There are much easier ways of earning a living.

Getting organised as a backbencher

I returned from Ireland after a week of walking and swimming in order to organise my new life as a backbencher. Jessica Drewery, my secretary in the House of Commons, is a wonderful woman. We had worked in the same office every weekday whilst in Opposition. Then for six years we had exchanged papers daily, talked on the phone infrequently, and had lunch together once a month. Suddenly I was once again dumped on her lap. Since the interview when I suggested that Blair was being reckless in rushing to war and that I would resign if there was no second UN resolution, I had received thousands of letters and emails, first of love and support, then of hate for not resigning, then a growing number saying I was right to stay. Just opening all this mail, and answering the phones and trying to ensure the constituency work did not get neglected, was a nightmare. We take pride in answering all my mail promptly, so that required a big effort, and then another enormous correspondence began following my resignation, including lots of moving letters from people working in DfID, at the UN, in the World Bank and some of the leaders of countries with whom I had worked. On top of all this, she had me full time again – diary engagements, a new office to organise, and more typing. Jessica must have wondered what hit her, but she handled it all with enormous aplomb.

Invitations to write, review books, speak and appear on the media rolled in. I did not have a clear plan. I simply thought that I had left government in order to speak the truth and participate in a discussion on what had gone wrong in Iraq so that we could learn lessons and correct our mistakes. I started to read voraciously – books about the history of Iraq, the Middle East, Islam, al-Qaeda and the publications of the neoconservatives. I also followed events in Iraq very closely and am grateful to the various experts across the world who have included me in their regular updates.

As I settled into my new life, the events leading up to war were going round and round in my head. I followed developments in Iraq very closely and agreed to give evidence to the Intelligence and Security Committee and the Foreign Affairs Select Committee inquiry into the decision to go to war in Iraq. As I prepared myself to give evidence, it became clearer and clearer to me that the Prime Minister had engaged in a campaign of half-truths and deception in order to get us to war.

Deception and war

For example, after I returned from Ireland, I had received a letter from a member of the public enclosing a transcript of President Chirac's remarks on 10 March 2003. I had, after some doubt, accepted Blair's word that Chirac had said he would veto any second resolution and made impossible agreement on the Chilean compromise, as I said in my letter to the PLP before the vote to authorise war. I remember saying to Blair, 'But he can't have said this' but being assured that he did, and asking my private secretary to find out what Chirac said but she was only able to find quotes from the press. I had talked to Kofi and he had said it was not just the French. Then Blair, Brown and Straw had come together and said time and time again that Tony Blair's promise of a second resolution could not be fulfilled because Chirac would veto any resolution. Tony had talked a lot about the Chilean compromise which was supposed to list the six tasks that Iraq must complete to comply with 1441. He said he could have achieved this and won more time, if the French had not threatened a veto. At the time I wanted to believe him. It is a very serious matter to reach the conclusion that your Prime Minister has deceived you and the country about a matter as serious as the taking and sacrificing of human life. But as I read and reflected, I became convinced that the Chilean compromise had never been going to succeed and that this was not the fault of the French.

In early June 2003, I thought I should put my conclusions on the record in the House of Commons. I therefore spoke in a debate on Iraq on 6 June.

I said in that debate:

> The conclusions that I have reached about the way in which the Prime Minister misled us in order to rush to war in Iraq are serious indeed. I am well aware of that. I wish that I had not reached those conclusions, but I fear that they reflect my opinion and I need to put my case. Obviously, loyalty to one's Government is an important quality, but loyalty to the truth is a higher imperative.
>
> The Christian teaching on just war . . . and I understand that the Muslim teaching is very similar, unsurprisingly – says that the cause must be just, the remedy proportionate,

the war winnable, and that there must be no other way of putting right the wrong. The problem with the war in Iraq is that the possibility of resolving the problem in another way was not exhausted. It was therefore not a just war.

The Foreign Secretary said at the time that we had to threaten force to avoid the use of force, and I agreed with that. That was his paradox. I agree that that is how we got 1441, but then came the contradiction. We were told that we had to go to war because we had troops in the desert, but we had deployed them in order to try to avoid war. That is explained only if there was a date to which we were working.

I then went on to outline the US Churches' initiative to avoid war and concluded by saying

> The Prime Minister told us that we could not get a second resolution because the French had said that they would veto any second resolution. A member of the public sent me the transcript of the Chirac interview, and it is plain that he said clearly on 10 March that the Blix process needed to be completed and we had to see whether that could succeed in achieving disarmament, but if not, we would have to go back to the Security Council and the Security Council would have to authorise military action. We were misled about the French position, and the French have been vilified disgracefully, when it was not their position to rule out all military action. We will never know—

THE MINISTER FOR EUROPE (MR DENIS MACSHANE): Will my Right Hon. Friend give way on that point . . .

I have the French transcript of the exact words that President Chirac said. Nowhere did he say that he was ready to contemplate the use of force. What he said – I do not refer to the veto reference – was that if there was a majority of nine on the Security Council authorising war, France would vote no. [Hon. Members: 'Ce soir.'] Not 'ce soir'. That is in a different part of the interview. He said that France would vote no, and that killed the chances of a UN path to peace.

CLARE SHORT: . . . I have the words of President Chirac on 10 March. He said that if the weapons inspectors came back to the Security Council, stated that they could not achieve disarmament, and said:

> "'We are sorry but Iraq isn't co-operating, the progress isn't sufficient, we aren't in a position to achieve our goal, we won't be able to guarantee Iraq's disarmament", in that case it will be for the Security Council and it alone to decide the right thing to do. But in that case, of course, regrettably, the war would become inevitable. It isn't today.'

That is what Chirac said on 10 March.

We will never know whether, if we had pursued the Blix process and indicted Saddam Hussein, we could have liberated Iraq without the horror, chaos, death and suffering of war. As a result of the secrecy and the element of deceit in getting to war by that date, preparations for the post-conflict situation were inadequate. The Office of Reconstruction and Humanitarian Assistance, which was set up in the Pentagon to deal with post-conflict Iraq, was full of politics about who was going to be the new Government of Iraq. That was not a matter for that body: it should have been left to the UN to be done properly under a Security Council mandate. ORHA did not face up to or prepare for the Geneva Convention obligations: the keeping of order being fundamental, as well as the immediate provision of humanitarian relief and the maintenance of civil administration. There is chaos in Iraq, and some 70 people a week are dying.

. . . My time is almost gone, so I shall briefly explain the conclusions to which I have sadly come. We should have tried to resolve this crisis without military action if we could, but the grave accusation that I am making is that there was deceit on the way to military action. If we can be deceived about that, what can we not be deceived about? We must get to the bottom of this. The Government's record must be made absolutely clear, and there is a major lesson for our system of government. We must not make decisions like this. There must be better ways of making sure that information is properly used and decisions are properly made, especially when the lives of large numbers of human beings are at stake.

On 9 June, I wrote in the *New Statesman*:

It is clear from material in the recently published *The War We Could Not Stop* (Guardian Books) – which can only have been sourced from the Blair entourage – that by 9 September, Blair and Bush were agreed that there had to be military action in Iraq. My conclusion now is that Blair had promised Bush that the UK would support military action in September 2002, if not before, and that he set out to help Bush build a coalition with a target date for action of spring 2003.

On 19 June, I wrote in the *Guardian*:

Of course, there was evidence that Saddam had continued his experiments to develop chemical and biological weapons and had ballistic weapons beyond the permitted range – this was why the weapons inspectors' work had been blocked and sanctions had continued for 12 years. But the spin was that there was an imminent threat from these weapons and from developing links with al-Qaeda. This was designed to get us to war by the spring and to suggest that there was no time for the threat of force to be used to try to resolve the crisis without further harm to the people of Iraq.

Given this plan, the promise of a second resolution was an enormous gamble. Allowing Hans Blix, the UN chief weapons inspector, to complete his work clashed with the agreed date for war. And therefore we were deceived into believing that France had said it would veto any second resolution. The vilification of France and misrepresentation of its position was the fig-leaf for the failure of the second resolution. I am afraid I believed the Prime Minister when he pressed this account of France's position upon me.

On 17 June, I gave evidence to the Foreign Affairs Select Committee. Gisela Stuart, who is the MP for Edgbaston which borders my constituency, asked:

Q125 MS STUART: I think you repeatedly said that the Prime Minister deceived you, the Cabinet and Parliament – deceived you deliberately or deceived you on the basis of wrong information?

CLARE SHORT: I believe that the Prime Minister must have concluded that it was honourable and desirable to back the US in going for military action in Iraq and that it was, therefore, honourable for him to persuade us through the various ruses and devices he used to get us there, so I presume he saw it as an honourable deception.

I also said in answer to Greg Pope, MP for Hyndburn, that the way in which the decision to go to war was clouded in deception '. . . led to the lack of proper preparation for afterwards and I think that a lot of the chaos, disorder and mess in Iraq flowed from not having made the decision properly and made the preparations properly.'

And then on 21 July 2003, I was asked to review the book by Peter Stothard, *30 Days*, which was a record of Blair's handling of the run-up to war. He had been invited into No. 10, like a war artist, to record the Prime Minister's handling of these great events. It is a short book, but devastatingly revealing. It tells us that in September 2002, Blair's

analysis of relations between Washington, London and Baghdad was clear and cold. It rested on six essential points to which he and his aides would regularly return:

- Saddam Hussein's past aggression, present support for terrorism and future ambitions made him a clear threat to his enemies. He was not the only threat, but he was a threat nonetheless.
- The United States and Britain were among his enemies.
- The people of the United States, still angered by the September 11 attacks, still sensing unfinished business from the first Gulf War twelve years before, would support a war on Iraq.
- Gulf War 2 – President George W. Bush v Saddam Hussein – would happen whatever anyone else said or did.
- The people of Britain, continental Europe and most of the rest of the world would not even begin to support a war unless they had a say in it through the United Nations.

- It would be more damaging to long-term world peace
  and security if the Americans alone defeated Saddam
  Hussein than if they had international support to do so.

The logic of these simple points is clear. They are hardly profound, but they explain why we went to war. It boils down to the view that the US will inevitably go to war in Iraq and for some unexplained reason it is dangerous if they go alone, therefore we should try the UN but in any case go with them. The six 'essential points' to which we are told by Stothard the Prime Minister and his aides would constantly refer were never shared with the Cabinet.

The book clearly displays the contempt Blair's inner team have for most other groupings in the political system. The following quotes are taken from the Stothard book. They show a horrible cynicism amongst the Blair entourage at No. 10. They refer to the Cabinet during whose meetings 'A messenger sits guard to ensure that none of the people outside, the people who really run this heart of government, makes too much noise'. The Parliamentary Labour Party who were pressed and charmed and persuaded to vote with the government on 18 March are sneeringly dismissed as 'the people who see themselves as leaders of the country'. And there is a 90th birthday party held at No. 10 for Jack Jones, the former General Secretary of the Transport and General Workers' Union who as a young man fought in the Spanish Civil War against Franco and who helped keep the 1974 Labour government in place and refused a seat in the House of Lords because he did not believe in unelected office. The book tells us that at the party Tony Blair says, 'You owned this place once. . . . Yes, you owned this place once. It's not quite like that now. But it's very good to see you here', and their attitude to the Labour Party's National Executive Committee is 'barons who have been cleverly deprived of their power, but to whom ritual respect must be paid'.

But perhaps the most cynical attitude of all involves the UN role in post-conflict Iraq. On 25 March, (Lady) Sally Morgan is quoted as saying, 'Yes, we want more Kofi. We seriously have to Kofi now.' We are told Labour MPs like 'a Kofi plan'. 'We'd better Kofi this', means we had better obscure this bit of military planning with a good count of humanitarian waffle. 'Let's speak Kofi is what the mood in London demands.'

This reading and writing and scrutiny of the evidence was leading me to more and more critical conclusions. The No. 10 spin on any former minister that criticises the government is that they are doing so because they are bitter. Thus all criticism is dismissed as badly motivated. In fact, the Iraq crisis makes me extremely sad rather than bitter, but the more I read, the more stunned I was that our Prime Minister could take us to war in such a way. I believe this raises very serious questions for the Labour Party and British Constitutional arrangements. But as I voiced my concerns, a strange atmosphere developed in the PLP. Some, normally described as rebels, continued to be friendly. But others, the Blairites, who had previously greeted me warmly and pressed me to attend dinners and meetings in their constituencies, looked through me with a sense of deep antagonism. I was surprised by this. I did not expect the Blairites to like what I was saying but expected them to respect my right to make my views clear. But their message was that I should stay silent and support whatever the government said. I had assumed that on leaving government, I was free to speak the truth. But the attitude of my colleagues made it clear that this was not the case.

The death of Dr Kelly

I was in my constituency, driving to a meeting, when the news came through on the car radio on 18 July that Dr David Kelly had been found dead. This was a terrible development. I am afraid Dr Kelly's tragedy was that he got tangled up in the war that Alastair Campbell launched against the BBC.

It is important to remember that the broadcast on the *Today* programme by Andrew Gilligan, which later became so notorious, was made on 29 May, long after Baghdad had fallen. And it took Alastair Campbell until the end of June, when he appeared before the Foreign Affairs Select Committee, to make a public fuss about it. There was no question of any threat to national security. Gilligan simply suggested that the government knowingly exaggerated the threat from WMD and that the dossier issued in September had been 'sexed up' in order to help make the case for war. The evidence made available during the Hutton inquiry, and even more clearly in Lord Butler's report, supports Gilligan's claim. Susan Watts, the Science Editor of *Newsnight*, showed in her evidence to Hutton that Dr Kelly did say the intelligence was being exaggerated under pressure from Alastair Campbell. John Scarlett, the Chair of the Joint Intelligence Committee, made clear in his evidence that the claim that WMD could be used in forty-five minutes referred to battlefield weapons only. The forty-five-minute claim originated from one source only and was played up strongly in the media – no doubt with Alastair Campbell's guidance. The Butler Report said it should not have been used as it was. I conclude that Gilligan's story was basically true and that the constant pressure from No. 10 to strengthen the dossier and the words used by Blair in the Commons suggesting a 'clear and present danger' that the Butler Report questions do amount to an exaggeration of the intelligence to an extent that the public were misled. The No. 10 line after the Butler Report was to constantly repeat that Lord Butler was not questioning the Prime Minister's good faith. Maybe so, but I am afraid it is clear that the Prime Minister did knowingly mislead, and my own explanation for this is that he must have considered it 'an honourable deception'. My conclusion is that Alastair Campbell launched his attack on Gilligan in order to divert attention away from the question of whether the country had been deceived in the rush to war.

It is notable that the leaders of the intelligence services, senior civil servants, the Prime Minister and senior staff at No. 10, the Secretary of State for Defence and his Permanent Secretary were all closely involved in the hunt for Gilligan's source. Dr Kelly was closely interrogated about whether he had said what Gilligan claimed. There is a serious question here, as to whether the resources of the state were misused in order to attack a journalist, who said no more than other journalists had written, simply because he had irritated and embarrassed the government. Once Dr Kelly came forward and said he had talked to Andrew Gilligan, the power of the state was focused on using Dr Kelly to get Gilligan. Dr Kelly's wife has described what this did to her husband. We politicians volunteer for the role, but when the press is after you and No. 10 briefing against you, life can be hell. And I am sure that the briefing describing this dedicated international expert as merely a middle-level technical officer hurt him to the quick.

Dr Kelly found the pressure of No. 10, the Ministry of Defence, the Chair of the Joint Intelligence Committee, the Foreign Affairs Select Committee, the threat to his pension and job, and 'being treated like a fly' too much to bear. I think most people would break under that strain. To use Dr Kelly in this way – to get at the BBC – was I fear a real abuse of power.

The Hutton inquiry

The Hutton inquiry had a dual effect – the fact that it was conducted in public and all documents were made available on the internet, exposed to public scrutiny much of the behaviour of No. 10 in the run-up to war. The fact that Hutton's report was completely uncritical of the government and criticised the BBC so strongly stunned the whole country and was widely denounced as a whitewash. The Prime Minister had said that the claim that he knowingly exaggerated the threat from Iraqi chemical and biological weapons would be a resignation issue. The evidence supplied to Hutton made clear that the threat had been exaggerated – not least the forty-five-minute claim. But Hutton absolved the government of all blame. Blair survived, but his reputation was badly damaged and his country ceased to be able to trust him.

Like many others, I listened to Lord Hutton's broadcast of his conclusions and was amazed. Tony Blair bounced into the Chamber of the House of Commons looking very happy and mightily relieved. Cherie was reported in the press as having said they were having sleepless nights in the run-up to publication. My view, like many others', is that the report was an outrage. The Gilligan story was basically true. Dr Kelly's job description required him to brief journalists. He told them that the dossier had been hyped. Gilligan's report embarrassed the government. The government machine was put to work to find Gilligan's source. Dr Kelly came forward when he knew he was under suspicion. When questioned, he had played down what he said. He was therefore pushed in front of the Select Committee and the media to support the government's case. When he knew that Susan Watts had a tape of their conversation, it was probably the breaking point. He took his own life after he had been put under unbearable pressure to save the government embarrassment. The irony was that although Hutton absolved the government, his evidence led the country to another conclusion. Whilst the establishment stood together, the people thought otherwise. Once again I found myself in agreement with the people and in a very unfamiliar Labour Party, where we were expected to celebrate the outcome of Hutton and brush away the concerns of the country. I am afraid that I withdrew from my commitment to participate in a *Newsnight* programme to discuss the report. I was already under pressure for my criticisms. This would get worse if I said what I thought of Hutton.

Call for Blair's resignation

My conclusion was that the government was deeply dishonoured, the world dangerously divided, Iraq in trouble, the Middle East further destabilised and al-Qaeda strengthened. The only way forward that I could see was to persuade Tony Blair to step down and then we could face up to the mistakes that had been made, get a new leader and correct what had gone wrong. My view was that Blair could do this with dignity and, once he stepped down, he would be respected for having gone voluntarily and honoured for his other achievements. He was also so massively popular in the US, he would be in a position to command a very good income giving lectures and with his book. He was still a relatively young man, but by stepping down he would put himself in a good position and enable the government to start to correct the errors made in Iraq and restore the honour of the Labour Party. I said on a number of occasions that I thought Blair should step down, but it was soon made clear this was not permitted. The style of our Prime Minister has become so Presidential that even to suggest that it might be time for him to step down was treated as sacrilege.

Tony Benn has often said that the Labour Party is traditionally fractious with its leaders, but lets them stay as long as they want, in contrast to the Tory Party which is deferential but moves them on when it is ready. It seems that even the fractiousness has now gone from Labour and that Blair has a right to go on and on and be obeyed for as long as he wishes, whatever the consequences. Loyalty is a good quality, but when it is called into play to cover up a string of serious errors that flow from too great a concentration of power in the office of the Prime Minister, then loyalty is being abused. My problem is not Tony Blair himself, but the terrible errors that have been made in Iraq and the Middle East and other areas of policy because of the breakdown of our constitutional arrangements and the concentration of power in No. 10.

I know that others share these concerns but there is a real fear of speaking out in the PLP, partly out of a wish to be loyal and not to rock the boat, but also for fear of what might be done to those who dare to express their anxieties.

Foundation hospitals

Another of Blair's second-term, ill-thought-through ideas –
foundation hospitals – came before the Commons on 8 July. I sat
through the whole debate and tried to be called to speak, but I was
not called, a new experience for me of being a backbencher in a
party with a large majority where it is difficult to get to speak. I
had to make do with making my view known in an intervention.
Frank Dobson (the first Secretary of State for Health in the
1997 government), who had not been critical since he left the
government, made clear his total opposition. David Hinchliffe, the
MP for Wakefield, who was Chair of the Health Select Committee,
whose inquiry had shown how hopelessly ill-thought-through
the proposal was, was also strongly opposed. The NHS had suffered
eighteen major reorganisations in twenty years. It was true there
was too much central control and too many targets; the answer
was not major reorganisation, but a slimming down of targets and
decentralisation, working with the people who keep the NHS
running. John Reid, who was by now Secretary of State for Health,
summed up the debate in a very cynical way. He basically said,
the Tories are opposed, so it must be right – an appeal to tribal
loyalty in response to a debate where many Labour members had
expressed detailed concerns. I then, for the first time in my life,
voted against a Labour government. The result was that the government won with a majority of only 17.

Labour conference

I attended the Labour Party conference in Bournemouth at the end
of September 2003 as I have for more than twenty years. I spoke at
many fringe meetings. But the conference was quite different from
any I have known. The previous year there had been great passion
over Iraq. In Bournemouth there were a few protesters outside the

cordon but very little protest inside. The *Tribune* meeting which used to be a packed rally was a modest affair. Gordon Brown caused a flurry when he made a strong Labour speech, ending with 'best when we are Labour'. This got strong applause, but hostile press briefing started immediately suggesting that he was trying to upstage the Prime Minister by appealing to the left.

The atmosphere at this conference was very strange. It felt as though the stuffing had been knocked out of the party. I watched the leader's speech from my hotel. I knew if I went into the hall, the cameras would pick me out if I did not clap. In every previous year I had sat with the Cabinet when it was compulsory to clap whenever there was a ripple of applause. The speech was unremarkable, except for the ridiculous suggestion that Tony had no reverse gear, clearly imitating Mrs Thatcher's remark, 'You turn if you want to, but the Lady's not for turning.' The clapping was nevertheless ecstatic, one woman member stopped me in the street to say how hard it had been to be in the hall and not join in. It is notable, however, that Iain Duncan Smith got more applause and a longer standing ovation at his conference shortly before he was replaced.

People used to contrast the vibrancy of the Labour conference to the stage-managed Tory conference. I am afraid the difference is fast disappearing. Somehow the spirit of the party has been broken. Very large numbers of long-standing members have left. Membership is now just over 190,000, the lowest since the 1930s. Those who have left were angry about Iraq and other things, but also saw the democratic structures of the party being crushed and therefore concluded there was no point in staying to fight. One MP, who worked for many years in a trade union in which there was a strong Communist grouping, said to me that the Whips are finding it increasingly difficult to get MPs to speak in the Commons. He said it was like the democratic centralism he had seen amongst the Communist group in the union. There is no point in speaking when you are expected to toe the party line and no one is listening. How very strange all this is. The party is crumbling and miserable, but the leader's speech has an ecstatic reception with young faces placed behind him and clappers leading the applause. 'New Labour – New Leninism' was the thought that came into my head after I watched the leader's speech at the 2003 conference.

Top-up fees

The next dishonourable policy bounced out of No. 10 and forced through a reluctant PLP was top-up fees. In January the Higher Education Bill came before the House of Commons. I spoke in that debate and voiced my opinion:

> As has been said in the Chamber before today, asking Labour Members to vote against the manifesto on which each of us was elected to the House is a serious matter. It is a breach of trust with the electorate and a breach of a solemn promise. It is also politically foolish. People are more and more cynical about politics and politicians, and these events will increase that cynicism and undermine the public's confidence in our party and its promises in a serious and troubling manner.
>
> We must ask what is the reason for such a serious breach of our promise. Why must we rush through the Bill even though it will not take effect until after the next election? We are told that we need more resources for higher education – that is agreed across the House – so that we may reach the Government's target of 50 per cent of young people going to university. However, facts outlining the progress that we have made during recent years and the increased resources that the Government have made available for higher education show that the case for rushing, in a manner that will breach our manifesto commitment, completely falls. The figures show that during

the years of the Tory Government there was considerable progress on the number of young people going to university. The proportion went up from 12 per cent of the age group in 1979 to 34 per cent in 1997. Last year, after continuing progress under our Government, the figure reached 43 per cent. There is no need to panic about the 50 per cent target because we are making good progress towards that objective.

We are told that universities are desperately short of money. It is true that they need more money and that they suffered badly during the Tory years, as did most of our public services. Between 1989 and 1997, the universities suffered a drop in funding of 36 per cent per student. So that enormous expansion in participation was paid for by the universities, and they did not get enough investment to reward that very important expansion. But the downward trend was reversed in 2001, and the Government have committed more money to higher education.

Spending on higher education will rise from a total of £7.5 billion in 2002–03 to almost £10 billion in 2005–06 – a real-terms increase of 6 per cent a year. So it seems to me that, yes, we have got an issue to solve, because of course we want every young person in our country who wants to go to university, and is capable of doing so, to be able to do so. I am sure that we will go beyond the 50 per cent target in time, as our country develops and there is more and more access to quality education. But we have not got a short-term crisis, and all this proposal, which is such a serious breach of our manifesto commitment, will bring in is less than £1 billion, which will not solve the long-term funding needs of the higher education sector.

I then referred to the threat that these changes would lead young people in deciding which subjects to study and to a choice of career and profession on the basis of debt, money and cost. I suggested that we surely did not want to live in that kind of country and wanted access to higher education to continue to include those who wanted to study subjects like medieval history, poetry or philosophy.

I continued:

> This seems to be really questionable and incompetent policy-making, and we have to ask where it has come from. I am afraid, as I said in my speech when I resigned from the Government, that we have seen in our second term a pattern of very surprising proposals. I do not know whether they come from the bowels of No. 10, or some of the advisers that circulate around No. 10, but they are not consulted on or publicly discussed, and they are then driven through the House with appeals to the loyalty of Labour Members to vote against things that they know to be right. We have seen that over and again, and it leads to bad policy-making. If we are to have a more presidential style of government, we must have a more independent Parliament that can say, yes, we are loyal to our Government and our party, but we will vote them down when they are wrong.

Spying on Kofi Annan

On 25 February 2004, criminal charges for breaching the Official Secrets Act against Katharine Gunn were dropped. She had worked at GCHQ, the agency responsible for government eavesdropping, and had leaked a document to the *Observer* which showed that the US had asked the UK for help in bugging the offices of the non-permanent members of the Security Council to assist the effort to persuade them to vote for a resolution to support war in Iraq. Her lawyers had indicated that they would raise the issue of the legality of the war and the Attorney-General's advice as part of her defence.

And then suddenly it was announced that the charges that had been brought against her would be dropped, just before her case was due to come to court. This decision received considerable media coverage and it was widely thought that the charges were dropped because the government did not want the question of the legality of war and the Attorney-General's advice to be raised in court. The *Today* programme asked me to comment on the dropping of the charges and I agreed to do so.

I have described earlier how, when I talked on the phone with Kofi Annan about the situation in Eastern Congo, we had gone on to talk about Iraq and the attempt to get a resolution authorising war through the Security Council. As we talked, Kofi had made clear that he was opposed to this and I had felt worried about the conversations ever since, because a note of the conversation would be obtained by the intelligence services and circulated in Whitehall. I was worried that this would lead to hostility to Kofi Annan and at the time I feared that there might be a smear campaign against him. There had been various attempts to smear Dr Blix because his second major report to the Security Council indicated that the weapons inspectors were getting growing co-operation from the Iraqis and this was thought to have made it more difficult for the US and UK to bully the Security Council into supporting a resolution for war.

In my mind, this was unfinished business. I had decided that I ought to inform Kofi that transcripts of his conversations as well as draft papers were circulated by British intelligence. This had been going on since we came into government and probably before. It may well have been a hangover from the Cold War. It had seemed odd, but basically harmless during the time that we were working closely and very supportively with him; but it became positively insidious when we were engaged with the US in manoeuvring and bullying to try to get Security Council approval for war at a pre-ordained date. I knew the transcripts of phone conversations were closely monitored because a senior intelligence official once came to see me and asked if we could speak alone. He pointed out that after I talked to Kofi from Kigali I had referred to something I could only know because I had read previous transcripts of calls to the Secretary-General. He was not hostile in any way, just asking me to be careful. This meant of course that my calls, like all the others, had been carefully monitored and analysed.

Given that we were now manipulating at the UN and acting to undermine Kofi Annan's work, I decided that the fact that we were spying on his office should be brought to public attention. I had been pondering what to do for the best. I had thought of writing to Kofi Annan, or sending a message, but decided it would not help to tell him he was being spied on when there would be little that he could do about it. Since the issue in the Katharine Gunn case was the proposal that we should bug the offices of members of the Security Council, it seemed the right time to bring the issue to public attention so that the practice would be brought to an end.

I therefore accepted the invitation from the *Today* programme to comment on the Katharine Gunn case and took the opportunity to reveal the fact that we were also spying on Kofi Annan's office. Following my interview, all hell broke loose. The No. 10 machine went into overdrive to attack, undermine and smear me. The Prime Minister said my action was deeply irresponsible and the briefings said I would be expelled from the Privy Council, charged under the Official Secrets Act and have the Labour Whip withdrawn. I received a threatening letter from Sir Andrew Turnbull repeating these threats and warning me to take no part in further interviews. Members of the public sent me copies of scurrilous responses they had received from their local Labour MPs when they had complained to them about the UK spying on Kofi Annan. Much of the press took the No. 10 line, as they so often do, but my office was inundated with letters and emails of support. And wherever I went on bus, tube or in the street, people would greet me very warmly, express support and ask me not to be crushed by the pressure.

I was surprised by all of this. There is no doubt that my allegation was true. It is completely ludicrous to suggest now the Cold War is over that anyone or any legitimate British interest is put at risk by my revealing that the UK spies on Kofi Annan's office. I was not attacking the Prime Minister. He does not engage much with detail: I doubt that he reads raw intelligence and my guess is that he did not know. I think they responded in this way because they were embarrassed by the disclosure and thought they could use bogus claims about national security to silence me on this and the other things. I had seen the viciousness of their machine before, but this time it was unleashed at full blast.

Nothing at all came of the threats about the Privy Council or Official Secrets Act, as I knew they would not. Following the suggestions in the press that the Whip may be withdrawn, the Chief Whip asked to see me. I had been a member of the Labour Party for more than thirty years, an MP for twenty-one years, ten years a member of the National Executive Committee and six years a member of the Cabinet. But because I disclosed that the UK was spying on Kofi Annan's office, I was threatened through the media with withdrawal of the Labour Whip which would mean I would cease to be a Labour MP and presumably that I would not be allowed to stand as a Labour MP at the next election.

These were very serious threats, but I was determined not to back down. I had quite deliberately revealed that the UK was spying on Kofi Annan's office. It was incredible that I was threatened with a criminal prosecution and possible expulsion from the Labour Party for doing so. I made clear to the Chief Whip, Hilary Armstrong, the MP for Durham North West, that I was not willing to come to see her if she planned to have press outside the door and to accompany the meeting with another smear campaign. We therefore agreed to meet when the dust had settled a little, in her office in the Cabinet Office in Whitehall. She said that I was free to disagree with Tony over the Iraq war but, under the Standing Orders of the Parliamentary Labour Party, no personal attacks were allowed. I said that I was not engaging in personal attacks, but it was clear that the Prime Minister had used deceit to get us to war. She said this was not true, and I said I thought the evidence overwhelmingly clear. I pointed out that I had already made my views clear in my evidence to the Foreign Affairs Select Committee which was published and had put these views on the record in the House of Commons. I made it clear that I was unwilling to resile from these views whatever her threat. After some discussion we agreed that she would send me a letter acknowledging that I would not resile from my stated views but had said that I had no need to constantly repeat them now the issues I had raised were so firmly in the public domain. She said she wanted to share her letter with the Parliamentary Committee. I said that was fine but if the letter said that I could not say what I knew to be true, I would reject it. We then negotiated an agreed text. But in the usual New Labour way the press was briefed that I had been rebuked, although the letter said no such thing.

Even more nasty was the briefing to the press that I was in danger of de-selection in Ladywood. There was no substance in this, but the question it raised was what they had in mind. I was born and grew up in my constituency. I have been the MP for twenty-one years. I have worked hard locally throughout that time and am strongly supported by the overwhelming majority of members of the Ladywood Party and by people in my constituency. Perhaps it had been decided that I had become a nuisance and that they would manipulate things to try to get rid of me. In any genuine expression of the views of party members this would be impossible, but one never knows what the New Labour machine might attempt.

These kinds of practices make me think more and more about the democratic centralist analogy put to me by one of my friends. We now have a ruthless party machine run tightly from the centre. There is a line to be taken and phrases to be used. Everyone must toe the party line. Occasionally, new policy positions are explored and then dropped by the centre and everyone must follow suit. The followers are expected to follow unquestioningly. The policy-making machinery of the party is manipulated from the centre. Candidates are pushed forward from the centre. The press are a crucial part of the operation but in this case don't even need to be owned by the party. Perhaps they plan to expunge me and people like me from the photos!

The Butler Report

Blair was very much hoping that the Hutton Report would be the end of discussion of the rush to war in Iraq. But agitation in the US about the failure to find WMD and therefore questions about the quality of intelligence led to the President establishing a Commission of Inquiry. This left Blair exposed, and he therefore decided in early February 2004 to establish a committee to review the intelligence on weapons of mass destruction. It was asked to investigate the intelligence available on WMD in countries of concern and on global trade in WMD. As part of that work it was asked to investigate the accuracy of intelligence on Iraqi WMD.

The committee was chaired by Lord (Robin) Butler, former Head of the Civil Service; it was to include a former Chief of the Defence Staff and a former Permanent Secretary in Northern Ireland. In addition, Blair proposed Ann Taylor, Labour's former Chief Whip, who chairs the Intelligence and Security Committee which scrutinises the operation of the intelligence services, and the Conservative and Liberal Democrat members of the committee. The Lib Dems refused to be represented because there was no remit to examine political responsibility for the use of intelligence. The Conservative Party originally agreed to be represented by Michael Mates, who was a former defence minister. They later withdrew their co-operation and he served in a personal capacity.

The report was published on 14 July 2004. It produced a summary of the available intelligence and made it clear that the Prime Minister's claim that there was a clear and present danger from Iraqi WMD was an exaggeration. They said the claim in the November dossier that Iraq had the capacity to use WMD in forty-five minutes, which led to widespread suggestions in the media that Cyprus or even London was under threat, should not have been included. This led both Greg Dyke, former Director-General of the BBC, and Andrew Gilligan, both of whom had resigned from the Corporation after the Hutton Report, to say that they thought the Butler Report had vindicated their position over the original Gilligan broadcast.

The report informed me for the first time that UK policy on Iraq was reviewed in March 2002 in the light of Bush's 'axis of evil' speech and other comments emerging from the US. Officials considered that there were two options – a toughening of the existing containment policy and regime change by military means. This review and toughening of policy was not made known to the Cabinet. The report also revealed that the Attorney-General had not relied on intelligence to say that there was legal authority for war. The Attorney had apparently initially said that there was no case for war on the basis of self-defence or imminent threat. I presume that was the point at which I had been told by my officials that the Attorney had said there was no authority for war. However, following the passage of Security Council Resolution 1441, which led to the return of the weapons inspectors, Foreign Office legal advisers disagreed about whether there was legal authority for war without a further UN resolution, and one of them later resigned. Butler tells us that on 28 February, the Attorney-General gave his advice on the question and put it in writing on 7 March. This advice was not made available to senior officials in Whitehall or to the Cabinet. We are told that there was legal authority for war on the basis of the history of UN resolutions. This remains contentious. Professor Philippe Sands QC pointed out in his memo to the Foreign Affairs Select Committee on 1 June that

> The reliance on Resolution 678 [the original UN resolution passed at the end of the first Gulf war] is selective. That resolution was plainly intended to remove Iraq from Kuwait. It did not provide for the overthrow of Saddam Hussein's government, in express terms or otherwise.

He also points out that writing in his memoirs in 1995, Colin Powell is explicit: 'The UN resolution made clear that the mission was only to free Kuwait . . . the UN had given us our marching orders, and the President intended to stay with them.' And that Sir Peter de la Billière, who commanded British forces in the first Gulf war, had expressed a similar view: 'We did not have a mandate to invade Iraq or take the country over.' The same point is made by John Major, who was Foreign Secretary and Prime Minister when Resolutions 678 and 687 were adopted. Writing in 2001, Mr Major noted that

> our mandate from the United Nations was to expel the Iraqis from Kuwait, not bring down the Iraqi regime . . . We had gone to war to uphold international law. To go further than our mandate would have been, arguably, to break international law.

However, contentious as the Attorney-General's opinion was, he did not give the final authority for war. He required 'the Prime Minister, in the absence of a further United Nations Security Council resolution, to be satisfied that there were strong factual grounds for concluding that Iraq had failed to take the opportunity to comply with its disarmament obligations under relevant resolutions of the Security Council and that it was possible to demonstrate hard evidence of non-compliance and non-co-operation with the requirements of Security Council Resolution 1441.' This opinion was not shared with the Cabinet.

We can now see why there was a smear campaign against Dr Blix when he reported increased Iraqi co-operation to the Security Council on 14 February 2003. At this meeting, Dr Blix described his inspectors' capability and said they had found no WMD, only a small number of empty chemical munitions. He said many prohibited weapons were not accounted for, but went on to say, 'One must not jump to the conclusion that they exist. If they exist, they should be presented for destruction; if they do not exist, credible evidence to that effect must be presented.' He went on to say that the United Nations Monitoring, Verification and Inspection Commission (UNMOVIC) had gone to look at sites suggested by international intelligence agencies and found nothing there. His message was 'that Iraq had taken some steps that could be the beginning of active co-operation'. Mohamed El-Baradei reported on nuclear capability and said that there were no 'unresolved disarmament issues'. It was at this meeting that Mr Ivanov, the Soviet foreign minister, suggested that UNMOVIC and the International Atomic Energy Authority (IAEA) should submit their work programme to the Council, including a list of 'key remaining disarmament tasks'. He suggested this would give objective and specific criteria against which Iraqi co-operation could be measured.

It was this constructive suggestion which would enable Iraq to know exactly what it had to do to comply with UN resolutions that was taken up by UNMOVIC and by the UK, and is referred to by Tony Blair as the 'Chilean compromise'. In his statement to the House of Commons on the Butler Report, Blair said:

> Through all the conversations that I had with Hans Blix, he never once suggested to me that Saddam Hussein was complying fully. He used to say, 'Well, he's co-operating a bit,' and I would say, 'That's not enough,' and he would say, 'Well, you know——.' Then came the argument that we should give him more time, and I said, 'Okay, let's give him more time, but tied to an ultimatum. If we don't tie it to an ultimatum, he's never going to do it.' That is why the decision had to be taken on 18 March, as opposed to some weeks later, as it could have been if an ultimatum had been agreed to. France and other countries made it clear that, whatever happened, they would issue no ultimatum. That was their decision, but it meant that, on 18 March, we were faced with either another UN resolution that would have been meaningless, or taking action. That is what we did.

But Dr Blix's careful account differs from that of Tony Blair. He tells us that he consulted Colin Powell and said that UNMOVIC and the IAEA could put together such a list of precise demands that Iraq must fulfil to solve the various remaining disarmament issues. He asked for a deadline of 15 April. Colin Powell said this was too late.

Nevertheless, Blix prepared a draft resolution for the Security Council as well as a background paper which he showed to Sir Jeremy Greenstock, the UK Ambassador to the UN. In his background paper, Dr Blix suggested that eleven weeks was a rather short time to conclude that disarmament could not be achieved by inspection backed by the threat of force. He suggested the Security Council set 'an explicit time line' and a number of benchmarks to be attained by Iraq rather than a catalogue of open issues. His draft requested that UNMOVIC/IAEA submit by 1 March a list of key points, which were the remaining disarmament issues along with a list of things Iraq must do to resolve them. These were referred to as 'the benchmarks'. His draft resolution also demanded the elimination of all missiles identified as proscribed by UNMOVIC. It requested that the inspectors should report to the Council by a specific date set by the Council and stipulated that if the Security Council were to conclude that Iraq had not fulfilled what was demanded of it, inspection would be terminated. The implication was clear, Dr Blix says, that this would mean the Council authorising war.

On 7 March, Dr Blix reported to the Security Council 'a substantial measure of disarmament by Iraq with the destruction of large numbers of al-Samoud ballistic missiles'. It was of this that Dr Blix said to the Security Council: 'We are not watching the breaking of toothpicks. Lethal weapons are being destroyed . . . The destruction undertaken constitutes a substantial measure of disarmament – indeed, the first since the middle of the 1990s.'

It is perhaps worth spelling out what a substantial amount of disarmament this meant. The al-Samoud, a massive missile seven metres long and weighing two tons when armed, was being destroyed, without the slightest obstruction or even complaint from the Iraqis. Major Corrine Heraud, a French woman who served as the chief weapons inspector for UNMOVIC in this operation and who had also served from 1996 with UNSCOM (the United Nations Special Commission), has said that the level of co-operation from the Iraqis was unprecedented, something that she never would have expected and did not encounter during the 1996–98 inspections. Each missile cost more that $1 million, which was a large sum considering the difficulty that Iraq encountered in buying materials and parts, due to the UN sanctions. Seventy of these missiles were destroyed by the inspectors.

We have also been led to believe that France was unwilling to contemplate any ultimatum to Iraq. In fact, France, Germany and Russia presented a memorandum to the Security Council saying that the priority should be to achieve full and effective disarmament of Iraq peacefully, and that the conditions for the use of force had not been fulfilled. They proposed that the inspectors should submit their work programme on 1 March. This should contain the list of key remaining disarmament tasks in order of priority and would clearly define what was required of Iraq. The inspectors would report to the Council at any time if Iraq interfered with inspection or failed to comply with its obligations. They were to report every three weeks and submit an assessment after 120 days. They urged that inspection be given the necessary time and increased resources, but stressed that 'they cannot continue indefinitely'. On 5 March the foreign ministers of France, Germany and Russia met in Paris and declared that disarmament of Iraq through inspection *was* possible, and that inspection was 'producing increasingly encouraging results'. They repeated that 'these inspections cannot continue indefinitely'.

On Friday 7 March at the Security Council, Dr Blix reported some considerable progress in Iraqi co-operation including the destruction of the ballistic missiles. The French, German and Russian ministers put forward the concept they had advocated in

Paris. The German minister asked what was the point of preparing for inspection for two and a half years and then giving inspectors only two and a half months to work. The French minister said that a deadline of a few days for inspection was merely a pretext for war, but that he was ready to shorten his own proposed deadline of 120 days.

Dr Blix reports that his refusal in his 7 March speech to 'assume that items unaccounted for might exist' displeased some people in Washington. The *New York Times* reported 'a senior administration official' as saying that 'the inspections have turned out to be a trap . . . We're not counting on Blix to do much of anything for us . . .' Blix goes on to say that, 'unlike the US/UK, the inspectors did not believe they had conclusive evidence that Iraq had weapons of mass destruction. This strengthened the widely held view that at any rate Iraq did not constitute a threat that had to be dealt with immediately by force. If armed action would be needed, it could be authorised later.' He also concluded that 'the US administration swung from seeing the inspection reports as potential assets in underpinning a future demand for armed action to identifying them as an impediment, the authority of which the US needed to undermine'.

Dr Blix suggests that there was a moment while the benchmark concept was being discussed when it seemed that the UK might separate from the US position, but it became clear that the US was not willing to support the benchmark idea and the UK dropped it. Blix makes clear that the French could accept a shorter time limit for the attainment of key remaining disarmament tasks but did not favour a resolution that would give automatic authority for the US and UK to claim the benchmarks had not been met, and therefore declare war without a return to the Security Council. Blix felt that the French and several other members of the Security Council were worried about a scenario in which they might accept the resolution and Iraq might attain a first set of benchmarks, but the US would launch its war anyway. This would mean those who had accepted the resolution had joined in authorising war. The French impression was that the US had decided on war in January, and France did not want to bless it.

The non-permanent members of the Security Council felt that achieving the benchmarks before 17 March was not a serious proposition. They looked for a compromise. They suggested a draft which would list the benchmarks similar to those the British had prepared and would extend the time given for the attainment of the benchmarks to three weeks or thirty days. Blix says this was clearly a more realistic paper than the British one, 'except that the time allowed went beyond what the US would tolerate'. And there was another vital point. Blix says that President Lagos of Chile explained to him on the phone that the 'six elected members of the Council were of the view that it was for the Council collectively to assess whether Iraq had attained the benchmarks and to decide on further action. They were not willing to let the Council abdicate this prerogative. The US, on the other hand, was not ready to drop the claim of a right to go it alone.'

This was the crucial gap within which the UK could have brokered a compromise. But again, the UK was not willing to take a different position from the US and therefore had no influence. It is clear from Blix's reporting that the account of the Chilean compromise that the Prime Minister gave to the House of Commons when responding to the Butler Report on 14 July was misleading.

He repeated his claim during the House of Commons debate on the Butler Report on 20 July. He said in response to my intervention:

> To answer my Right Hon. Friend the Member for Birmingham Ladywood directly, I agree that it would have been better to let the inspectors have more time, provided that we had a UN resolution for them to operate under

which laid down a clear ultimatum to Saddam that action would follow if he did not comply with the benchmarks that I agreed with Hans Blix at the time. However, as I think I explained to my Right Hon. Friend at the time, the problem was that some other countries made it clear that they would not accept any resolution containing an ultimatum.

We have seen that the record is clear that other members of the Security Council were willing to give an ultimatum, but not to give a right to the UK and US to decide whether the resolution had been met. As we have seen, Dr Blix is very clear that the Security Council favoured an ultimatum, but not automaticity. Blair is wrong to claim that there was not support for an ultimatum. He seems to be using the word 'ultimatum' to mean a resolution that gave authority for the US/UK to declare war without going back to the Security Council.

It came as a complete surprise to me that the Prime Minister gave his unequivocal view in writing on 15 March that the requirements of Resolution 1441 were being breached. This exchange of correspondence was kept from the Cabinet. Paragraphs 383–6 of Butler tell us that:

> Following the end of negotiations in the United Nations on a further Security Council resolution, the Legal Secretary to the Attorney-General wrote to the Private Secretary to the Prime Minister on 14 March 2003 seeking confirmation that:
>
>> . . . it is unequivocally the Prime Minister's view that Iraq has committed further material breaches as specified in paragraph 4 of Resolution 1441.
>
> The Prime Minister's Private Secretary replied to the Legal Secretary on 15 March, confirming that

. . . it is indeed the Prime Minister's unequivocal view that Iraq is in further material breach of its obligations, as in OP4(18) of UNSCR 1441, because of false statements or omissions in the declarations submitted by Iraq pursuant to this resolution and failure by Iraq to comply with, and co-operate fully in the implementation of, this resolution.

We have been told that, in coming to his view that Iraq was in further material breach, the Prime Minister took account both of the overall intelligence picture and of information from a wide range of other sources, including especially UNMOVIC information.

The Attorney-General set out his view of the legal position to the Cabinet on 17 March, by producing and speaking to the Written Answer he gave to Parliament on that date.

For me, this is the most important revelation from Butler. I knew the intelligence had been exaggerated to suggest an immediate threat. I knew that Cabinet discussions had not been properly informed and there had been no collective decision-making. But I did not know that the Attorney-General had said that there was legal authority for war on the basis of an unequivocal statement from the Prime Minister that there was no other way of securing compliance with Resolution 1441. On the basis of Blix's account, it is impossible to accept that the Prime Minister was correct, and it is clear therefore that legal authority for war was achieved on a false prospectus.

The third term

Sometimes it is suggested that all is basically fine with the Labour Party, that Iraq is the only problem, soon it will settle and the public will get bored and we can go on and win the next election (pencilled in for spring 2005, although it does not have to take place until June 2006). There is a general presumption in the Labour leadership and amongst political commentators that Labour will easily win. Despite a very poor performance in the European and local elections of June 2004, and the two by-elections in July, the view continues that this was just a protest and that Labour was well set to win the election. This lack of respect for the unease expressed by the electorate seems to me both wrong and deeply unwise. But also it is clear that the electorate do not want a Tory government. What I believe they want is a decent Labour government, full employment, good public services and a commitment to social justice at home and abroad. But there is a deep unhappiness about Iraq, top-up fees and the general style of the government. There has also been a big loss of trust in Blair which has arisen over Iraq but now extends much more widely.

I found it hard to understand why the government was not more concerned about the disgruntlement amongst the electorate until I attended a presentation by MORI analysing the consequences of the local and European elections of June 2004. They pointed out that the distribution of the electorate and the workings of our electoral system means that there is now a massive bias in Labour's favour. Thus in the 2001 election Labour obtained 26,031 votes for every seat it won in the House of Commons, the Conservatives 51,060 votes per seat and the Liberal Democrats 92,583 votes per seat. The conclusion of the presentation was that Labour would probably win the 2005 election with a majority of 100, despite the mood amongst the electorate. Current projections are, for example, that if 42 per cent vote for Labour and 42 per cent for the Conservatives, Labour would have a majority of 70. Obviously, Blair is aware of these projections. This helps one understand his complacency. I suspect it may also persuade the Tories to start to consider the case for electoral reform.

7

WHAT IS TO BE DONE?

There is no doubt that the world is in serious trouble and that the UK has become part of the problem. It is impossible to correct what has gone wrong unless we admit how serious the problems are and agree that we need to find different solutions.

Our most serious immediate problem is that the Middle East is burning with anger and increasing numbers are joining up to a loose network known as al-Qaeda because they are coming to believe that the only way to secure justice and resist state violence is through the use of violence. This anger is spreading across the Muslim world and large regions are at risk of continuing violence and instability. The mishandling of Iraq and the failure to establish a Palestinian state alongside Israel, as promised in the Oslo peace accords of 1993 and then the Road Map to a Palestinian state published in 2003, has intensified the problem.

The challenge of poverty

The most serious long-term problem facing the world is the desperate level of poverty and inequality and the linked threat to the sustainability of the earth's environmental resources. Over a billion people live in extreme poverty, with insufficient food, no access to health care, education, clean water or sanitation. Nearly half of the people of the world are very poor, living on less than the equivalent of $2 per day for all their needs. We are continuing to lose environmental resources at an alarming rate, forests are being decimated, fish stocks depleted, lands overgrazed and deserts spreading. Global warming is now an established reality and its threats very serious worldwide. The consequences will be very harmful for people in all countries but as ever the poor will suffer most. To take one example: Bangladesh, one of the poorest countries in the world, stands to see its population grow by 50 per cent and to lose one third of its territory over the next 30 years. World population will continue to grow until it stabilises in 2030–50 at 8–9 billion people. This is a potential 50 per cent increase on the current world population on a planet which is already under strain. Ninety per cent of the new people will live in developing countries. The people of the 49 least developed countries, who are the very poorest in the world, currently number 668 million but will reach 1.7 billion by 2050.

The new consensus

In the late 1990s and the early years of the new millennium, there was a growing international consensus that these levels of poverty and inequality were the greatest moral challenge and the greatest danger the world faced. The Millennium Assembly of the United Nations which was called to mark the year 2000 was attended by more Presidents and Prime Ministers than any previous UN meeting. It agreed that reducing poverty was the world's top priority. It was at this meeting that the world adopted the Millennium Development Goals (MDGs) which committed all nations to work together to systematically reduce poverty. The agreed goal was to halve the proportion of people living in poverty by 2015. Of course, halving acute poverty is not enough, but we are working against a moving target. If a billion people successfully lift themselves out of poverty by 2015, population growth means that they will be replaced by a billion new people. The challenge is enormous but at least the world will have learned to work together to begin to eliminate extreme poverty. The agreed goals also recognise that poverty will only be reduced sustainably if there is a commitment to reduce income poverty, provide education, health care, clean water and sanitation.

The evidence is now clear that the single most powerful force for development in any country is the education of a generation of children, including the girls. In the poorest countries, girls tend to be denied education, yet girls who have been to school, even if just to primary level, transform their country as they grow up. They marry later, have fewer children who are more likely to survive, they increase family income and are better at accessing education and health care for their children. Similarly, it is now understood that access to basic health care is an essential investment in development. The poor of the world are not a static group of people. They work enormously hard and pull themselves up by their own efforts. But constant ill health of a breadwinner or a child causes income to drop or the need to sell animals and tools to pay for health care, and throws them back into poverty. The urgent need is for basic healthcare systems which can provide immunisation, treatment for diarrhoea, and access to contraception as well as treatment for malaria and TB, and testing, advice and where possible anti-retroviral treatment for HIV(Aids). Much of the public debate has focused on the cost of drugs and there have been some improve-ments, but most poor people in the world have no access to basic health care so even free drugs will not reach them.

HIV(Aids) is a serious threat. It is causing great loss of life and economic loss in Africa and is spreading rapidly in Asia and Eastern Europe, but countries like Uganda and Cambodia have created models of success in containing and reducing the threat. In the case of Uganda infection rates of 12 per cent in the 1990s reduced to a national prevalence rate of 4.1 per cent. The upsurge in TB is serious and linked to the rising levels of HIV(Aids). But malaria also kills more than 1 million people a year, mostly children and pregnant women, and causes enormous ill health and loss of ability to work. In order to contain the spread of more virulent forms of malaria we need new drugs and better sanitation. As we know from our own squalid cities at the time of the Industrial Revolution, the biggest improvements in health came from access to clean water and sanitation. Currently, 1 billion people lack access to clean water and 2 billion people, in a world of rapid urbanisation, lack any sanitation.

Obviously the setting of agreed targets does not of itself deliver progress but it did help to galvanise the world and provide a clearer focus for development efforts in each country and at a global level. The world is currently on track to achieve the target of halving income poverty, largely because of progress in Asia and particularly China. Progress is being made against other targets, but not fast enough and, despite progress in some countries, Africa, overall, is still getting poorer.

Following the Millennium Assembly, the World Bank, IMF and the Regional Development Banks adopted the MDGs as the measure of development progress. The Development Committee of the OECD, where all the donors of aid come together, also committed to the targets. This provided, for the first time, a worldwide agreement upon the purpose of development and on how to measure success.

And then in Doha in November 2001 at the first Ministerial meeting of the WTO since the disastrous meeting in Seattle in 1999, the world agreed an agenda for a trade round which would make trade rules fairer for poor countries. This was an enormous breakthrough. It came after the attack on the Twin Towers and before the mistakes of the 'war on terror' when the world felt the need to commit to more justice in order to contain the threat of bitter division.

At Monterrey in Mexico in March 2002, the UN convened a conference on Financing for Development. There was agreement that the private sector should be the engine of growth and that the state must provide the framework to enable economic growth and development to take place. The OECD countries also promised an increase in aid, in order to help poor countries create the conditions necessary to generate economic growth and development. The promise made at Monterrey amounted to an increase in international aid of 20 per cent. This is insufficient – an extra $50 billion is needed if the world is to meet the MDGs – but it was a turning point after ten years of continuing decline in aid spending by the US and most European countries. It is notable that world-wide spending on aid stands at $68 billion (£40 billion). Worldwide spending on arms is over $1,000 billion. The US alone spends more than $400 billion per annum on arms and less than $16 billion on aid.

The final advance in building the new consensus was the UN meeting on environment and sustainable development held in Johannesburg in September 2002. This was intended to monitor progress, ten years after the original UN environment conference in Rio. Although media reports of the outcome were critical, my view is that the meeting was a considerable success because the environmental movement shifted from a rich-country perspective calling for conservation to a commitment to guarantee development for all and to share the earth's environmental resources more fairly and sustainably.

DfID and I have been closely involved in building this new consensus and also the improved development model which focused on building competent state capacity rather than charitable projects or one-off investments. Also, John Prescott and Margaret Beckett worked hard to help build agreement on the Kyoto Protocol which was designed to get the rich countries to move first to contain the growth in greenhouse gas emissions as a first step in reversing the cause of global warming.

There is no doubt that the problems of poverty, loss of environmental resources, global warming and all the suffering and turbulence these problems cause, is an enormous challenge facing mankind. From 1997 onwards, the UK government helped build a new international consensus designed to face the challenge and in that, I believe, we were entitled to take some pride.

Failed states and conflict prevention

Alongside the new consensus on development there was a growing understanding that weak states, and prolonged civil war, caused enormous suffering and instability and created a barrier to development. In Sierra Leone, Sudan and the Democratic Republic of Congo, DfID had worked with the UN and others to help bring wars to an end and start the long, patient process of nation-building. In Uganda, Rwanda and Mozambique we had worked with others with some success to help decimated nations rebuild. In East Timor and Kosovo, we were engaged with the UN in supporting rebuilding.

Kofi Annan was driving a programme of UN reform and the UK were strong supporters. This meant increasing the effectiveness of the various UN development agencies. DfID provided funding to the agencies on behalf of the UK. The UN agencies are greatly respected and trusted in developing countries but often bureaucratic and less efficient than they might be. DfID negotiated partnerships with all the organisations we funded, aimed at increasing effectiveness in return for improved funding.

On conflict, serious efforts were made to learn from the failures in Somalia and Rwanda. The Brahimi report commissioned by Kofi Annan was submitted in August 2000 and put forward far-reaching changes in UN peacekeeping operations. It set out an agenda for improving the effectiveness of the UN and the international system to achieve conflict resolution and prevention. DfID and the Foreign Office were strongly committed to the detailed implementation of the Brahimi report. In addition, the UK was committed to reform of the Security Council which clearly needed to change to reflect the changes in the world since the end of the Second World War. And, following Kosovo, the report of the International Commission of Intervention and State Sovereignty commissioned at the request of Kofi Annan had given us an agenda for a new framework for intervention for humanitarian reasons.

The consequences of 11 September 2001

Thus before 11 September 2001, I was feeling hopeful that we were beginning to build an improved international system committed to justice and development in which the UK was playing a central role. Then the attack on the Twin Towers took the lives of nearly 3,000 people, stunned the world and humiliated and hurt the greatest power on earth. This was not the first attack on US targets by al-Qaeda but the attack on the World Trade Center and the Pentagon was so spectacular and so humiliating that it was bound to generate a strong reaction. At first the world stood strongly together. Across the globe there was a deep sense of solidarity with America. The UN Security Council, with universal support, established a system to require every country to tighten up on efforts to tackle al-Qaeda. Tony Blair became very active at this time in helping to establish an international coalition to deal with the al-Qaeda training camps in Afghanistan. It was at this point that wise policy would have been to commit to a just settlement in the Middle East and the fostering of international co-operation to deal with the al-Qaeda threat.

But instead mistakes were made. The first was the failure to provide for the proper rebuilding of Afghanistan by demobilising the militias of the warlords and supporting the building of an Afghan state that would deliver development and progress to its people. And then there was the disastrous detour of the attack on Iraq led by neoconservative preoccupation rather than a serious analysis of the threat from al-Qaeda.

This led to the shattering of the international consensus and the strengthening of al-Qaeda, as is now widely acknowledged. Following these mistakes we face the real danger of decades of conflict between the Muslim world and the West. This will cause suffering for all of us and has already diverted the world from the need to focus on reducing poverty and promoting sustainable development. This is in my view a massive failure of leadership and the prospects are very gloomy unless we can create a new commitment to greater justice and equity as the only basis on which the post-Cold War world can be managed.

The challenge of the post-Cold War world

I am afraid that when we celebrated the fall of the Berlin Wall and Nelson Mandela's release from prison in 1989, we thought a period of great advance was inevitable. We did not appreciate then how confused and destabilised the international system would be by the end of the Cold War and how difficult it would find it to establish a new world order. During the Cold War era, which lasted for two generations, order was kept through the promise of Mutually Assured Destruction. The division between the Soviet bloc and the West ran through every area of tension in the world. Conflict was contained because of the risk that it could escalate into a conflagration between the two blocs, which had the potential to destroy the world.

But once this balance of fear was destroyed, there was little order to take its place. The Balkans descended into ethnic conflict as Milosevic and other old Communist leaders used ethnic nationalism to keep themselves in power. The response of the international system was slow and muddled. Terrible atrocities were committed against all ethnic groups – but those who suffered most were the Muslim people of Bosnia, who experienced mass rape, vicious prison camps and the slaughter in 1995 of over 7000 Muslim men and boys in the UN 'safe area' of Srebrenica.

India and Pakistan had been at odds over the territory of Kashmir since the time of Independence when the ruling Maharajah opted to join India, but 80 per cent of the people were Muslims, and most wanted to be part of Pakistan. This led to conflict which was brought to an end by UN intervention and the promise of a referendum. This was never honoured. The two countries came to blows again in 1965, and over Bangladesh independence in 1971. But the conflict was contained, largely because India was close to Russia and Pakistan to the US and China. But in the post-Cold War world, conflict within Kashmir has escalated with terrible loss of life, and both India and Pakistan have acquired nuclear weapons. War was narrowly averted in the summer of 2003.

Various conflicts broke out in the former Soviet Union; the most bitter was that in Chechnya, another Muslim people whose demand for independence was savagely repressed. The situation in Afghanistan and Central Asia has already been described. The region remains unstable, the people are suffering and they are a Muslim people.

Africa also saw a big increase in conflict and civil war at the end of the Cold War. The West and the Soviets had armed and supported their surrogates in Africa in the Cold War years. But as the Cold War ended and the Soviets and the West withdrew from interest in Africa, many countries with bloated armies and weak states collapsed into civil war. As a result, we saw war spreading in Somalia, Sierra Leone, Liberia, Rwanda, Burundi, Zaire and else-where. The post-Cold War international system no longer felt its self-interest was at stake and did little to intervene. For Africa the problem is desperate poverty and weak states, collapsing into civil war. But Africa also has a substantial Muslim population and a deep sense of grievance. There have been a series of attacks on US and Israeli interests in Africa since 1998. In Algeria, a bitter civil war erupted in 1991 after an Islamist party won the first round of elections and the second round was cancelled and Algeria became a military dictatorship. The war has cost 100,000 lives.

Latin America, which is the most unequal continent, saw a period of democratisation and advance in the 1990s as it threw off the military dictatorships that had been supported by the US to prevent communism expanding from Cuba. But as the Millennium arrived and the poor of the continent made clear that democracy and economic reforms may have pleased the international community, but have not improved their lives, tension has begun to grow again. The war in Colombia has been prolonged by drug dealing which has also started to endanger the Caribbean.

More recently a civil war erupted in Nepal, in which the international community took little interest, and the peace process in Sri Lanka which made progress for a time after more than twenty years of civil war has collapsed and the ceasefire is now under strain. And Indonesia's progress towards peace and democracy is looking fragile.

Thus long before 11 September 2001, the post-Cold War world was unstable and divided and there was clear evidence of a growth in the Islamist resistance movements fuelled by poverty, corrupt authoritarian governments and aspirations for an overthrow of an unjust order and dreams of a future of justice and peace based on the teachings of Islam.

The growth of al-Qaeda

This state of the world provides the background to the growth of al-Qaeda. It was established by Osama bin Laden and the groups that had fought, with US and Saudi support, to overthrow the Soviet-supported regime in Afghanistan. After the first Gulf War, Osama bin Laden dedicated himself to overthrowing the Saudi regime, which he saw as decadent and pro-Western, and to removing US forces from the land of the Muslim holy places. Increasingly, the US was seen as the enemy, and al-Qaeda was able to rally support across the Muslim world because of the sense that

Muslims were suffering in many lands but particularly because the US unconditionally supported Israel and its repression of the Palestinians and propped up corrupt and authoritarian regimes across the Middle East.

This is the backdrop to the terrible attack on the Twin Towers and the dreadfully misconceived declaration of the 'war on terror'. The reality is that it is impossible to prosecute a war on terror. It is like declaring a war on war. All war uses violence and violence creates terror. We have religious, moral and legal teachings on when war is just but those who are strongly committed to the use of military force cannot consistently argue that the use of force by the poor and dispossessed is always wrong. The obsession with terrorism, which is a tactic – the tactic of the powerless – has made it harder in a whole range of contexts to analyse sensibly its roots in injustice.

Similarly, all are agreed that the French Resistance was right to fight Nazi occupation. The Americans were right to resist British colonial rule. It follows that the Palestinians have a right to resist occupation. International law recognises a right to resist in such circumstances. This does not mean that it is ever right to target civilians, and there is little doubt that the first non-violent *intifada* won stronger international sympathy than the second, but for the US to argue that any state or person that supports Palestinian resistance to occupation is a supporter of terrorism, is an unacceptable nonsense.

And so this so-called 'war on terror' is becoming a very dangerous game. If there is no commitment to international law and justice, then might is right. The US has more military power than any other nation in the world. But we have seen in Afghanistan and Iraq that military power alone cannot create stable states and it certainly cannot make the US secure. If the war on terror continues on current lines we are heading for decades of continuing violence and bloodshed which will inflict terrible suffering and instability across the world.

Religious fanaticism

There is a danger of a new global divide with a growth of fanaticism in all the world's major religions leading to an era of bitterness and conflict, reinforced by religion. It was Gandhi who said, 'An eye for an eye makes the whole world blind.' Yet today, Osama bin Laden, George Bush and Tony Blair all tell us that we are engaged in a battle between good and evil and thus justify the killing of large numbers of innocent people. There is a very real danger that the current attitude to the growth of the al-Qaeda network and the 'war on terror' is exacerbating the problem and acting as a recruiting sergeant for terrorism.

If we are to do better in dealing with the anger that is feeding the growth of al-Qaeda we must face the reality that even when it comes to the terrible tally of loss of innocent life, the story is being distorted. If we take all the attacks on Western targets resulting in death between September 2001 and up to February 2004 and add in the Madrid bombing, the total according to Iraq Body Count is 3,575. This includes 2,976 in the Twin Towers, 202 in Bali and 200 in Madrid and 14 other incidents. But as many as 13,000 non-combatant civilians have died following the invasion of Iraq – 7,356 during the war and the rest thereafter. There have also been more than 3,000 civilian deaths in Afghanistan. On top of this, we have the continuing tally of civilian deaths in the Israeli–Palestinian conflict. The estimate is that the Israeli army has killed 2,750 Palestinian civilians in the three years up to February 2004 and 892 Israeli civilians have died at the hands of Palestinian bombers in suicide attacks. The terrible consequences of this unending conflict is reflected in a survey of children carried out last year by the Gaza Community Mental Health Programme, which showed that only 2 per cent of the children displayed no symptoms of post-traumatic stress disorder; and that a quarter aspire to martyrdom. 'Children think it is better to choose how they die. They would rather die a bomber's death than be killed on the street by a missile,' said a doctor at the programme.

If we go beyond this to think about the deaths of Muslims in Bosnia and particularly Srebrenica, the savagery of the war in Chechnya and the terrible loss of life over the last ten years in Kashmir, we might begin to understand that very many Muslims, who are absolutely clear that their faith can never be used to justify attacks on civilians, feel angry that the West appears to value Western lives very much more highly than those of Muslim civilians.

The Washington-based Pew research centre completed a second survey of public opinion in Britain, France, Russia and Germany and four large predominantly Muslim countries in March 2004 (The Pew Global Attitudes Project). It found that anger against the United States is pervasive and that Osama bin Laden is viewed favourably by 65 per cent of the people in Pakistan, 55 per cent in Jordan and 45 per cent in Morocco. Even in Turkey where bin Laden is very unpopular, as many as 31 per cent say that suicide attacks against Americans and other Westerners in Iraq are justifiable. Majorities in all four countries doubt the sincerity of the war on terror and see it as an effort to control Middle East oil and to dominate the world.

The image of this resistance and of al-Qaeda that is being propagated is highly misleading. It is not a tightly organised group of conspirators that can be defeated as soon as Osama bin Laden is captured. It represents a millenarian set of ideas which have been taken up by bin Laden, and have adherents across large parts of the Muslim world. Al-Qaeda is seen as a response to the constant humiliation and suffering of the Arab and Muslim people who, its followers say, must engage in sacrifice, martyrdom and spectacular violence in order to awaken the masses and thus reinstate the honour of Muslim civilisation, and the values of justice for which Islam stands.

Of course, such nihilism is immoral and irrational, but if we are to counter it we need to understand it and ought to reflect on our own experience. Millenarianism has a long history in Christian thought. This does not mean it is right, but if we study the history of such movements in the West, we might better understand why a movement like al-Qaeda could acquire such strength. It is notable that millenarianism has always been a strong current in US Christianity.

There is also a grave danger in the anti-Muslim prejudice which is being fanned by the current approach to the war on terror. It ignores the fact that the fundamentalism, or fanaticism, that distorts Muslim teaching and is inspiring a loose and growing network of angry young Muslims, is mirrored by new fundamentalist and fanatical movements in all the world's major religions. The Christian Zionists, who are a significant part of President Bush's political alliance, support an expansionist Israel because they believe there has to be a Jewish state in the whole of historical Palestine before the Messiah will return. Jewish settlers, illegally occupying Palestinian land in the West Bank and Gaza, cite the Old Testament when asked for their title to the land. And in Gujarat in 2002, fundamentalist Hindus engaged in mass murder, rape and pillage against local Muslim populations. We need to give much deeper consideration as to why religious fanaticism is on the increase in the face of the uncertainties of the post–Cold War, globalising world. A new global dividing line seems to be emerging between bitter and divisive or generous and inclusive interpretations of the major world religions.

Britain in particular ought to bring a wiser historical understanding to these problems. As I suggested earlier, the errors of the early response to the 1970s IRA campaign with internment acting as a recruiting sergeant for the IRA, taught the important lesson that terrorist movements require support from the people from whom they emerge. There are no quick fixes once such movements are in place, but a commitment to justice is essential to undermine local sympathy and build the necessary alliances to defeat them. And in the case of al-Qaeda, this means we must reach a just settlement to the Israeli/Palestinian conflict which is the root division between the Arab and Western world. We must create a non-violent route to justice and development in the Middle East; re-establish the commitment to poverty reduction and development worldwide and then try to re-establish the agreement there was immediately after 11 September 2001 when there was a worldwide determination to co-operate and defeat the perpetrators of such a terrible crime.

There is currently a mood of dismay and despondency across the world, and yet we are living at a time when humanity has the capacity for a greater advance than has ever previously been possible. It was the Industrial Revolution that created the material potential for the abolition of poverty in Western Europe and North America. But following these technological advances, people had to organise to demand the right to vote and create trade unions and political parties dedicated to sharing that wealth in order to remove gross poverty and inequality and share out the abundance there is today. Globalisation, which is simply an increased integration of the global economy, has the potential, the capital, the technology and the knowledge to create a similar uplift worldwide. We now have the technological potential for a worldwide assault on poverty, but the current leadership of the world appears to be incapable of grasping this prospect.

Poor leadership

My diagnosis is that we are suffering from a serious problem of mind-lag in the political leadership of the world. Those in leading positions in politics, the media and the civil service, rose to the top in the old order. We are living at a time of very great historical change – the end of the Cold War, an integrated world economy, new communication technology – which is driving rapid change everywhere. The old elite seem to be incapable of understanding the change that is taking place, of responding to the challenge of the new era and of understanding that a commitment to equity, development, the rule of law and universal rules is the only way to make the world safe and sustainable.

It is notable that the Clinton administration was reluctant to embrace the Kyoto protocol, the International Criminal Court, the treaty banning landmines and even the Convention on the Rights of the Child. Perhaps it is difficult for the only remaining great power to understand that an international order based on fair rules and equity is in everyone's interest. And it is notable how the Bush administration rushed to replace the old war on communism with 'the war on terrorism'. It was as though they were incapable of imagining a world of multilateral co-operation founded on the rule of law. They needed a new enemy in order to understand their role in the world. This is not to say that the threat from al-Qaeda to the US is not very serious or that the attack on the Twin Towers was not a terrible crime, but a response that declares a generalised war on terror is a nonsense and, as we have seen since the wars in Afghanistan and Iraq, doomed to failure.

The special relationship

The question of why Tony Blair accepted and supported Bush's response to the events of September 11 will be debated for many years to come. It is notable that in doing so he set aside the advice of his Foreign Office, party and country. My own view is that the concentration of power in No. 10, the habit of thinking about policy in terms of announcements and media manipulation and a hubristic pleasure in being the only world leader who could deal as an equal with the President of the US, led Tony Blair to make an error that deeply damaged his premiership and will blight his reputation for ever more. But that said, it is notable how every post-war Prime Minister apart from Ted Heath made the 'special relationship' a centre point of their foreign policy. Peter Riddell's book *Hug Them Close*, published in 2003, tells very clearly how

British Prime Ministers of all parties are somehow obsessed with their relationship with the US and pretend to themselves that it makes Britain more powerful than it is. It does seem that the 'special relationship' is part of a UK which, in the words of Dean Acheson, who was US Secretary of State from 1949 to 1953, 'lost an empire but has not yet found a role', and is instead pretending to itself that being close to the US gives the UK a powerful role on the world stage.

The question of Britain's role in the world, and our relationship with the US and the European Union needs much deeper debate. The Conservative Party, the Blair government and much of the media criticise anyone who questions the 'special relationship' as being anti-American. I do not accept this. I believe that the US, traumatised by September 11, has lashed out and made terrible mistakes and any real friend would have told them they were doing so. The tragedy of Blair's support is that he encouraged the US into gross errors which have made it hated across the world and al-Qaeda a stronger threat.

The UK and the US will always have a relationship of shared language and history, but to believe that this gives the UK some special influence over the US is delusional. There is no serious relationship that gives the UK any special role or influence. As we have seen in Iraq, the UK was simply the fig-leaf and did not change the course of events. Some argue that the alternative for the UK is to commit to the EU as a counterbalance to the power of the US. Blair insists that the UK is a bridge between the US and EU, but over Iraq he demonstrated a total incapacity to act as a bridge. My view is that the EU is similarly muddled about its role. I agree that it can act as a counterweight to the US but it should be clear that it must not attempt to become an alternative great power. The EU should act as an exponent of development, and multilateralism, supporting a strong UN and fairer international environmental agreements and trade rules. Its performance at the World Trade Organization talks in Cancún in September 2003, and the poor quality of its development effort, means there is much work to be done if the EU is to take on such a role. In the meantime, I believe the UK should make these values the centre of its foreign policy and use all its seats on the world stage – Security Council, EU, World Bank, IMF, Commonwealth, etc. – to this end. Britain should later look to work with allies that share these values and thus help to move the EU forward, improve the operation of the IMF and World Bank, make the Commonwealth more relevant and the UN more effective. This would be a foreign policy through which Britain could make a distinctive contribution and in which most British people would take a lot of pride.

The way forward

I believe that it is quite easy to see the way forward in the Middle East. Delivering the policy would take time and face difficulties, but the principles on which it should be based are very clear. As I say to my Muslim constituents when we discuss these matters, the Muslims of the world do not have a different view from the rest of the world. The people of the UK, of Europe and of most of the world agree that the suffering of the Palestinian people is unbearable and strongly support a settlement based on a two-state solution. The Palestinian and Israeli people also support such a solution. The problem we have is an inadequacy of Israeli and US political leadership. There is a tendency to blame the lack of progress on President Arafat. He is not above criticism as the people of Gaza have made clear, but it is wrong to suggest that he cannot be a partner for peace. In our own country the problem is – despite his promises – the failure of Tony Blair to use the influence he had in the US, because of their determination to act on Iraq, to get progress on Palestine.

The present difficulties that the US faces in Iraq, and their growing need for international support, creates the possibility of the world uniting to demand progress in establishing a Palestinian state and a genuine commitment to hand Iraq over to the Iraqis rather than an interim government selected and backed by the US. If this is to be achieved, there needs to be a shift in UK policy. If the UK were to unite with the rest of the EU, Russia and China, the alliance would be very influential. At a time when the US is increasingly vulnerable because of the mishandling of Iraq and cannot afford to be isolated in the Security Council, a shift in UK policy in order to achieve a better future for the people of Iraq, and the establishment of a Palestinian state could be very powerful. This should be accompanied by an agreement that all WMD, including Israel's nuclear weapons, should be removed from the Middle East. Such progress would lance the boil at the centre of the Middle East conflict and open up the prospects of an era of progress and development in the region.

There is no doubt that getting the US to shift its policy towards Israel and Palestine will be difficult. Democrats and Republicans share an unbalanced view of the Middle East. This is reflected in the vote of the US Congress on 23 June 2004 by 407 to 9 to support Israeli Prime Minister Ariel Sharon's plan to withdraw from Gaza but to annexe large sections of the Palestinian West Bank, seized by Israel in the 1967 war. This vote supported Bush's letter endorsing the Sharon plan and thus destroys the internationally agreed Road Map and challenges the UN Charter which forbids any country from expanding its territory by military conquest. When Blair visited the US in April 2004, he appeared to give endorsement to this plan. It was Blair's seeming endorsement of the Sharon/Bush plan that caused more than fifty former British diplomats to issue their open letter to Blair on 29 April 2004. They said they had watched with deepening concern the policies which Blair had followed in the Arab–Israel problem and on Iraq and called for a return to the Road Map to a Palestinian state. They described the Sharon/Bush plan as 'one-sided and illegal' and said it would cost yet more Israeli and Palestinian blood. This led, on 4 May, to fifty retired US diplomats issuing a public letter calling on President Bush to reverse his Middle

East policy. They stressed that they were 'deeply concerned at his endorsement of Sharon's plan to deny the right of Palestinians to return to their homeland and to retain five large illegal settlement blocs in the occupied West Bank'. They went on to say that President Bush had put US diplomats in an untenable position by ignoring international laws declaring Israeli settlements illegal and undermining the Road Map. They called for a return to American traditions of fairness and said that the Israeli–Palestinian conflict is at the core of the problems in the Middle East. However, the UN has welcomed the commitment to a withdrawal from Gaza and called for the plan to be made consistent with the Road Map. If the UK government were to shift back to our original bi-partisan position, we might put ourselves in a position to be able to help modify the Gaza plan and help drag the US back to respect international law and a two-state solution. Without the UK, the US would be left completely isolated at a time when it needs allies.

Without progress on establishing a Palestinian state and a firm commitment from the US and UK to withdraw from Iraq, to give full authority to the UN to help the Iraqis form their government and invite other countries to help them establish security, I fear that al-Qaeda will continue to grow. If this is the future, the Middle East will become more unstable. This will continue to divide the international community, weaken the UN and potentially, through the effects on oil production, damage the world economy.

Beyond the Middle East, the world must urgently get back to a focus on reducing poverty and promoting sustainable development, ending conflict, rebuilding weak states and overcoming the catastrophes that global warming and all its consequences are likely to bring to the world.

Tony Blair was, I believe, sincere in his commitment to focus on Africa in his second term. He did call lots of meetings, ask for briefing and argue the case for Africa at G8 meetings. This generated much bureaucratic activity by the G8 special representatives but I fear it did not produce many results. Similarly the recently announced

Commission for Africa which Blair has established at the prompting of Bob Geldof is unlikely to do much harm, but I fear little is likely to come of it. We have passed the point when Commissions chaired by European men are likely to resolve Africa's problems. What we need is a strong focus on resolving conflict, rebuilding weak states, better trading opportunities and improved economic and social development across the continent. Africa is too often treated as an object of charity. Instead, we need a partnership to rebuild a continent deeply damaged by European intervention, to enable it to escape from its deepening poverty. Such action is essential for the sake of its people, but also in the self-interest of Africa's neighbours in Europe. If failed states such as Afghanistan threaten global interests, a failed continent is a much greater threat.

Crumbling constitution

As I have tried to argue, the mistakes on Iraq and support for the US 'war on terror' are the most spectacular and serious manifestations of a deep malfunction in the British political system and in British constitutional arrangements. Under the Thatcher government, but much more seriously under the Blair government, the checks and balances of the British government system have broken down, leading to a pattern of ill-considered policy development and deep mistakes in both domestic and international policy-making.

The central problem is that the electoral system is producing governments with massively distorted majorities in the House of Commons. Mrs Thatcher won 44 per cent, then 42 per cent, and 42 per cent of the vote. If we take into account the turnout, this reflected the support of 33 per cent, then 31 per cent and 32 per cent of the people. Yet she had majorities of 43, 144 and 107 in the Commons and inevitably hubris developed, together with a failure to consult and listen, and she and her party came to be despised by the electorate.

Exactly the same thing is happening under Tony Blair. As I have shown, in 1997 the votes of a minority of the electorate produced a majority of 179 in the Commons and, in 2001, the votes of one in four of the electorate created a majority of 167. The projections by MORI of the likely outcome of the next election show that this distortion is likely to continue.

The consequence of this is that parliamentary majorities are taken for granted, Parliament is downgraded and ignored, the power of the Prime Minister is enhanced and the Cabinet sidelined because the Prime Minister does not need the help of the Cabinet to keep his majority in the Commons.

Prime Ministerial patronage is very powerful in the British system. The Prime Minister appoints the Cabinet and 91 other paid Ministers and Whips, and the Whips control appointments to Select Committees, foreign delegations and permission to attend events outside the Commons. It is reasonable, especially with such large promotion prospects, for everyone to aspire to ministerial office, but the only way to rise is to obey and not rock the boat and thus sycophancy thrives. In addition, the Prime Minister nominates appointees to the House of Lords; under the Blair premiership the numbers appointed have been higher than under any previous Prime Minister, with 268 since 1997 (125 of them Labour).

In addition to the power of the distorted majority and the power of patronage, Blair has broken down many constitutional arrangements through his very informal decision-making style. I have described how the Defence and Overseas Policy Committee did not meet to consider UK options towards Iraq and how the whole Iraq strategy was decided informally by Blair and his personal entourage of advisers. This way of making decisions enhances the personal power of the Prime Minister but reduces the quality of decision-making. I believe it is this way of proceeding that produced the disastrous approach to Iraq, but also ill-thought-through policy on issues such as foundation hospitals, top-up fees, asylum and crime, and now proposals for 'choice'. Clearly choice is a good thing as the focus groups are telling both Michael Howard and Tony Blair, but public-sector reform cannot succeed on the basis of headline-grabbing slogans. One of the great problems of Blair's approach to public-sector reform is that it has been accompanied by centralisation of control and a proliferation of targets and bureaucracy which has undermined morale and thus the commitment of staff, which, alongside the increase in public investment, is essential for quality public services.

In the case of the Blair leadership there has also been a total preoccupation with managing the media. This is the founding inspiration of New Labour and the explanation of the enormous influence of Alastair Campbell and Peter Mandelson. Previous Labour governments have been damaged by media hostility and it is a perfectly worthy aim to manage the media better but, as the book on Alastair Campbell by Peter Oborne and Simon Walters published in June 2004 demonstrates, for Blair the media was the primary consideration and it took over from Parliament and Cabinet as the force to which he held himself accountable. This inevitably led to an obsession with spin, an economy with the truth and ill-thought-out announcements. As John Smith said, governments should decide what the policy should be and then present it as well as possible. Under Blair, presentation was the primary consideration and of course he is very good at it, but an obsession with short-term presentational considerations leads to poor policy-making.

The final distortion that has led to a deterioration in the quality of British governance under both Thatcher and Blair is their idea of leadership. Both Prime Ministers have seen strong leadership as domination. This is an unattractive leadership style but also it is incapable of mobilising and changing big organisations and meeting complex policy challenges. Good leadership draws people together in a shared endeavour. It forges agreement on the best way forward and then decentralises power and creates structures that encourage all to contribute to the task in hand. It is this kind of leadership that achieves large advances because highly motivated people working together for a common purpose create highly effective organisations. Thatcher's psychology is probably different from Blair's but my instinct is that it is an insecurity in Tony Blair that causes him to operate in this way. Unfortunately, it has diminished the effectiveness of the government and the quality of public-sector reform.

The Labour Party

Blair's approach to the Labour Party has been even more brutal than his attitude to the British Constitution. He has displayed quite openly his lack of affection for the party he leads. What has been less commented upon is how the democratic structures of the party have been eroded and broken down. The original Labour Party constitution brought together a federation of organisations all governed by their own rule books and constitutions into a party governed by rule and democratic decision-making. After the turmoil of the 1980s, there was a general will to reduce conflict and amend Labour's constitutional arrangements to create new methods of decision-making based more on consultation and less on resolution-passing. These reforms were beginning to be put in place under the Kinnock and Smith leaderships but under Blair they have been used to corrode the democratic structures of the party. This is one of the reasons for the slump in membership. Members left rather than stayed to fight because their democratic influence had been considerably reduced. The National Executive Committee is now a pale shadow of its former self, policy is written by ministers and their special advisers and policy forums are allowed to express an opinion but the process is heavily managed and they have limited capacity to determine the outcome. Manifestos are written in No. 10 and increasingly candidates for the European Parliament and even Westminster are selected centrally and manoeuvred into place. Local councillors continue to be selected locally, but their discretion has been narrowed as power is sucked more and more to the centre.

Conclusion

My sad conclusion is that the world is in deep trouble and that conflict and bloodshed are likely to continue for decades unless we can achieve a change of direction. The UK government – a Labour government – has played a central role in the mistakes that have brought us here and this has happened partly because British constitutional arrangements and the democracy of the Labour Party have been grossly undermined.

However, I believe it is possible for us to start to put things right. A settlement in the Middle East could be achieved if the US can be persuaded to change its unbalanced policy towards Israel. Given the UK role and the US need for international support in Iraq, a change in UK strategy could bring considerable benefits. The UK should also use its international influence to focus its efforts on the reduction of poverty, the promotion of sustainable development and facing up to the risks of global warming.

At home, we are richer than our great-grandparents would have ever dreamed of. And yet there is a growing disgruntlement and coarsening of society. People in Britain work longer hours than the rest of Europe. Those in well-paid jobs find themselves under enormous pressure and strain. Those in less well-paid employment who have returned to work with the benefit of Labour's tax credits find it difficult to cope with their basic bills and obligations and live under constant financial strain. Inequality is growing despite a considerable effort to reduce child poverty, largely because the wealthy have become even more wealthy. Debt is very high and pension provision inadequate to provide a secure future for many of our citizens. The quality of life is deteriorating and though public services are improving there is a general demoralisation amongst those who work in them.

All this demonstrates that material wealth and consumerism are not enough to make people fulfilled and happy. People need more than selfishness and greed to satisfy the best of the human spirit. A commitment to a fair society and a more just world and the opportunity to help build such a future has inspired a century of Labour Party activism. It is a deep irony that, at a time when the values of the Labour Party and the Social Democratic tradition worldwide are the answer to disgruntlement at home and bloodshed and conflict internationally, the Labour leadership is moving away from those values. The undermining of the UN and international law is the most spectacular example of the move away from Labour values. The obsession with the need to inject market forces into the public services, lack of concern about inequality and illiberality on questions of criminal justice and asylum are others. The central-isation of power and undermining of democratic process also undermines the traditions on which Labour has built. Labour has always believed in the equal value of each human being, the duty to share wealth, technology and knowledge to care for all. But we have also understood that material wellbeing is not enough. The human spirit needs to treasure nature, culture, creativity and caring. We have always believed that the best way of organising society is through a universal franchise, a mixed economy and the rule of law. We have also been, since our beginnings, strong internationalists and supporters of the UN and international law. These are values that speak to the human spirit and can hold the world together. It is imperative that those who treasure such values, and in particular members of the Labour Party and those who have left the party or ceased to vote Labour, should come together and insist that these values are reinstated at the centre of British politics. It took 100 years for British history to build the Labour Party. We cannot allow its values to be trampled when they are desperately needed to find a way through the crises we currently face.

ACKNOWLEDGEMENTS

I am grateful to my friends Ruth Bundey, Nigel Fortune, Ian Martin and others who wish to remain anonymous, for reading and commenting on my draft. They provided valuable feedback and corrected mistakes, but the basic judgements and mistakes that remain are entirely my own.

I am also enormously grateful to Jessica Drewery whose fast returns of my manuscripts enabled me to keep up the momentum of my writing and meet the deadline. She is a marvel and I am immensely grateful to her.

INDEX